The People of the New River

To the generous people who
granted us interviews and their families;
and to the memory of our parents:
Elmer L. Cooper, Kate Ross Cooper,
James I. H. Lambert, and Mary Cox Lambert

The People of the New River

Oral Histories from the Ashe, Alleghany and Watauga Counties of North Carolina

by Leland R. Cooper *and*
Mary Lee Cooper

CONTRIBUTIONS TO SOUTHERN APPALACHIAN STUDIES, 5

McFarland & Company, Inc., Publishers
Jefferson, North Carolina, and London

CONTRIBUTIONS TO SOUTHERN APPALACHIAN STUDIES

1. *Memoirs of Grassy Creek.* Zetta Barker Hamby. 1997
2. *The Pond Mountain Chronicle.* Leland R. Cooper and Mary Lee Cooper. 1997
3. *Traditional Musicians of the Central Blue Ridge.* Marty McGee. 2000
4. *W.R. Trivett, Appalachian Pictureman.* Ralph E. Lentz. 2001
5. *The People of the New River.* Leland R. Cooper and Mary Lee Cooper. 2001

Library of Congress Cataloguing-in-Publication Data

The people of the New River : oral histories from the Ashe,
    Alleghany and Watauga counties of North Carolina / [compiled]
    by Leland R. Cooper and Mary Lee Cooper.
        p.   cm.—(Contributions to southern Appalachian studies ; 5)
    Includes bibliographical references and index.
    ISBN 0-7864-1190-2 (softcover : 50# alkaline paper) ∞
    1. New River Valley (N.C.–W.Va.)—Social life and customs—20th
century—Anecdotes.   2. Country life—New River Valley (N.C.–W.Va.)
—Anecdotes.   3. New River Valley (N.C.–W.Va.)—Rural conditions
—Anecdotes.   4. New River Valley (N.C.–W.Va.)—Biography.
5. Ashe County (N.C.)—Biography.   6. Alleghany County (N.C.)—
Biography.   7. Watauga County (N.C.)—Biography.   8. Interviews
—New River Valley (N.C.–W.Va.)   9. Oral history.   I. Cooper,
Leland R., 1926–   II. Cooper, Mary Lee.   III. Series
F262.N6 P46   2001
975.6'83—dc21   2001041053

British Library cataloguing data are available

Manufactured in the United States of America

Cover photograph by Robert Franklin

McFarland & Company, Inc., Publishers
  Box 611, Jefferson, North Carolina 28640
  www.mcfarlandpub.com

ACKNOWLEDGMENTS

We are especially grateful to Annabel Colvard Hunter Harrill, a true daughter of Ashe County, who gave us encouragement, information, old photos, and who showed us many historical sights and much beautiful scenery, and to J. Edward Harrill for his support.

Our thanks to Pam Blevins, who interviewed her grandmother, Beulah Blevins; to Annabel Harrill, who interviewed her cousin, Dean Colvard; and to Dean Colvard, who shared with us portions of his 1972 interview with his mother, Mary Colvard;

— to Teresa Isaacs, who faithfully and sensitively transcribed the interviews from our tapes;

— to Art Rex, who, through his mapping expertise, placed the interviews in their proper setting along the New River;

— to the members of the Blue Ridge Writers Group, who were always helpful and understanding in their critiques of our work;

— to the staff of the National Committee for the New River;

— to Jo Greene and the staff of the Ashe County Library;

— to the people of the Riverview Senior Citizens lunch group;

— to the friends and neighbors who made suggestions of persons for us to interview: Al Corum, David Edmisten, Molly Gambill, Johanna Gorham, Clara Gray, Annabel Harrill, Robert Hartsoe, Tom Lawrence, Neal Lineback, Nenie Midyette, Thomas Bruce Mock, Joe Morgan, Iris Morphew, Joyce Osborne, Eloise Price, Nell Sutherland, Mack and Ruth Vannoy, and Patrick Woodie;

— finally, to all who shared their photographs, many of which are family treasures: Edmund Adams, Beulah Blevins, Imagean Brackins, Ken and Jo Caraway, Dean Colvard, Russell and Peggy Colvard, Bob Cornett, Joyce Davis, Nellie Mae Edmisten, Bruce Eller, Molly Gambill, Clara Gray, Ben Harrison, Robert Hartsoe, John Jackson, Kenneth Jackson, Polly Jones, Marye Lineback, John Little, Gina McCoy-Hopper, Bruce Miller, Iris Morphew, Carol Wade Colvard Noronowicz, Ed Reed, Virginia Price Roberts, Nancy Scott, Bill and Lula Severt, Sam Shumate, Charlotte Stanley, Bart and Patsy Stewart, Nell Sutherland, and Ruby Trivette. (Recent photographs are by Leland R. Cooper, except where otherwise indicated.)

This has been a community effort. If we have failed to include someone, please accept our apologies.

Newcomers

Fred Chappell

We are the youngest children of the river
Which suffers us to return to it again,
      And yet again,
In preparation to be changed forever
As if newly from the hand of the Giver
      We came without stain,
      Clean as the rain.

Let us refresh the source that freshens us,
For from our source we cannot far remove,
      Cannot farther move,
Without distressing an ancient bond that is
The ligature between the eternities
      In which we live
      In which we love and live.

By river light we read our history
And watch ourselves become part of the land,
      Apart from the land,
As we embrace a mutual destiny
Or abrogate the solemn fealty
      That keeps us bound
      To our native ground.

The river flows away beneath the sun
But bears the sun upon it and the stars,
      The coursing stars, at night.
The river's flame, the sky's long gleam, are one,
Commingled, twinned, as are the world and man:
      Let both emerge to sight
      Reborn, forgiven, new-clothed in light.

Written by the Poet Laureate of North Carolina to commemorate the designation of the New River as one of the American Heritage Rivers and read by the poet on July 30, 1998, at ceremonies in the Boggs community of Ashe County, North Carolina.

TABLE OF CONTENTS

PREFACE

This book is about people who live or did live primarily in the North Carolina section of the New River. Thirty-three individuals (14 women and 19 men) told stories about themselves and described how things were when they were growing up. Most of them were in their 70's, 80's, or 90's at the time they were interviewed. The oldest among them have memories that cover most of the twentieth century.

We had just completed a collection of interviews in the Pond Mountain community of Ashe County, North Carolina, and were considering other areas in which to begin another project. On July 30, 1998, President Bill Clinton came to Ashe County, and, in ceremonies held on the banks of the New River, declared it the first of the American Heritage Rivers. Vice-President Al Gore, North Carolina Governor Jim Hunt, Congressman Richard Burr, and others participated in the ceremonies. The crowd was estimated to be some 12,000 persons.

Some time later, Robert Franklin, president of McFarland & Company, Inc., Publishers, suggested that the people who live or grew up near the New River would be good subjects for interviews. We agreed, then set about determining the procedures to be followed.

Along with our first visits and interviews, we felt the need to absorb as much about the river as possible. The fall of 1998 was sunny and balmy, so we traveled and photographed many sections of the river, both North and South Forks. In addition, we read several books, magazine articles, and newsletters from the National Committee for the New River.

We did not use a scientific method or academic model in selecting the people to be interviewed. We started by asking the proprietor of a grocery store in Creston to tell us something about the community. He did that, recommended two women, and told us how to get in touch with them.

It often happened that the person interviewed would recommend someone else who fit the description of the people we wanted to interview — that is, older people who had grown up on or lived a long time in the vicinity of the North or South Forks of the New River in North Carolina. That person

1

then might recommend someone else, and often introduce us in person or by telephone. Chance also played a part in our meeting these people. In one case, we met an acquaintance in the supermarket. He asked what we were doing, and when we told him, he described how his mother had lived many years on a farm through which the river ran. In another instance, we met a friend on the sidewalk in Boone. He told us about his mother, who had a similar background in another county. As the project neared completion, we had a list of 40 additional persons who had been recommended to us.

In many ways, the lives of the people were similar as they were growing up. Many of them lived on farms of varying sizes. Most lived on what they raised. Corn and wheat were staples and both were ground at local mills to make bread. Vegetables and fruits were eaten fresh in season and preserved in a variety of ways. Meats, especially pork and beef, were preserved, as well as deer meat, fish from the river, and even bear meat.

Families were large (some having as many as 16 members) and work was hard. It really was from "sun to sun." Everybody worked and families were close.

But it was not all peace and harmony. In a way, the life of the river resembled the life of the people. There were destructive floods, not only in 1916 and 1940, but at other times within the memory of the people interviewed. The winters were cold. One person recalled the river freezing to a depth of 18 inches, and when the ice would begin to thaw and break up, the chunks would pile up in the curves of the river to the height of a sizable building.

Everyone remembered the snows of 1960, when very heavy snowfalls over a period of several weeks did not melt because of the extreme cold and accumulated to over 90 inches. Farm animals suffered as well as people. The region was declared a disaster area, and food for both animals and people was flown in by helicopter.

Some of the people interviewed told stories of sickness, accidents, and death, sometimes violent and tragic. Some of the men interviewed were survivors of World War II.

A controversy arose in the 1970's when a large power company wanted to dam the New River and flood thousands of acres of its valleys, including homes, churches, and schools. Forces against the dam were assembled and the plan was eventually abandoned.

The education level of the people ranged from what they could get in a one-room school to master's and doctoral degrees. Some of them left the area when they reached adulthood, especially during the Great Depression and World War II, when a family could not be supported on a farm and jobs nearby were hard to get. They went to West Virginia, Pennsylvania, Michigan, Delaware, Maryland, and other places. Some stayed away for years and only came back when the farming situation improved, jobs became available, or they retired here. It was not unusual to find that someone, who had been gone for years, had returned to renovate and operate the old home farm. Several of the book's subjects have gained prominence in public life and are recognized throughout the state and region.

Our motivation in collecting these interviews has several parts:

(1) Each of the persons interviewed has a unique story to tell and each is a bit of history. If the stories are written down and included in a collection, this history will be preserved and will be available to the descendants of the subjects and to others.

(2) Many people welcome the opportunity to collect their memories and put at least a portion of their recollections on paper. Our project encouraged them to do this.

(3) Scholars may find the interviews useful for their research and study in a variety of academic areas, especially the social sciences.

(4) Reading the stories may encourage others to write their memoirs and, especially younger people, to interview their relatives and record their words for future generations.

(5) Knowledge of what life along the New River was like in the past should inspire today's citizens to preserve and protect its beauty for the future.

For us, the task of traveling around the river basin and talking with a number of congenial people has been enjoyable. We considered it recreation.

Oral history is a time-honored method for passing information from one generation to another.

In the electronic age, messages can be sent anywhere in the world in seconds, and at little or no cost. But there seems to be no better way to preserve and collect stories of the lives of individuals than by interviewing them, recording their interviews, and transcribing these into written form.

Our approach to conducting and recording the interviews was essentially the same as we had used before, except that we were not always able to visit and talk with each person before we visited for the interview. In such a case, we asked someone who knew the person to be interviewed to telephone him or her and explain what we were doing. We would then call and explain the proposed interview and ask the person to think of some stories to tell us. Then we would make an appointment for a visit.

At the appointed time, we would arrive with two small tape recorders. The second one was a back-up in case of a malfunction of the first. Actually, we had to use the back-up only once. That was when we opened the briefcase to begin recording and found that the recorder that we usually use was not there. We had left it at home, so the back-up saved the day.

We would have the subject talk for about 45 minutes, or more if it seemed appropriate. Then we would take the tape to be transcribed. The person who did the transcribing was asked to make the typed copy as close to the spoken words as possible. After some minor editing, the revised copy of the interview was sent or delivered to the person interviewed for making any corrections or changes. The person was also asked to see if he or she had any old photographs of the subject and family, especially those showing activities along the river.

In wording and content, the interviews remain about the same as when the people spoke them. We chose to use the individuals' own words as much as possible, as they were using their everyday language, and it is natural and comfortable for them. It is probably the same language they grew up with and have used most of their lives. Actually, it is little different from that found in other places. There are some words, phrases, and expressions that may be unique to this region; these will be preserved for the future in these conversations.

Several of the people we interviewed earlier have passed on, and their families have their statements to remember them by. One high school girl came to see us after her great-grandfather's death. She had read his interview and said it "sounded just like him," and wanted to get a copy of the tape, which we gave her.

We celebrate the lives and stories of these people, as we feel sure the families, friends, neighbors, and even readers in faraway places will join in doing so, too.

It is our hope that this collection of conversations will help preserve our sense of time and place for the future as well as for the present and past.

INTRODUCTION

The New River has its beginnings at two springs in Watauga County, North Carolina. One of these is in Blowing Rock, which is the beginning of the South Fork of the river, while the other rises near Pottertown to begin the North Fork. After flowing for several miles, both have gathered enough water from springs, creeks, and other tributaries to be called rivers. The two flow through Ashe County and come together to become the New River just south of the Virginia line and continue in a northerly direction through the high plateau of North Carolina and Virginia, the deep valleys of West Virginia, and through the New River Gorge in West Virginia. There it joins the Gauley River and becomes the Kanawha River, which continues to the Ohio River at Point Pleasant.

The course of the New River is by no means a straight line; it has many twists, curves, and bends where the water finds its way around the mountains and hills.

Bishop Augustus Gottlieb Spangenberg, one of the first to explore the region, describes the winding of the river in a diary entry in December 1752, cited in Fletcher, *Ashe County: A History*, page 9:

> We were completely lost and whichever way we turned we were walled in. Not one of our company had ever been there before and path and trail were unknown — though how can one speak of path or trail where none existed? We crossed only dry mountains and dry valleys and when for several days we followed the river [New River] in the hope that it would lead us out, we found ourselves only deeper in the wilderness, for the river ran now north, now south, now east, now west, in short to all points of the compass! Finally we decided to leave the river and take a course between east and south, crossing the mountains as best we could.

The Bishop and his party were looking for 100,000 acres of land upon which he could settle a group of people (now called Moravians) who were seeking economic security, religious freedom, and freedom from persecution. Though they returned to the Yadkin area and established their colony

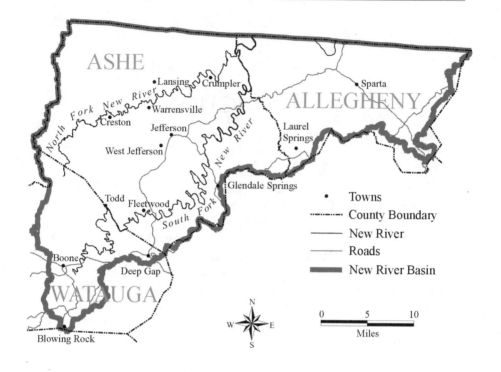

Source: Appalachian State University, GIS & Image Processing Lab, Art Rex, 2001.

there, the Bishop said he had never seen more beautiful land than the area that is now Ashe County.

The Ancient New River

Ironically, the "New" River is often if speculatively said to be one of the two oldest rivers in the world, the other being the Nile. No one actually knows how the name came to be applied to the river, though there are many theories. Morrison, page 11, *New River News,* mentions several:

> Hanson, in *Virginia Place Names,* says Dr. Thomas Walker named the New in 1750 for a ferry operator of that name. However, Augusta County (Va.) court records, as early as 1745, identify the river as the "New River," clearly predating Walker's explorations.
>
> Wilson Good ... wrote: "Indians called the stream Kanawha, spelled in various ways. They slurred the first syllable and emphasized 'nawha' pronouncing it like the German word for new. Hence the German folk began to call the river by that German word, translating it into New when speaking English." The German word for "new" is "neu," which sounds like "noy."

Morrison gives the following as his choice:

> In March 1642, the [Virginia] Assembly passed an act that referred to Walter Austin, Rice Hoe, Joseph Johnson, and Walter Chiles who petitioned "the Assembly in June 1641 for leave and encouragement to undertake the discovery of *a new river* (emphasis added) or unknown land bearing west southerly from Appomattake river..." (As far as anyone knows, this expedition never went forward.) This act uses the word "new" in the sense of recent awareness. Did Virginians commonly refer to this westward flowing river as "a new river" until its discovery when they began calling it "the New River"? That's my guess.

However, Schoenbaum, *The New River Controversy,* page 5, states the following:

> Legend holds that the New River received its present name from the father of Thomas Jefferson, Peter Jefferson, who surveyed the valley in the eighteenth century. The most likely explanation for the name is that the New was the first river travelers encountered that flowed "behind the mountains," beyond the Eastern Continental Divide.

As the real origin of the name is not known, and will probably never be known, each person is free to choose.

Even where motor traffic travels beside the river and across highway bridges, the landscape lies in pastoral peacefulness. The space of about 60 miles through which the river runs in North Carolina is marked by diversity. The South Fork builds up volume as it flows through several settlements around Blowing Rock and Boone, through valleys and around hills and mountains into and through Ashe County. Here the South Fork actually flows alongside a mountain for some distance, then finds the end and turns around it and goes in the opposite direction for about the same distance until it encounters another mountain. Then it turns and heads back in the original direction.

The twisting and turning of the river was very confusing to the early explorers. In one instance, a party of explorers left the river and crossed a mountain to find what they thought was another river, flowing in the opposite direction. Actually, it was the same river, the one we now call the New.

Both parts of the river flow somewhat slowly past pasture lands with clusters of cows and calves grazing, corn fields, vegetable farms, tobacco patches, acres of Christmas trees in orderly rows, and, in one stretch, high rock cliffs bordered by woodlands managed by the Park Service.

Stately farm houses, large enough for 10–15 people or more in past generations, still watch over the fertile river bottom land. Smaller homes of vacationers, weekenders, and full-time residents nestle among the trees, as well as beside the river. Some of the newer homes are placed on top of the hills and ridges and look down on the river.

The North Fork of the river is formed at a spring of water emerging on the west slope of Snake Mountain, which probably gets its name from the resemblance of the series of peaks to the undulations of the reptile. The settlement where this is found is called simply "head of the river" by those who live nearby. It is in the vicinity of Pottertown in Watauga County.

Beginning at this higher elevation, the stream moves swiftly down the valley through Sutherland, Maxwell, Ashland, Creston, Fig (Riverview), Clifton, and Dresden. Along this stretch the river is accompanied by a paved road, most of it Highway 88. It is well-populated, and has a number of houses with a variety of types of architecture. A number of creeks of all sizes enter the river from all directions.

The People

For centuries the rivers and valleys have been used for transportation as well as for habitation.

Considering its great age, archeologists believe the New River may have been inhabited by several different cultures back as far as 10,000 B.C. or before. As described by Schoenbaum, they are: the Pleistocene, the first modern man to appear on the continent, and the Paleo-Indian or big-game-hunting tradition. Members of this culture were nomads who wandered around following the big animals such as the giant bison, mammoth, mastodon, and camel. Evidence of this culture can still be found in broken projectile points, apparently for spears used in hunting. The Archaic period featured a hunting-gathering culture which left many artifacts to show their increasingly complex way of life; woodworking tools, stone vessels and the whole range of projectile points have been found.

From about 5,000 B.C. until the arrival of the first Europeans in the sixteenth century, various Indian cultures moved in and settled on the flood plain bringing in maize (corn) and other food plants and establishing the agricultural base for a more permanent habitation and a tribal community. Relics of these cultures include pottery and ceramic figurines, some of which have been found in their burial mounds. (Schoenbaum)

When Hernando de Soto and his party passed through Western North Carolina in 1540 on their expedition to the Mississippi River, the first contacts between Europeans and the Cherokee Indians were established.

During the first half of the eighteenth century, most of the contact between the Native Americans and Europeans was with hunters, trappers, and traders who had no intention of settling in the mountainous region. Some of them carried on a profitable trade with the Indians, exchanging guns, ammunition, tools, and trinkets for furs and other items.

Before, during, and after the Revolutionary War, the population began to increase. Sometimes the trappers and traders would carry word of the possibilities for farming in the highlands and would seek out land for other people, especially family and friends. Because of the richness of the soil and convenience for farming, the river bottoms were the first lands to be taken.

Settlers continued to move to Western North Carolina for several decades, claiming or buying land in the river valleys whenever possible. Many moved from the Piedmont area of the state, while others were from the North and even the South. Their ancestry was German, Irish, Scotch-Irish, Scotch, English, and a scattering of other nationalities.

Descendants of some of the early settlers still live in the same areas where their ancestors lived, and some are on the same land their families have occupied for well over a hundred years.

The Interviews

ROSE GAMBILL, 98

July 19, 1999

*At her home near Sparta on the Farmer's Fish Camp Road.
Her daughter, Johnsie McIntyre, is present.*

I was born March 9, 1901. We lived on a farm in a family with eight children. We enjoyed life. I went to a little country school house just across the hill over there. It was the Gambill School House. Everybody in this area was a Gambill. I went to the Gambill School House to the seventh grade and then we had to board and go to Piney Creek. Back then you didn't have a car. It'd take us most of a day to go to Piney Creek and back. Now today you can make it in about an hour and a half. We went in a buggy. It was about eight miles. Then you went to Boone, that was high school, after the seventh grade. I didn't go any further than high school. I went to Piney Creek to high school and Boone for summer courses. I went in the winter, too. It was called Appalachian Training School back then and I was preparing to be a teacher. I taught for two or three years and then I got married.

I taught seven grades in one room, boys bigger and almost as old as I was. That was at the Gambill School House. The building is not there now. That was in 1908–09 when I started school. There were more boys and girls in class than one teacher needed. I had seven grades.

When I went to Boone to school I would come home on holidays, maybe Thanksgiving and Christmas. It took two days to go up there and back. Dr. Dougherty was the head of it. That's where I met my husband. He and my brother walked home and carried a suitcase one time for Christmas. My brother put his trunk on the train and sent it to Galax at Christmas. He didn't like school. He decided if he'd go to Turkey Knob to school and stay with my sister, he wouldn't have to go back. But my husband went back. Neither one of them taught. They were farmers. I was raised just up the road here and my husband lived in that little white house down there.

One Sunday afternoon we went out to the river and my husband's folks lived in that house down there [by the river]. He came down there where we were. Of course, we went to school together and we were friends. He walked us home that night and from then on. After two or three years, we got married. We had two daughters, Johnsie and Nancy. Nancy lives in Sparta and Johnsie's home is in Albemarle. She came back when my husband died. Her daughter lives in her house and she lives with me. So it's good for both of us.

When I wanted to go to my mother's I would get on a horse with Johnsie behind and Nancy in front and ride across that river. That's the only way I had to go.

I remember the first car I ever saw. We lived back up the road, a good ways from the road. We were playing out there in the yard and I saw this car go down the road and I thought it was a buggy that didn't have horses. When my brother Rob Gambill — I was a Gambill and married a Gambill — bought this new car on Friday he just drove it home. On Sunday he was going three or four miles to see this girl and I went with him. We picked up another girlfriend that went with us. He'd just had the car from Friday to Sunday, so he didn't know much about it. As we came back home, she was driving and she hit a tree. He didn't know how to drive either. She was going slow. She didn't hurt it too bad. But my husband and I, this was before we were married, and we were riding in the back seat, our knees hit the back of the front seat and we had some sore knees.

After we got married in 1926, I stayed home with my children and helped on the farm. We grew corn, beans, potatoes, onions, and cabbage. We had cattle and sheep. We sheared the sheep and sold the wool. Back then we didn't go to the store to buy much. We grew it on the farm.

JOHNSIE: I remember hearing them talk about one winter that was such a bad winter the river froze over solid. I don't know why the cattle were on the other side of the river, but Daddy brought a herd of cattle over on top of the ice and people were driving wagons and horses across the ice. I believe it got colder back then than it does now. I remember when Daddy and I went skating on it. They had a ferry down at Forest Forge.

ROSE: After we got the bridge, he turned the ferry loose and let it go down the river. One time the water was too shallow for the boat to come to the bank, so he had to drive the cattle out in the river and they put the gate down and drove the cattle onto the boat. That river, twice in my lifetime, has been up to the steps of that house down there. It didn't get in the house, just up to the front steps. We didn't lose anything, any cattle or outbuildings. The branch was so high that they couldn't get across to the barn. They called a neighbor that lived down here then on the other side of the branch to go and open the barn door and let the horses out. The water was getting in the barn. When they opened that gate, those horses ran to the top of that hill before they ever stopped. They knew which way to go. That was in 1916.

There wasn't much difference between the floods of 1916 or 1940, I don't think. I didn't live down there in 1916 but I did in 1940. There was a big haystack below the road in that meadow and it washed that haystack away. That was in 1940.

JOHNSIE: It was in 1929 the Depression came. My grandfather, who lived down here, was a cattle trader and her father that lived up here both dealt in livestock. Her father had contracted lots of cattle and he really lost about everything he had. This property was a land grant to a Mr. Long and my great-grandfather bought it from Mr. Long. Mr. Long is buried right along the fence up the river there. We still have the land grant. My great-grandfather was Robert Gambill.

ROSE: He had four sons and he gave them all a farm, 250–300 acres apiece.

JOHNSIE: He was the register of deeds in Ashe County back in 1850, somewhere along there. I have lots of his papers. There were three brothers that moved here from Culpepper, Virginia. Two of them stayed in Wilkes County and Martin [Gambill] moved to Ashe County. I don't know if you're familiar with Gwynn Gambill and where his place is near the river. That was the old Martin Gambill place, on New River.

ROSE: There were two Martin Gambills. My great-grandfather was named after my great-great-grandfather Martin Gambill.

We had a small boat. The river bottom was rich land. You can put those bottoms in corn every year. That bottom has been in corn ever since I've been here. It's regular corn. Up here you can't have corn in the same place year after year.

JOHNSIE: We used to find a lot of Indian relics down by the river. There's a real sandy area over behind the old house. We've found some arrowheads and Daddy found some pottery after the flood and brought it to the house and put it on the porch. The next time he looked, it had just disintegrated.

For the social life around here, the young folks went from house to house. They had parties every time they turned around. I know I've heard my mother talk about making molasses and a group of young people just came in and she and her sisters had to leave her mother and one other person making molasses while they went home and entertained, had a party.

ROSE: A crowd of young folks came in to have a party and you wouldn't know they were coming. We square danced. The Gambills didn't do much singing because they are not musically inclined. The Methodist church is right up here. It's been there a long time. Then there's a church across the river. Where I was raised, just up the road here, we'd go up to Independence [Virginia] more than we did to Sparta. But when I got married and lived down here on the river, we went to Elk Creek church. It was a Baptist church.

Flooding near low water bridge near Farmer's Fish Camp Road, probably in the 1980's (courtesy of Marye Lineback).

We had a little one-teacher school house just across the hill over there. We had box lunches and things like that at school. You'd take a box and they'd put it up to the highest bidder. They didn't have a name on it, but they had a way they could find out. We'd put chicken, sweet potatoes, cakes, and pies in the boxes. We decorated the boxes with crepe paper and ribbons, some of them fancy. It was something about like a shoebox. Whatever box you had, you'd wrap it up pretty. Everybody would stay and eat then and the fellow would get to eat with whosever box he bought. Sometimes, a boy would want that girl and somebody else would buy her box. It may have been their boy friend that would buy their box.

JOHNSIE: Life on the farm when I was little growing up was pretty self-sufficient. We grew wheat for flour. There was a water wheel across the river. My father and Cleve Gambill and Earl Farmer that lived across the river got electricity for several years from that. We didn't get electricity until 1947. When we wanted to wash, we'd call and tell Earl to turn the water wheel on. We couldn't all wash at the same time. We'd have lights and radio at night, but when Earl got ready to go to bed, the power went off. There was a line from the wheel to our house. It was also a mill where we could get corn ground. I don't know what happened to the old building.

Farmer's Fish Camp used to have cabins and rented the cabins to people and Mrs. Farmer cooked; she was a good cook. She'd serve country ham and eggs and gravy and fresh vegetables. That was a very popular place. He would pole the boat for the men to fish. The cabins are gone. Mother used to have an interest in a couple of the cabins. She would go and change the beds and sweep up. That was a way of earning a little spending money.

Also, she raised turkeys. In the spring of the year one of those hens would have a nest on top of that hill and another one on top of this hill. You'd have to watch them to find the nests. Then you'd have to gather eggs every day. Then she would set them. She'd train those turkeys to go up in a tree to roost so the foxes wouldn't get them. That was a merry chase.

ROSE: It was about the only thing you could get any money out of.

JOHNSIE: My grandmother had chickens. She raised chickens and sold the eggs. She would sell butter in town. This was back before I can remember, but back in the '30's when my grandfather got in so much debt, if she had not worked like she worked making cheese and butter and raising chickens and doing things like that, I'm sure they probably would have lost the farm.

ROSE: My grandfather was in the Civil War. He fought for the South.

JOHNSIE: I'm not sure where he went. He was in prison for a while at Abingdon, up near Washington. My aunt had letters and I don't know what happened to those letters from him while he was in prison. Her grandfather went to the Civil War so his sister's husband could come home while their baby was born. So he went and served in his place and, while he was there, he got captured. But he came home eventually. He came home and married and had a family. The children loved their grandfather. There were eight children in her family. Their father was out trading cattle all the time.

But every child loved their grandfather. He died not long after my aunt was born. We have his bed upstairs. When another baby was born, and one was born about every two or three years, he would take the next one and sleep with it.

ROSE: A big family has more fun than just one or two. We'd go to school at Boone or Piney Creek. Over here you could go to seventh grade and then you had to go away from home to go to high school. My oldest sister went to Boone, she and two more girls, stayed seven months without coming home. It'd take two days to go to Boone back then. I can't remember how they went. But anyway, they took the wagon from home and took their trunks up there. They stayed seven months without coming home. You had to have money to go to Boone then. We paid and stayed in a dormitory. It was hard on my mother and father to send us to school. Of course, some got married before they finished high school.

JOHNSIE: Daddy got his first tractor in 1947. It's down there in the tool shed. Up until that time, he had four work horses, did everything with a horse and wagon and plow. That table was down in the old house and it was my great-grandmother's table. It was two feet longer than it is now, but it was in the old kitchen down there.

ROSE: She died in 1902, so that's over a hundred years old. This chest was given to my mother when she was married. Her daddy made it. It was in February, 1895. It's nice and makes a nice coffee table, too. We refinished this table. It was about three feet longer and we cut it off. It didn't have that edging around it.

JOHNSIE: I remember my grandmother telling about this, before she was married and came down here. Her grandfather Robert lived in a log house just about where the road is. They had a few slaves during the Civil War. They sent the slaves with the meat and the foodstuff down on the river bank to hide, so the soldiers coming through would not steal what they had to eat.

Over at Mother's house, they had a wooden churn, one you pushed back and forth. It was like a rectangle. It would hold several gallons. I've heard her mother say that you'd get a bolt of material and she'd make all of them a little summer dress out of that one bolt of material. My grandmothers on both sides would knit stockings. Mother said they got a new pair of stockings every year for Christmas. The shoemaker would come around once a year and make shoes for everybody and stay about a week.

ROSE: Mama kept knitting on hand all the time. Every time she'd sit down, she'd be knitting. They made all the boys and girls clothes. We'd go to the country stores and buy the cloth. I can't remember if anyone had a loom and did weaving.

JOHNSIE: I do not know why people did not die from botulism or something because they would kill chickens and take them to market.

ROSE: I never could wring a chicken's neck. Somebody else had to chop its head off. My daddy bought turkeys and they dressed them up here in an old house, scalded them, and shipped them on the train.

JOHNSIE: And he's driven turkeys and pigs to Elkin.

ROSE: They had boiling water and scalded them and dressed them and hung them up down in the old barn and put them in a wagon and took them to Galax. You had to do lots of things to get a little money back then.

JOHNSIE: I guess it didn't kill anyone. Down at the old house we had a spring that ran in the springhouse all the time with a trough that ran through to keep the milk and butter cold.

ROSE: I can remember when we had to go to the spring, 'cause I got a spanking once. My brother and I had to go to the spring. Daddy sent us to the spring to get water for the night. But we got to playing until it got dark and we went and got the water in the branch. I don't remember how he found out about our getting it out of the branch. That was before we had pipes to the house. We had a springhouse just out back and had a trough dug out of a big tree and the water ran in that to keep the milk. We had no refrigerator. We had to buy crocks to store the milk in. I guess they cost about as much accordingly as they would today, 'cause we didn't have much money to pay for them. Things were different.

There's lots of differences in then and now. There were several of us in the family and my dad traded and was on the road most of the time and Grandpaw stayed with us. He'd go up in Ashe and buy cattle and then ship them to Galax and he wasn't home a lot.

JOHNSIE: They owned land on the river over here. They always liked for corn hoeing time to come because they could go with Grandpaw to hoe corn and play in the river. They'd have to hoe the corn before they could play in the river. They'd take their lunch with them.

Her mother was a great herbalist. She dug roots.

ROSE: She made tea for colds, boneset tea. Mayapple was to build up your blood. Sulfur and molasses, they'd give it to us at night for colds.

JOHNSIE: My grandmother that lived down here had to have her teeth out. A neighbor pulled them. I don't know where she got her dentures. I don't know if we had a dentist around here. Anyway, a man across the river pulled her teeth.

My grandmother would pick dock leaves and mix it with leafy greens in the spring. She doctored a lot at home. She was a great cook. Talking about doctors, with her last baby, when she was about six and one-half or seven months pregnant, she had kidney problems. The doctor didn't think she or the baby would live.

ROSE: He took her to Roanoke, I guess. The baby just weighed about three pounds. Dr. Smith said there wasn't one out of a hundred that would raise that baby. She died last year, she was about 70 years old. Her mother got along all right with the kidney.

If we wanted to go shopping for a new spring hat, we had to go to Galax or Mouth of Wilson. We had to have a new hat every spring. The milliner would make them and trim them for us.

I was small. I didn't go much myself. It would take two days to go to Galax and back in a wagon. We had to camp out. A girlfriend and I went with someone to get us a spring hat. We camped just this side of Galax. We slept in the wagon and he slept on the ground. The wagon had a cover on it.

JOHNSIE: I remember Daddy's brother telling about going to Galax. He went by himself in the winter and he stopped to camp and it started snowing. He was on his way back. So he got wet during the night and as soon as it was daylight, he got up and hitched the wagon and came on home. He said he was the nearest frozen to death that he had ever been. The wind was blowing; it was snowing; his clothes were wet.

ROSE: We'd usually take some kind of meat, like sausage or ham, with biscuits and cornbread. We didn't eat out then. We didn't have money. There weren't many places you could eat out.

JOHNSIE: My sister still has a provision box. It looks like a small chest.

ROSE: Times are a lot different today than what they were then. I remember seeing my first car. There was a house down at the barn and a couple lived there and they had the first radio. They owned this farm and had no children and they had more money than the rest of us around here. We didn't have a TV. Radio was the first mystery.

JOHNSIE: The first car, the doctor had it, and he went to see Mr. Cox. Mr. Cox really had to have everything new that came along, so he talked the doctor out of his car. He learned to drive in the loft of this barn down here.

ROSE: He locked the door to that barn and learned to drive upstairs in that barn.

JOHNSIE: I've forgotten what his horse was named, Solly, or something like that. The car was going and he couldn't stop it and he would say, "Whoa, Solly, whoa, whoa." He had the first radio and the first gramophone.

ROSE: He had the first of everything. His name was Bill Floyd Cox. We bought this farm from him.

JOHNSIE: They used to go up to Mr. Cox's and hear election reports. They were interested in politics. They had to hear the election results.

ROSE: Now radio was a mystery. They might have had some fights around the voting places. I think they'd get drunk. At election they'd get pretty hot down there sometimes.

JOHNSIE: People used to give people a drink to vote a certain way. Maybe still do. It's pretty evenly divided between the parties now, but I think years ago it was more Democrat.

ROSE: We've had some pretty big snows. Probably 1960 was the biggest one.

JOHNSIE: That was when they had to airlift hay up to Ashe County. Mother said that Papa used to take her to school on a horse when there'd be a big snow. Snow didn't stop them from going to school.

ROSE: One time we were going to school on the horse and some of the bigger children were walking. They came down behind the horse and it jumped and threw us right off in this big snowdrift.

JOHNSIE: That was a fun day at school when you could go sledding during recess. I remember you telling about the time that all the kids got on a sled, a pretty good-sized sled and rode down that hill and went right into the barn and the sled was torn all to pieces.

They [Appalachian Power Company] tried to flood this area for a dam, which was the reason we didn't have a paved road until last summer. They'd pave the road as far down as the dam was supposed to cover. It was on the other side of the river about half a mile. The old house [by the river] was supposed to be under 40 feet of water, or something like that. We were very much against the dam. Floyd Crouse was probably the most instrumental person that prevented [highway] 77 from coming this way and prevented the dam. It took a lot of work for years and years [to stop the dam]. It really did hamper the progress of Alleghany County because the dam bought up so many farms. These farms weren't active for years, just allowed to grow up. A lot of the farms had been bought and they were owned by Appalachian [Power Company]. Nothing was done with them. Maybe they were rented for cattle or something. They just became grown up because nobody really cared to look after the land. Of course, Appalachian didn't lose because during this time the value of the land went up so much. It was not good for the county, just waiting to see what was going to happen with the dam.

So, we didn't get the road paved. Robert Barr was in the highway department. He had promised Daddy a road up here, but because of the dam it didn't get built then. They started it and paved maybe half a mile down from Elk Creek, but they stopped where the water was supposed to start.

Even though we won, it was not good, the waiting was not good for the county because lots of the owners of these farms were paid a reasonable amount at the time they sold, but they had to go buy something. Then by the time Appalachian got ready to sell the land, it was so much more valuable. So they did not lose money. The only people that benefited were those that sold water rights. There were some people that sold their water rights and kept their land. So they got something for nothing. Highway 77 was supposed to come right across this ridge up here. Floyd Crouse lobbied because it would take so much land from an already small community. There were a few people who were for it. Most of the landowners were not.

ROSE: I have six grandchildren and 11 great-grandchildren.

JOHNSIE: This week her youngest grandson is expecting a baby. By week's end she will have 12 great-grandchildren. He is Nancy's son.

My children and Nancy's are not far from the same age and, at one time, we had seven children under four years of age.

ROSE: They all come to visit at holidays. We have a full house when they all get here and a lot of noise.

James Bard, 95

February 23, 2000

At his home north of Jefferson on Highway 221.
Mr. Bard lives alone, except for his black cat Chad.
Because Mr. Bard is hard of hearing,
Chad goes to find him when there is a knock at the door
or when the telephone rings.

I was born near the New River in 1904 on the eighth day of December. I helped my daddy on the farm till I was 17 years old.

I'm going to tell you the most scariest thing that ever happened to me. I was about seven years old. We lived right on the New River. We had a farm. I wasn't old enough to take a gun out, but I slipped my daddy's shotgun out all the time. I had to cross the river to get over where my buddies lived who were a-going with me. It was about the 15th of December and I was crossing this river in the boat to get over with my buddies. I got about half across and I seen a whole bunch of partridges, about 25 to 50 of them, an awful big gang, and I couldn't help but shoot at them. I was so anxious to shoot at them partridges, I up and cut down on them. The mush ice was running in the river and the first thing that hit was my head in the water. At that time I couldn't see and I got around to where I could see and I swum around in the mush ice till I could get a-hold of the side of the boat. I never did get that shotgun. It was 12 feet deep right where I lost it. That was a kind of an unfavorable scene for me to go through that.

I never got a whupping, but I got a hell of a talking. We's building a new house and we's putting sheet roofing on it and they had to have tools to put it on with. Dad was gone to get the tools that morning. So when he come back, I knowed or I thought I was going to get a whupping for certain. I was a-dreading to see him come and when he come in the house, my mother told him about what had happened, and he said, "It's a wonder he hadn't a-drowned

21

James Bard and his cat Chad in 1999
(courtesy of Patsy Stewart).

and he's lucky to be here." He said, "Where's my old shotgun?" I said, "It's down there at the bottom of the river." I never thought about trying to get it out. He said he'd get a pole and fix it and go down there in the morning. It was about 12 foot deep and he never could find it. The mush ice was running. When winter was over with, we still couldn't find it. The river cleared up where you could see the bottom everywhere, but we never did find the shotgun. It was covered up in sand, of course.

The mush ice was the ice that was flowing down the river. It would be in big pieces, in sheets. I'd a-drowned if I hadn't been in that because I couldn't swim then. I held on to the ice. I got my head out and I paddled around till I could get to the edge of that boat and then I got back in. It was a close call.

My mother was a Phipps. They lived right this side of Jefferson. They moved out of Watauga County. They was a family with 12 people and he bought this land up here right out of Jefferson. It was about 125–130 acres. My grandpa and grandma and uncles, they died there, and three of my aunts; they're dead, too. My family's about gone. Mother and daddy, their picture is on the wall right over there. They were buried at a cemetery at Nathan's Creek, just down the road from here. They's three of us children, one girl and two boys. My brother, he's all tore up when my mother and dad passed away, and he never did get over it. He's got 150 acres of bottom land, river bottom down there. His boy lives down there and farms it, him and some more fellows. They see that my brother's took care of good. Somebody has to stay with him. That's a hard job this day and time, to hire somebody to stay with you. I don't care if you've got money.

I've got two daughters and two boys, me and my wife. My youngest boy got into this here pine-growing business, Christmas tree-growing business. He was an electrician. He put up these here high lines like goes down to the coast where we get our power from. He built and worked on them all the time. He wanted to make some money in the pine business. He had a farm with about 100 acres in it, and he's always in a hurry. He'd come home on the weekends. He worked a crew with around 30 men; he was the boss of them. Mount Airy is where the head man of it was, and my son just worked under him. When it come time to spray them pines when they was growing, he was in such a hurry, he put this tank on his back and he never got it tight. When he started using it, it started leaking. It was a hot July. It got his back wet and I happened to be going over there that morning and never got to leave here until way up nearly 12 o'clock. I asked his wife where he was. She said he was up on the hill a-spraying pines. I went up there and he was a-spraying them. It was awful hot that morning. In less than two months, he got sick. We took him to the best place money could buy, Duke University, but he had a big knot under the hide, right against the brain, it formed right there. They operated on him and he never did know much after that. That spray was poison. It had to be to kill the bugs and everything. That was the end of him. He was an awful good worker, a good boy. His name was Blaine.

My other son's name is Blair. He lives up here just the other side of West Jefferson, just about three or four miles up the road there. He was into the business, too. He worked for this company BREMCO for 35 years that makes this juice [electricity] that comes here. He retired from that, then he went into the pine business, but he paid more attention to what he's doing.

Then I've got a daughter, Patsy. She works for the health department. I've got one more girl, Polly. She married a fellow that's got some money and they've got a place in Florida. They go down there every winter. They leave about the middle of October. I talk to her every week. Her husband is getting in bad shape. They've got a home over here. She lived and worked in Indiana for about 25 or 30 years.

My wife's been dead about 15 years. She was a Bare. She was from around here.

I was going to tell you about moving the mill across the river on the ice. It was a sawmill. This Panson man was a fellow that I worked for when I was little, helping when I didn't have to help my daddy. I helped him with a sawmill. He liked to sawmill. He went out in Oregon where that big timber is and he stayed out there for, I think it was, 12–14 years, and operated a big one of these sawmills that cuts going and coming. When he quit out there and decided to come back, a company by the name of W. M. Ritter over in Virginia and West Virginia was just a-cleaning up. They'd bought all that timber and cut it and got the lumber and they had these big sawmills. He bought this sawmill as he was coming home, and he hired it hauled down to the river. He lived across the river. Back then the water was about five foot deep most anywhere you come to it. They had decided to wait until spring like. At the time the river froze over, plumb up and down the river everywhere, solid. They sawed a hole in it to see how deep it was and it was five

James Bard walks over property in Scottville area in the mid-1960's (photo by Bart Stewart).

foot deep froze then. So they just went and hauled the sawmill, the big boiler and everything that goes with it. The snow was about, or over, a foot deep. It was an awful bad winter. They just went out and cut two big pretty good-sized locusts and they peeled the bark off of them on the bottom and they made a sled out of it and loaded this boiler on it and took a big yoke of cattle and hooked them old steers to it. They pulled the nails out of their shoes they had on and they put ice nails in the place of them. The heads stuck away down there. There was just two big ox, they'd weigh about 1,800 pounds apiece. They pulled that boiler right to the place and then they went back and got the mill. It was a big old long boiler, about 14 foot long. He cut all the timber off the land that he had and then he bought other land and timber. That's all he done. He loved to sawmill. He had a big farm but he never farmed it much. He just liked the sawmill business. That was here in Ashe County, just down the road about three miles. The time was about 1916. That was during World War I, I remember that now.

I was too young to go to the war. My daddy didn't have to go because there wasn't nobody in the family but me at that time and everything had to be looked after, this, that, and the other. He was a farmer altogether, my daddy was. We raised mostly corn. There wasn't no tobacco; well, everybody had a little patch of tobacco to use theirself. He chewed tobacco. They didn't raise much tobacco, but he raised corn in the river bottoms. We made everything that we eat but coffee and soda and sugar. He raised his hogs. He killed four and five big hogs and he just sold enough of the hams to buy him some pigs back. He was a farmer that was pretty well-to-do when he passed away.

I worked in the coal mines in West Virginia for 31 years. It's 105 miles from here and I'd come home about every two weeks. I took my wife out there with me. Oh, she was going to stay with me. We got out there and the house was along a creek and just across that creek was a railroad. Just above there was where they dumped the coal and where them old engines were a-backing in and backing out, hauling the coal away from there. It was just about every day or every other day. Every time she washed, that coal dust settled on her washing. She started raising hell about that. She said she believed she'd just as soon live back here and if I wanted to work out there, all right. I'd come home as often as I could. So I done that. The pay was good. I always worked for this Panson that had the sawmill. He knowed all about machinery and I helped him a lot. I went to helping on a coal-cutting machine when I first went in there. I knowed the man that was operating this big mine. He was from Ashe County. He'd come in a-fishing every year. That was back when I was just a boy and I'd help him catch his minnows to fish right out of this creek, right down here. So he give me a good showing, the boss did, and I made good money all the time.

Yes, I had to go down in the mines. The first day I worked, I did. That was a little scary, but after you've been there long enough to know when you're in danger and when you ain't, why, it ain't no worse than it is, it's not as dangerous as it is on this here dadburn road around here with a car. It's getting outrageous. I still drive yet, but I've got to catch a clear day and when I'm feeling good before I get out on the road any more.

Oh, yes, I had the black lung disease, I've still got it. That's what's going to take me away from here. Yeah, I cough it up every morning. I get a payment because I have that disease. The government has to pay so much, and the coal company pays so much. They can't doctor that much now. They ain't a dern thing they can do. What I done, I didn't do like some of the rest of them, operating machinery in there. They made a mask that you could wear. You had to stop about every hour and take your dinner bucket, the bottom part of it had water in it. You turned it up a little and you could wash that thing [the mask] out and then put it back on. They'd laugh at me and every damn one of them people's dead.

I washed out my mask. It was a mask that fit over your mouth and it was rubber and had a big old piece that you had to breathe through. It was wet and it would catch the most of the dust and you had to wash that dust out right quick. It didn't take but about four or five minutes. They'd laugh at me. I said, "Now you just better be a-laughing the other way." They didn't like it too well the way I told them, but I didn't care. If they wanted to laugh, they could laugh. They're dead and been dead, every one of them. The fellows would want me to take them out there and get them a job in the mines, and I told them what to do about that. If they got to working around a loading machine or a cutting machine, to wear that mask, and if they don't, "Why, I'll have to haul you back dead one of these days." They put a mask on. I'd see whether they did or not. I'd ask the boss and I'd tell him, "You'd be better off to make them all wear it." They started to pass a law and some of them didn't want to wear them at all. You just let them go to hell then. They died out, them people did. It just got so much on their lungs they couldn't breathe and they just died. Now that breathing business, buddy, when you get to messing with it, you ain't going to stay here if you don't do something about it.

I was here for the flood of 1940. I'll tell you about that, and in 1916 there was one then, too. We just had got through in them bottoms. They wanted to let the grain dry in a shock. It got real dry before you put it in a stack. And this flood come. It come from nearly three-quarters of a mile to the house where we lived, from the river. It come under that floor. We got one horse out and hooked him to a sled and hauled out 28 shocks of wheat, that's all we saved out of that whole thing. We had to untie it and spread it out on a sunshiny day and we saved about 50 bushels. That's all we saved out of the whole thing.

People didn't jump in automobiles and go ripping around all over the country every day. They worked back then, everybody did. They wasn't no playing about it. Back in that day they worked.

When I was a boy they was school houses on this side of the river and they was one across the river. There was Dog Creek School down here and Ore Knob School across the river. The school teacher had to go right by our house and cross the river. He had to cross the river twice. He walked across the hill by our house over to the school. We was pretty good boys, but then me and one of my buddies was a little slow when the bell rung. When the bell rung after dinner for us to get in the school house, why, me and this boy was a little late a-getting in there. We was carrying on like two old boys will. This happened in the winter time and it was cold as hell. Me and this boy, we was about two minutes slow a-being there when that bell rung. This school teacher, he thought he was running the whole damn state about it. He was one of these here big-headed fellows. He throwed big old dippers of water. He had them all ready when we come in and he throwed them in our face. That made me so mad. My daddy had that boat that we crossed the river on there going to school. I come in and was telling my daddy about it. The next morning, the mush ice was running and so I went and slipped a hand saw out and slipped down there to the river and cut that pole about half in two all the way around up about four foot of it, the pole that he used. Well, we was in the boat, me and the rest of the kids, and he bared down on that pole and it broke and he fell in. The first thing that hit was his head. The mush ice was running and it was cold as the devil. My daddy didn't like it when he throwed that cold water on us. He never said nothing to him about it, but he didn't like it worth a damn, I knowed. So he had to go right up by our house. He seen me a-coming back from down there a-carrying something but he didn't know what it was, my daddy. So when the teacher come walking up there with ice on him and cold as the devil, my dad got to studying and he went out there and they's still some sawdust in between them teeth of the saw. He knowed what I done. He said, "I can't blame you, I ain't going to whip you for it, but don't never do another trick like that." I never told him it was me, but he knowed when he seen that dust. He seen me a-carrying something but he thought it was an old stick or something I'd picked up. I was a-carrying the saw under my coat, bringing the saw back to the tool shed.

Pauline Price, 94

September 22, 1998

At her home, Rich Hill Farm, on the New River near Warrensville. Her daughter, Virginia, and Virginia's husband, Tom Roberts, are present, along with Eloise Price, her daughter-in-law, wife of Joe Gwyn Price, her son.

My earliest remembering is back beyond 1912. I was borned in 1903 at Sutherland below the Methodist Church that sits on top of the hill there. That has had a great deal to do with my young life and my old life, because I'm still a member of the Methodist Church.

My mother was a Sutherland and, you know, the Sutherland Methodist Church was a great support of my father and an uncle of his, Mr. Hardin, that owned at this early age the parsonage. No, it wasn't the Methodist parsonage either, because it's always been at Creston, but the homeplace is there at Sutherland. Bunk Sutherland bought the house in 1912 from the Hardins that built it. It's a brick house and the only brick house in the community at the time it was built. There's several more scattered through the area now.

My dad was from down here about Warrensville. His name was Martin Rowan Shoaf and his Martin name came from his mother's people. His mother was a Martin from down below Statesville, and Rowan was the county he was born in. Dad married Ola Sutherland in the Sutherland community in the upper end of the county. Our home is still there. Mama was Ola Sutherland Shoaf, and her daddy was Thomas Houston Sutherland. His uncle that has a big house below him was Alfred Sutherland. As far as I know the two daughters of Charlie Sutherland owned that place. That's as far as I know, but I lose connection because they live in Boone and I live in Ashe County and we don't see one another. Charlie's two daughters are Charlotte Stanley and Joyce Davis.

My daddy's daddy was a Baptist preacher. How he convinced mama that the Sutherlands ought to be Baptists is more than I ever understood. But she never did join the Baptist Church. She stuck to her Methodist religion all through her life. My dad came up and bought a little ... well, it wasn't a little store, because back then this was a big establishment. He'd send a wagon every week to Shouns, Tennessee, to pick up his grocery supplies that he needed every day to feed back to his customers.

We called it the Deep Hole [Depot]. He sent two horses with a wagon every week to Shouns, Tennessee, to pick up his supplies from the railroad. Back then, they had been getting groceries from Mountain City for many years before that. My brother Jack was two years younger than I, but he was one of these smart guys. He knew a little bit of everything. He proved it because before he died he had a manufacturing company building furniture in Rome, Georgia. My brother was excited to get to go when the two horses with a wagon and driver went to pick up supplies at Shouns, Tennessee. That was a little station just below Mountain City, just out on the edge. When he got back he said, "Well, Sis, there's no deep hole. It's just a house, and the train comes and unloads everything they've got on the train right there. We put it on the wagon and bring it back to Sutherland." He said, "Why, Daddy is a rich man."

All children have special things that they like in a store. Well, there was one box of Cracker Jacks out of all of them that had a nickel in it. We searched every box until we found the nickel. We took the nickel to my daddy and said, "Here is a nickel out of this box of candy." He said, "Well, I guess then you're entitled to the box of candy." We took the box and went under the porch floor to divide the candy.

The first year Jack went to school, I think Mae Brown that lived at Trade was the teacher. Jack walked home from the school with some Cornett boys. The Cornetts lived just below us. We had two settlements. The Potters lived above my granddaddy Sutherland, a house almost in Watauga County. The Watauga line extends just beyond his house and Pottertown was there. But Cornett town was down here at the Methodist Church below us and that whole community was nothing but Cornetts. As they came home from school, he walked home with some of those Cornett boys and they said, "Jack, have you got a match in your pocket?" He said, "Yes, I've got some matches." They said, "Well, let's see if this stuff will burn." They gathered some broom sage and brought it to him and he set it on fire. He dropped it and the whole field caught afire. The next Sunday, the preacher knew about the fire and he knew the boy was in the church and so he opened his sermon, saying, "Well, you know I understand you had an excitement this past week, that one of you boys set the broom sage field on fire." Jack raised up in the seat where he was and he said, "Yes, pastor I set that broom sage field afire."

We had a school close by, just below the church. I went to school there one or two years and then they moved it up the road where the Sutherlands lived. The house is still there; that was back before 1912.

I graduated from school in Bristol, Tennessee. My mother and daddy had a store at Sutherland but in 1912, somebody, I don't know who it was, induced Daddy to sell his store and go to Mooresville, that's this side of Charlotte, and put up a store. There he had a shoe store. After we moved from Mooresville, we came to Bristol, Tennessee. We went to school when we got to Bristol; we went to the Tennessee school. The Tennessee/Virginia state line goes through the town. We lived on the Tennessee side, never on the Virginia side. But we played football with Virginia every Saturday. We had a good connection because as a rule we won, but they never held it against us, the Virginia people. They were always kind and let us march up and down State Street.

I went to college at Virginia Intermont. That's on the Virginia side of Bristol. It's still a good school. As I walked up the street I went by a house that had a parrot that could talk very good. She'd holler, "Polly wants a cracker," every time we'd go by. Sometimes we'd holler, "All right, we'll bring you one back tomorrow."

How did I meet my husband? He was at Emory and Henry. That's just above Bristol on the Virginia side. Mama had a friend that lived in Emory and Henry, on the school campus; she had a home. She rented Gwyn a room and Mrs. Eller invited Mama and her family, Jack and me, up for a commencement exercise. Gwyn was one of her roomers. I think he was the only one she had at that time. I met him and he took me to the cemetery. He took me to a Sutherland grave, and I was surprised because I didn't know we had a Sutherland that had gone to Emory and Henry College. It was in May and the ground was just red with strawberries and he picked me some strawberries.

The Prices were proud of their name and it was well known that Granny Price didn't marry just an ordinary Englishman, that only one brother and sister had crossed the ocean with him to North Carolina, just before the Civil War. The brother was lost in the war, but George, that was Granddaddy's name, couldn't find where his brother was killed and buried, and never did find him. His sister married a man from Mooresville and went to Asheville, N.C., and then in the years that followed that, they lost contact with one another. That was a good many miles away from here to Asheville, N.C., and it is today, a good little ways.

When we were dating, I remember I baked Gwyn a chocolate cake. My brothers Bob and M. R. liked my chocolate cake so much that they took it to the back porch, the whole cake on the cake stand, and sliced them a good-sized piece of cake. They were sitting there with a plate in each hand eating

Gwyn and Pauline Price, Rich Hill Farm, 1991 (courtesy of Virginia Price Roberts).

my cake that I fixed for Gwyn. I was so proud of that cake. Gwyn finally got a slice.

We got married — I guess it was 1924. We got married in Bristol and came to live in Jefferson. That was when he was teaching school; he was the principal at Jefferson. He had a boys' dormitory and a girls' dormitory. The girls' dormitory was on the school grounds; the boys' home was on a hill above the school. It had six rooms upstairs and six rooms downstairs and it made a nice place for the boys to live. They went to the girls' dormitory for their meals. Years later the boys didn't have their dormitory. They had to put one girl in the dormitory and she didn't have any more sense than to take the ashes out of the stove in a wooden box and put them in her closet. Sometime in the morning they looked out and that boys dormitory was afire. Joe Gwyn was born in the boys' dormitory.

Then we came up on the farm. We moved here because Granny Price had died and she had three boys, but only one had married. The other two were bachelors and stayed bachelors. Uncle Roy, he was a rich man. He lived in Shreveport, Louisiana. We came to the farm because Granny Price had three boys and nine girls. The girls didn't want the old farm. Daddy Price was the only boy that Granny had that married, and he had three children, a boy and a girl and a boy by the first wife. Then in 1919 Daddy married again and by this wife he had a girl and two boys. Ruth Graybeal and Todd were his children, and Mary Carolyn, Joe, and Tom Price were his second wife's children.

While Gwyn was teaching, REA [Rural Electrification Administration] of North Carolina became very popular and Gwyn in his first years did support the REA and was a great believer in the REA. The first thing he knew our governor had appointed him as chairman of the REA. He spent four years in Raleigh as chairman of the REA of North Carolina. The next governor appointed Gwyn four more years, and the third governor appointed him the next four, and it went through eight different governors that sent him to Raleigh as chairman of the REA. That established him as REA of North Carolina and he was known all over the state, because he represented nearly every county that had REA. In the beginning REA wasn't too well known, but Gwyn, as good a man as he was, had established rural electrification very well for the 32 years that he was chairman.

During most of that time, I lived on the farm with the two children. They didn't want to go to Raleigh to school 'cause they knew no one in Raleigh. They wanted to stay at home. So Mama stayed at home and kept the children, kept the cows, kept the whole farm.

Then the war came along. The war hurt every farmer in North Carolina, one way or the other. They took your help into the service or into factories. You see we still have the barns. We had a dairy for 32 years and were on the road every day selling milk in quarts and half gallons. We bottled plain milk and buttermilk. We churned cream, separated the cream from the milk to get the cream to make butter. Butter went sky high; everybody wanted butter, butter, butter. We couldn't keep butter, for our customers wanted it so much. We made chocolate milk by the gross. We sold chocolate milk even to the school children. The children loved chocolate milk.

The boy that did the milking lived across the river where my son lives today. His daddy had I don't know how many children, 10 or 12, I guess, because the house was filled and one of the boys worked for me since I was the only one at home. He helped milk the cows and helped bottle the milk and put it on cold storage. We had a big room that we put our milk in at night when we milked it and of a morning when it was milked to get the warmth off of the milk before we bottled it and shipped it out to sell. We had a boy that drove the milk truck that helped bottle the milk. The trouble was that he couldn't read and write. He could tally, but he couldn't write out the order. I had to go with him to collect the money at the end of the week. Then the war came and he got anxious to get into the service. So up to Baltimore he goes. That was heaven to him, and it was because what I was paying him was nothing to what he could get up there.

When Gwyn's grandmother died, she left her house and it was filled with

Flood of 1978 on North Fork of the New River at Rich Hill Farm destroyed the swinging bridge (courtesy of Virginia Price Roberts).

furniture. She had nine girls and three boys. You know those nine girls had to have everything granny had. They took everything that granny had. The house was wood. Granny Price got the homeplace when the mother died. Out here in the yard somewhere are the rocks that the chimney was made from. The house was made from two slave cabins put together. Granny put them together with a hall between them to separate the two rooms. She used one as her bedroom and living room and one as the kitchen and dining room.

The day our house caught on fire and burned, I had gone to substitute for one of Gwyn's teachers who had to go to Raleigh for some school matter. She had asked me to take her classes while she went to Raleigh so I went

Pauline Price (left) and Nell Sutherland quilting, 1995 (courtesy of Virginia Price Roberts).

with Gwyn that morning. I told my daughter Virginia Ruth that if she would stay in the house and not get out, I'd bring her a bag of candy. I had to leave her with a hired girl, Clara, but Clara had been with me for several years. She lived in the house with us. She had her room as we had ours. She had gone down to make hot chocolate and the men that were cutting wood out at the wood house came and said, "The house is on fire. Get Virginia Ruth outside." So Clara got her best winter coat — this was in the Thirties— and put it on her and got her out. There was no telephone then so Everett Roland drove to town to tell me. He lived between here and Warrensville, just beyond that store building that's empty now. We came on then to the house and it was gone. All that was left was the chimney in the kitchen and the one in the living room, the room that was the parlor and our bedroom. The neighbors got most of our furniture out. They were very helpful. They got my Haviland china out and set it out in the yard and broke only one teacup handle. They were very careful and that was just an accident. The fire started from the chimney. Birds had built a nest in the chimney out on the corner and the coal stove got too hot and started a fire in the chimney.

The children and I stayed for 32 years. Well, the last four years I was able to go to Raleigh. Mama lived in Bristol, Tennessee, and her health was very poor and I had to go back and forth. Back then we had a bus that ran from West Jefferson to Mountain City, Johnson City, Bristol. My grandchildren called it Granny Price's bus. Well, it was, because they would stop and pick me up at the highway and bring me back and leave me at the highway. So it was Granny's bus that took her to Mountain City, Johnson City, and up to Bristol. Changing buses and stopping to pick up people made it take all day.

When I was in Raleigh during the day I went to the senior citizens place. I got interested in weaving there. Here are one or two of my napkins. I have a loom upstairs. I learned to do oil painting. Those pictures there, this log cabin, and two pictures over there of birds, I painted. I do needlepoint, too. I've done eight dining room chairs for my daughter and dining room chairs for a grandson. I do quiltwork. I have done, I guess, 30 or 40 quilts. I've made one for each of the great-grandchildren.

Mrs. Price died on January 15, 2000.

TOM JACKSON, 91

August 23, 1999

At his home on the Tom Jackson Road
(just off Castle Ford Road), near Boone, N.C.
His son Ken is present.

I'm Tom Jackson. I married Ella Mae Jackson. She was June Miller's daughter and she died January 11, 1974. She was at Reins Sturdivant Funeral Home, the only funeral home in Boone then, and they told me that night that they's the most people there at the viewing that they'd ever had. When Ella Mae was in the Baptist Hospital in 1969 the nurses wondered why I wasn't there of a morning. Well, I didn't want to see her go in for an operation because I knew it'd be serious.

I honored my father and mother and I'm not sorry that I did, because Dad was a good man and Mama was a good woman. My parents' names were Frank and Minnie Jackson.

I remember growing up and living in that old house down yonder, that's where I was born. We had a farm. Farmers then grew three or four acres of corn. I was present over there in the field and they's a toad frog hopping out. I laid the hoe down on the ground like a snake and the frog took off in the water flying.

Our farm was not on the river. This is as close to the river as I've ever lived, only in that house down there, which is empty now. At the foot of the big hill there was a low water bridge. They have a high bridge there now.

Willard Norris was my friend and we worked together. He never would take pay and I never would take pay, because he would come down here and help me several days. Then I'd go up there and help him for several days. That's the way people did back then. He came one foggy morning, it was very foggy. We went up on the mountain. We's looking over and I saw something coming. At first I thought it was a gray squirrel, then it got a little closer, and I saw it was a fox. Then later I shot it and killed a fox. Willard went and picked it up and he says, "I want its tail." We went on down the ridge and somebody fired a gun back up here. That was called the Big Ridge. I said, "Somebody's shot our fox. Let's go back and see." Sure enough, that fox was laying off five or six feet to the left.

At the foot of Big Hill they's a deep channel on the other side of the river. Willard Norris would throw rocks in and drive the fish up and I would grab hook them. We'd take it turn about and we caught 22, 11 for each one. They were yellow suckers, eight to ten inches long. They's good to eat.

Tom R. Jackson at his home in 2000.

I used to cut cross ties for the railroad, me and my father, when I was just a kid. We hired Ed Jackson that lived across the river over there. I'd hew ties morning and evening and when I'd quit, I'd have to take my fingers and open them. They were stiff from gripping the handle.

The train came in to Todd one evening and I had a young horse. I's riding him. Every time the train blew, he would rare up. Well, I got tired of that and I got me a stick about the size of a hammer handle and when he started to come up, I give him a lick between the ears and that was the last time he ever come up.

I was a school teacher. I taught at Green Valley and Miller's School House. That was over here where the Baptist Church is. I was a county commissioner for Watauga County and was elected chairman. One time when I was chairman, they's a man named Clyde Eggers. He had a brother that was a lawyer, and he told me that I had the most friends in Raleigh that he'd ever seen. He didn't go down there to check on me, he said, but I had the most friends in Raleigh. Then I introduced myself as county commissioner and he said, "He's too modest to say so, but he's chairman." I was in the Legislature after I was a county commissioner. It was interesting.

The Legislature was wet then; they would drink liquor and I was dry. I voted for dry people all the time. They's a man named Elsie Whitaker from Goldsboro there and he had a bill in to raise the content of beer from three to six percent. He said, "Let's go out and vote." I voted Nay, which was

The seven Jackson brothers (sons of Jesse William Jackson) on the banks of the New River, South Fork, at the residence of Edward Jackson. Left to right: Robert, Frank, Ross, Thomas, Edward, James, and John. Frank Jackson, second from left, is the father of Tom Jackson and the grandfather of John Jackson (see his interview in this book). (Courtesy of John Jackson)

against it, and he was for it. When I looked around, he was gone. The Democrats won — the drys. When I was in the Legislature I helped to pass a bill to make the eighth month in the high school. I was in the Legislature just one term. That's all I wanted. It wasn't bad. It was good and I enjoyed the service there. But I didn't want to go back. It's better to be at home.

I was a county commissioner when the new courthouse was built. The committee was responsible for building the new courthouse and my buddies, Len Hagaman and Glenn Hodges, voted for it. Well, they's defeated. I wouldn't run because I knew I'd be defeated and it nearly killed them because they got defeated.

I taught all grades at the Miller School, but at Green Valley I just taught the fourth and fifth grade and Ellie Tugman taught the sixth and seventh. I was around when Watauga High School was consolidated and all the students were brought together in Boone. That was a little controversial at the time because Cove Creek didn't want to leave their school. But we worked with that to get it done.

When I was growing up I walked to Big Hill School. Etta Lewis was the teacher and she married a Lyons for a husband. She taught the best school that I've ever seen. She taught me more of the principles of education than any other teacher did, even when I was in high school or the two years I spent in college. I went to Elkland School at Todd for high school. Clyde Greene was my teacher and I liked him and he liked me. But they's a big boy there and he told him that he would throw him out the window. We's on the second floor. One morning it was cold, zero weather, and the ones that lived in town would go home and the ones that rode a bus would stay till bus time. Well, I rode a bus. I went to college at Boone (Appalachian State Teachers College).

Kenneth here is my only child and I'm proud of him. He takes good care of me. I have a great-grandson. Kenneth has a daughter and she has one son.

Now I go with Ken down to Winston-Salem to his home part of the time and he comes up here and lives a few days with me. I enjoy both. We need to be up here in the summer time. It's been getting pretty hot down there. Ken and I have a good garden here. He does most of the work. He bought seed down near his house quicker and better than he could get anywhere else. We've got some good vegetables out of it, but it's not a big garden. Ken's a good cook — excellent. He's clean.

There have been a lot of changes in our county since I was a young man. The schools have changed the most, for the better. I was attendance officer for the school for 10 years. Hamp Clawson lived over yonder near the highway and when I would pass there, if it was 10:30, I had to go in and eat with him. Verlie was a very clean cook and I enjoyed it. I had to travel around and find students that should be in school. I traveled in a car, a Chevrolet. That was the last work I did with the schools. Then I worked some in Boone at the post office department of the college.

I have been involved for a long time with the Bethelview United Methodist Church. It's up here about 8/10ths of a mile. I taught Sunday School for years and years. They's three boys in my class and they listened to me teaching for a few minutes, then they went to whispering and laughing. I looked at them and I saw my look make an impression on them. That was the last time that they tried to pull something over my eyes. They were teenagers.

It's hard to say what was the happiest time in my life. Gardening with Kenneth; he does the most of the work and he grows good crops and I appreciate it.

When we were growing up some of the games we played were running base and over the house basketball. The church and the school were the main socialization places. There'd be parties at school or church socials at the church.

One time we had a corn crop and the corn was up so high, and then the frost came on the seventh of June. Then the corn grew and the next frost came on the 10th of September, an early frost. It was an early frost and a late frost and we didn't make any corn. Dad carried the corn to the granary and put it up in the loft. In a week he went back and every ear had turned yellow. To get corn for a meal, to make cornbread, he got his corn from Newt Howell. He was related to Mr. Glen Howell down here. The reason he always had corn was the fog from the river kept the frost off.

CHARLOTTE STANLEY, 89, AND JOYCE DAVIS, 79

June 14, 2000

At the home of Charlotte Stanley in Boone.
Joyce Davis lives across the street.
They grew up in Sutherland near the New River.

I, Charlotte, was born in Watauga County, and my father, Charlie Clinton Sutherland, and mother, Addie Louise Shull, were married in 1909. Then my father went west to find a home to take Mother and me. He stayed a good little while looking for a place. He had a cousin out there who advised him to come back home and look after the land that his father had left him, which would be my grandfather, Thomas Sutherland. So he came back, and he and Mother moved in a little house that belonged to Will Lovill first, who was a lawyer, and then it belonged to Dr. Robinson. Daddy had not saved a great deal of money when he was out west but he had enough to build a little house on the farm, which was right across from my grandmother's.

I had to cross the New River, on a footlog, to get to her house. The footlog was a large tree trunk that had been hewn flat on one side. The New River was very narrow, but because of the floods it covers twenty feet or more now.

Daddy farmed and grew cattle. A barn was one of the first things he built. Mother had all kinds of things built for her work: a chicken house, a dry kiln for drying fruit. We also had a wood shed, pig pen, and corn crib. We were surrounded by all these out buildings. As a young child I had to go hunt the chickens and turkeys, feed them, and see that they were put up for the night. Foxes, weasels, and other wild animals would kill them if they could get in to them at night. A job I didn't like was hunting the cows and bringing them in to be milked. I can also remember carrying water from the

41

Joyce Sutherland (Davis) and Charlotte Sutherland (Stanley) in wheat field in front of house at Sutherland (courtesy of Charlotte Stanley).

spring which was a good distance from the house. We lived there until my grandmother was not able to stay by herself any longer, so we moved to her house to care for her and an uncle, Tilden. We made many trips across the New River.

I had a little sister named Joyce and I remember staying over at my grandmother's and then they came after me and said I had a little sister. She was born in that little house. I was real excited about that. I stayed there at Sutherland until I was in the 10th grade and they moved the senior class to Jefferson. Our mother kept the dormitory for two years until I finished high school.

The school at Sutherland was one of the best in the county. Sutherland and Helton were two of the best schools in the county, the only two that had much recognition at that time. We had a music teacher and Mr. Plummer was principal first. Then A. B. Hurt was principal and then I believe Mr. Duncan became principal and then they moved the school to Jefferson.

I wanted to tell you more about living on the farm and what we children did for entertainment. Mother's sister, Aunt Minnie, married Daddy's brother, Jim Sutherland, so we had double cousins and we would get together and play. It was always fun for me to go up there because there were more children; that was Lillian James's mother. We played all kinds of games and

The Sutherland Seminary, date unknown (courtesy of Charlotte Stanley).

I remember one funny thing. We were going to play baptismal service. Lillian and I got Louise, who was the smallest one, who was about five, I think, so we got her to stand across this little stream of water and we told her just to make herself real stiff and we would not let her fall in the water. But, of course, we let loose of her and she fell in the water. Aunt Minnie chased me home for getting Louise in the water, I remember that very well.

We had a cemetery for our little ducks and chickens and turkeys that died. In our little cemetery we would have little services and put up tombstones. We had a big lake right close to the house. It just formed really from the river, but we had ducks and geese. Mother had geese and picked feathers for feather beds. We would get the big old geese by the wing, which wasn't a very good thing to do, but we would play with them and then let them get into the water and go after them and we would have a lot of fun doing that. We would swing on the trees and limbs that would come down. When I went to school at Sutherland, that was one of the things we did at recess. They had those beech trees and they were real tough and we would swing on those.

Mother would make yeast bread a lot. I remember her doing light bread. If Daddy was working nearby, she'd always call him in to have some hot light bread. He would come from wherever he was working. She probably made it with potato yeast. I don't think they had yeast then.

We had all kinds of wild things that grew around us. We would gather blackberries and wild strawberries. We had lots of berries. When Mother had her first garden, she had little gooseberry bushes. Grandmother had currants, lots of currants, and when we lived at Grandmother's, Mother would make currant pie.

It was quite an experience to think about the change from then. We didn't have any water in the house or any bathrooms. But we didn't know that it was hard as no one had these other things, so we were all in the same boat.

We had lots of children when we would get together at school and we could have any kind of team. We'd have ball games and we had a men's basketball team, boys' basketball team, and I mean they were men, they were rough. We would win. One of my aunts was a large person and she would go and just yell for the team. They all enjoyed having Aunt Sophia and Uncle Joe. They didn't have children and so they loved sports and would take in all the games. The teachers boarded in their home, the Dixon girls, Cleo and Bonnie, and one of the Dixons that taught there, I guess he was principal when there were not as many teachers, or he taught there. I don't remember when that was.

JOYCE: I have several things I'd like to tell. I don't know how authentic or true they are, but they are things that I have heard. I think it's interesting how Granddaddy got the land. Now I have just heard this story a few years ago and I don't know whether it's true or not. It was said that Granddaddy loved land and that an Indian came upon him. Granddaddy had a beautiful white horse. The Indian claimed the land. They made signs and talked and the Indian said he would give Granddaddy the land for the horse. Now I had never heard that before. Several people who had lived in that section told me that they had heard that since they were small, but why we did not hear it, I don't know. It was the time when the Romingers, Mr. Marvin Rominger from the Peak, lived in that area. He was the father of Ruth and we were born the same day. It was her granddaddy, Hilton Rominger, that said he had heard that all his life about our granddaddy. So, it would have been in his lifetime.

We have never heard of any Indians being around there. Another thing that I heard was from Dr. Ray Derrick. He liked Daddy very much and he loved to talk with him. He said that he and Daddy were talking one time and he asked him how much land that Granddaddy Sutherland had owned. He told him 30,000 acres. Now, I can't imagine how much that is, but Granddaddy owned Sutherland valley. Our granddaddy was known as Red Tom because he had sandy hair. There's another Tom, a cousin, and he had black hair and they called him Black Tom. If you are going up through Sutherland Valley, you keep on going and you will come to a bridge with a creek and

Granddaddy sold Black Tom the property above that. That was partly in Watauga County.

CHARLOTTE: I remember sitting on the porch and my grandmother said, "Now if you just look around here, the top of the Peak Mountain and all the land that you can see from standing here on this porch, Granddaddy once owned." He wouldn't sell any land to anyone unless that he felt like it was somebody that would be a good neighbor. So he started selling, one was an Osborne, that was one of the first people I remember they sold some to.

JOYCE: I thought it might be interesting to know about Granddaddy's family. Granddaddy was considered an old bachelor, and it's always interested me that Grandmother was a Grant from Virginia and she was teaching in that community. She came there to teach and then she and Granddaddy married. He was in his forties. They had nine children, six boys and three girls. Our Daddy, Charlie Clinton, was the youngest. Aunt Minnie was teaching there in Sutherland and Mother came over for commencement and she pointed Daddy out to Mother. She thought he was the cutest little boy, so they ended up marrying years later. There are just the two of us. Our grandparents lived in a log cabin house that was on the property but I never remember it.

CHARLOTTE: Part of the old house is part of what has been added to the house now.

JOYCE: Uncle John Wilson, who was a Wilson from that community, built that house. We know that Aunt Jenny and Aunt Julia went to Martha Washington College over at Abingdon. Aunt Maggie, we think, went to Greensboro. None of the boys went to college. Granddaddy Sutherland was real interested in education and from the time I was little, he talked about Governor Aycock visiting. He had come to the home there and they talked about education. I don't know whether he had any influence on building that high school that was there or not.

CHARLOTTE: Senator Doughton, who was from Alleghany County, spent many nights at Granddad's house. They once told about him drinking the water out of the gourd and when he went to Washington he asked the boy to bring him a drink in a gourd. Of course, that was just a joke.

JOYCE: There are two little stories that I would like to tell. Every once in a while Daddy would get started on telling old things that I just loved. The boys were really pretty rowdy and imagine having six boys. I think they gave Grandmother a real hard time. Daddy being the youngest, he was kindly spoiled, I guess. He would like to run the ducks over in the mill pond. Grandmother didn't like her ducks run over the mill pond. One morning when he was sleeping late, he heard Grandmother (and he told me this) coming up the steps. He said she didn't come up the steps unless it was something bad. She had a hickory. She said, "Charlie, you better never run my ducks over the mill pond again" and she let him have it.

Uncle Boss and Daddy loved to go to Pottertown and get them a little liquor. They always had to take something to exchange for the liquor. Granddaddy had a lot of meat which was kept in the meathouse. They said they would get them a ham or a piece of meat to take up there to trade for liquor. Grandmother kept the key [to the meat house]. She wore about six petticoats and an apron or two over all of that. She looked much bigger than she was as she really wasn't a very big lady. It was Uncle Boss's business to try to get the key from Grandmother. He was watching for her to go into the meat house and when she did go in there, then Uncle Boss must have grabbed the key. In the meantime, Grandmother was in and out of the house and around and they couldn't very well slip in there. They always had a row of logs and wood right up above that house to carry to the house to heat the house. They had a fireplace in every room of that house. When they looked up, a dog had the meat they had hid in the wood and the dog came down with their meat. So, they had to postpone their trip to Pottertown.

When Mother and Daddy moved from the little house to Grandmother's, I was just about three years old but I can remember us moving to that house in a covered wagon. The covered wagon scared me and so Mother and I walked through the field. She walked with me through the field so I wouldn't be scared. The house is up on a hill and they had built a springhouse at the bottom of the hill. This was one of the hardest things and it was really hard on Mother because she had to do a lot of cooking and get the water up from the spring. Many times she'd be in such a rush and carry two buckets of water. She had said so many times that that was really hard on her. A lot of people would stop at that spring and get a gourd of water. That was away from the creek, and it's still standing there. It's looking pretty bad.

CHARLOTTE: There's no sign of where Mother and Daddy lived, there's no sign of where the spring was at that time, 'cause I used to carry water. Later, the water was pumped to the house. Where they pumped it from was up the other direction. I remember when I started to school, the road was terrible and there was a mud hole that went all the way across the road and you could climb on the fence and go part way around it. If it was a little drier, then you could kind of get yourself a place to step so you could get around it. It was terrible, the roads were just paths.

Some of the things I remember we did, Daddy had a little sled and it was just big enough for the three of us to get into and we would go to my uncle's and have a candy pulling, taffy pulling. One time we were going across the bridge right where my Uncle Joe lived and Mother yelled and we were almost off the bridge. It was cold and ice was in the New River. The old oxen whirled around and the whole little sled went right off in the water almost, just a little corner, and they finally got it back on. We would have a big time and we'd go down the meadow to their house and pull taffy.

In the fall of the year, we had a great time playing in the leaves up at Aunt Minnie's because they had so many trees. We'd go up there when they made molasses. I can remember having the stirrer go around and around and Fred and I would get into an argument about who would get to lap up the molasses.

We had the first cheese factory in Ashe County and it was run by Don Shull and he stayed with Mother and Daddy. He would tell me to come down and he would give me cottage cheese in the morning sometimes, and I loved that. To this day I love cottage cheese. Then Mother used to make it. She would save the milk, let it become clabbered, and let it heat slowly to make delicious cottage cheese.

As we became older, we went on Bald Mountain and that's where I met Jim on the way to the mountain, which is straight up from Sutherland, on a picnic.

We went together about seven years and I was also going with a boy from Virginia at that time. I would see him through the week and then I'd see Jim on the weekend. That wasn't very nice, was it? Then we were married at home on August 26, 1939 at the spot where some of the children of past generations were married. Granddaddy's brother lived there, Uncle Alfred Sutherland. This was the old house after Mother and Daddy moved from Grandmother's house. They said that was where my grandmother was married, that I stood in the same place.

When Jim retired and came back here, I taught at the Appalachian Elementary School here for about seven or eight years and retired in 1972.

I'll tell you about the floods, starting with 1916. That was a crisis, because my father had gone with his uncle to a Confederate reunion in Alabama. They served ice cream and it was the first ice cream he had ever seen. Daddy got typhoid from the contaminated ice cream. He became very ill and Uncle Doc Robinson came and said, "You have typhoid." He lost so much weight he became skin and bones and looked terrible. I remember Uncle Jim, Daddy's brother, came down to see him when he was getting better and had Fred, his son, on the horse behind him. When Fred saw Daddy he fell off the other side the horse, it scared him, as he had grown a beard and couldn't stand any noise. I was little and, I guess, running around, and Mother sent me up to stay with Aunt Minnie because Daddy was so bad.

The flood water came up close to the house. It seemed like it was water all the way around our house and there was a little branch and we had a little footlog to go across and the water came up to that little branch. I can remember seeing the water and Mother was just standing there so worried and crying. She said, "Everything we have is going to be washed away. There goes my big wash pot." She had a great big black iron wash pot and the man that lived on the farm was there and he said, "I can go get that." He had on rubber boots and he walked up there and pulled the wash pot in for her. She was so happy about that. The water came out over the land.

That was the worst flood until the flood in 1940 and it didn't damage that community like it did places in Watauga County. Jim and I had been home. He was in school at Chapel Hill and I stayed at the house for the first six weeks he was in school. I got afraid to stay by myself for some reason. He said, "Just come on and go with me back to Carolina." I went down there and he had come home to see about getting the school set up for the school year. The next time we came back we couldn't even get into Fleetwood, as it had washed the road completely out. It was devastating. That was when they found the child up in the tree. I stayed up there and Aunt Minnie couldn't come down to see Mother and, of course, she couldn't leave home. It was really hard for them at that time, as they were very close and shared so much.

Mother was a real worker and a real homemaker. She did all kinds of things, like canning and gardening. It was real hard for her after the move to Grandmother's because Grandmother always had a lot of people around at the old home. Joyce was talking about all the meat they had in the smokehouse. I remember them saying they would kill as many as 25 hogs a season. They ate so much meat. They kept lots of hogs and they were fattened on the chestnuts up on the hill. They had set out an orchard. My uncle had a wonderful orchard and they had all kinds of trees growing up there. Uncle Jim had all kinds of fruit, peaches, pears, and grapes.

I didn't tell you about going in the buggy. We'd been to my grandfather Shull's. We'd go in the buggy, just one horse, and go from Sutherland to Cove Creek and get there when Grandmother was putting the milk in the springhouse, so that was pretty early. We would leave home before daylight so you could see where you were going. The road was so bad and there was always a hill to go down that was so rocky. The wheels to the buggy were small and you would go back and forth in the buggy getting over those rocks. Then they finally got a road after we'd get to the Tennessee line. We would go up and down that Cove Creek and people would just be coming out of their homes, and Mother always wanted to talk and speak to everybody. Even after we got cars, she said, "I'm just tired of these cars. I never get to speak to anybody along the creek."

Uncle Jim died and Daddy tried to help Aunt Minnie with all the problems she confronted. The sad thing about it was that she had a beautiful team of horses; they looked like the kind that you read about. She had ordered a new cook stove and he drove the horses to Mountain City to bring the stove back. On the way back he said he just couldn't get them to go and when they got home and called the veterinarian, the horses had gotten poisoned on stagger weed. It was a weed with a purple flower. Both of those horses died. We all cried, everybody cried.

Left to right: unidentified person on left, John Wilson, Cardie Eggers, Charlie Sutherland, and daughter Joyce (courtesy of Charlotte Stanley).

I was going to tell about the ducks. We came from Grandmother Shull's and I had five little ducks. They were the cutest little things. I had the best time playing with them. I'd let them swim under water and get them out and feed them. Joyce loved little chickens and little ducks. We both loved animals and fowls. So, I came in just breathless, I was crying, and Mother said, "What on earth is wrong?" I said, "My little ducks, my little ducks." I was crying so that she went out to see what had happened. Joyce had loved them all to death.

JOYCE: Mother was always trying to find ways of making money and one big way she did was to grow and sell turkeys for market. At that time they would clean the turkeys. They'd either do it before Thanksgiving or before Christmas, and then you could get barrels and put them in. One time they had been killing and dressing the turkeys all day. I think maybe it was two days that they had worked on this, because it was going to be cold and that was a good time.

CHARLOTTE: They did geese, too.

JOYCE: It was a moonlit night and they had hung the dressed animals across like a clothesline and they would get up all different hours of the night to see if they were still there, that no one had stolen them. I can remember that scene today looking out the window and seeing those birds hanging two together across that line. They had to put props under it to hold it up. The next morning they would be frozen and they packed them in barrels and put salt over them. Then they took them to Mountain City on a wagon and shipped them by train up north. That was good money for them. Another thing about that, Mother did this for several years, and one time she was doing it to make money to bring water to the house by pipe. I cannot believe how much they made on the turkeys during that time and the amount that they went up was very, very little considering. After I was married and buying a turkey, I bought one for $5.50. They were raising and selling turkeys for about $5.00.

CHARLOTTE: I'll tell you a story about my grandmother making butter to sell. She took it to the store and the merchant said, "Aunt Mollie, we've had people putting potatoes in our butter and we've found some little stones in there, so we've been cutting the butter open to see if there's anything wrong." She said, "Go right ahead, just cut mine all you want to." This old lady in the store picked up her basket and went out. She didn't want them cutting open her butter.

There at Sutherland, they had everything right there. It was the up and coming place. As the store was sort of like a company store, they had a blacksmith shop, a tanning shop for hides, and they had the Sutherland Post Office. There was a whole row of buildings that they used for business. A cobbler was there and they had just about anything that you wanted at that time. It was right across from where we lived.

JOYCE: If you go up Sutherland bridge, across that, it's the first building that you come to on the left and is about to fall down.

CHARLOTTE: All of the other buildings are gone. The old store is gone, too. After you turn off and cross that bridge, the next bridge you cross, the house on the hill is where our father was reared. There's a little branch that comes down and joins the New River there at that bridge. There's a house there that was John Sutherland's. He was not Daddy's brother, he was a cousin. He's Black Tom's son. So, the house that you can see from right there on the hill is where Joyce and I were reared. It's the first house after you cross the bridge. Uncle Joe lived next in a great big house and Granddaddy's house was next, all in a row. There was a house between Grandfather's house and our house where we were reared and that was where my Uncle Joe lived. All of that belonged to the Sutherland family, all the way up for about two miles.

You want to hear about the Sutherland Methodist Church. I think the Hardins were the ones who took the lead in that and Grandfather helped. It was a big church at that time and if you could go in the church, there are pictures in there that tell. It was 1866, I don't remember the dates, but on the back of these pictures, there's a writeup about it, and they said that at that time this church had been shown in more places around the world than any church. So it's a very old church, but they still keep it going and some of the younger people, my grandson for one, give generously to that church. I asked how in the world they belong to the conference. I thought they were not in the conference any more, but they make their payments and are still in it.

There are few Sutherlands left. Up and down that valley, there's only one family of Sutherlands. The Sunday I went, I think there were about seven present. I played the piano there for 30 years, I guess, and it used to be a big church. We'd have big meetings and dinners on the ground and homecomings and that's the way they got what money they have. In July of this year, it's the 16th, I think, they have the homecoming and then different ones of a generation come and make good donations.

I have a copy of the Sutherland commencement. Daddy said he had an Ashe County girl and a Watauga County girl 'cause I went to school in Ashe County and graduated from high school. Joyce went to Watauga.

We used to have commencement that would last a week. We had declaration contests for the boys and girls. We had a play for the children, some kind of little operetta, and we had a music teacher. We had a play for the junior class, a play for the senior class, and then graduation. We had a lot of people in the school. There was a good enrollment.

JOYCE: Oh, I must tell this. I was always in their hair. See, I was a lot younger than our cousins and Charlotte. They had the best time. There wasn't anybody my age to play with, so I was always around listening. One year I remember that they would have storm parties. They would go from one house to the other. It came Christmas time and I remember them talking and chattering, she and mother, about what they were going to have. They were going to storm us at our house. I remember they were getting things together to eat, good things. I had never seen the maraschino cherries before and I thought they were the prettiest things. I remember having fresh celery, oh, that was the ultimate. After Christmas, you did not have those things. Anyway, they were going to have a big party and they put cornmeal on the floor to dance. It made the floor slick. They wanted to get rid of little sister. I remember Mother saying, "It's time for you to go to bed." I would go upstairs but I would not go to sleep. My eyes were big as moons, I guess.

CHARLOTTE: Jim looked up one time and saw her red hair hanging over the stair rail.

JOYCE: The boys were lined up against the wall along where the steps go. I didn't like it, I guess, because I wasn't getting any attention. I just reached down and got hold of this boy's hair and pulled it. Somebody looked over and I had to live with that for a long time.

CHARLOTTE: We had the first Victrola in the community and that was quite a thing. They would put the records on and then Daddy would see how far he could go and still hear the music playing, as if you would want it that loud. Everybody would come in and hear the Victrola. Then Mother and Daddy were real good as host and hostess for the young people. They would move the furniture all around and they'd have dances, square dances, something like that. I was barely big enough. I was about 10, I guess. A crowd would come and they'd play the Victrola and then we would dance. Mother and Daddy were always helping the young people out by going places and chaperoning.

JOYCE: They did have a really good time. When I got that age the valley was empty.

CHARLOTTE: When they took the school away, after that the community all just slipped out. I finished high school in Jefferson. I first went to Davenport College. The president came to our house and talked to Mother and Daddy. Mother wanted me to go to a girls' school. They sent me to Lenoir and I remember Daddy taking me down there. We just had a little old roadster and Joyce had to sit on mother's lap all the way to Lenoir. I had my clothes in a trunk and we started down the hill and I was driving then. I had on high-heeled shoes. Daddy saw somebody going down and he said he'd just ride with him and leave me to drive. I'd never been to Lenoir and going around those curves scared me to death. I was driving and after they'd gone two or three miles, he realized what he had done. He waited until we came on so he could drive. He said he shouldn't have left us there because I didn't know how to drive and I couldn't drive with those shoes on.

JOYCE: You had to put water in the car every three miles. I remember that water spout out there and there were two or three along the road there going down the mountain and we'd stop at every one and fill up the car.

CHARLOTTE: I remember we had an old Plymouth that wouldn't start and finally Mother had to push it. She came on the bus to see us when we lived in Englehard and the bus stopped and all the people got out to push the bus. She said, "I have pushed a car all winter and I'm not getting out to push the bus."

Jim was an educator. There was only one person who had his master's degree in Ashe County at that time, Troy Jones. Jim got his master's at Carolina. It was really something to get your master's degree in 1940.

I started teaching in 1939 at Sutherland. The school had gone down; there were only two teachers. I taught the first, second, and third grade. Then I got to be the principal of the school and taught sixth and seventh.

JOYCE: The real reason that she taught, she was in school at Davenport, and I remember this very well 'cause it was the Depression. I remember Daddy going through the hallway crying one night. I slipped upstairs and Mother was saying, "Oh, honey, we'll make it some way." He said, "But Charlotte won't be able to finish her schooling." And so she didn't [at that time but did later].

CHARLOTTE: I want to tell you about my first day of teaching at Sutherland. I came in and Mother and Daddy were sitting in the swing and Mother had her old guitar out. Daddy had a banjo. They were sitting there and when I came around they started laughing and playing

Charlie Clinton Sutherland, father of Charlotte and Joyce, April, 1967 (courtesy of Charlotte Stanley).

the guitar and the banjo and carrying on. They said, "We've made it now you have a job and you are making some money. We never thought we'd make it, but we've made it through." I remember saying to Daddy, I knew times were hard, and I said, "I don't want you to take all your money to send me to school." He said, "Honey, if it takes the finest steer on this place, I'll sell it and you are going to school." He always trusted me. He gave me a checkbook. Aunt Minnie said, "What did you give that child a checkbook for? Don't you know she'll break you up?" He said, "No, she won't." So he gave me a checkbook. When I really needed anything, I would make a check for it. I didn't spend any money that I didn't have to.

JOYCE: Another thing that happened during that Depression that was impressive and it's important, too. Things got so bad, and on the farm we had food but we had no money. I remember there was a man in another community, but Mother knew about it. She had been appointed to have whatever the government gave, which was corn meal and oil and maybe some flour and rice. They brought the food to Mother for the very needy and she dished it out to them. We were sitting on the front porch, just she and I one afternoon, and Mother looked around and she said, "Oh, my goodness, I am glad to see that man coming. He's coming here, I know. Honey, he has his leg off and that's his little boy." They had one buggy that was horse drawn. They came up there and she met him and she said, "I've been looking for you to come." He started crying he was so hungry. Mother went in and built a fire in the stove and cooked supper and they ate and she gave him what was his portion of whatever they had.

JOYCE: At Granddaddy's house they had a big fireplace and the pulls that held the pots. I think that mother did most of her cooking on the fire. I don't know about breakfast. I cannot remember a stove there at that time.

CHARLOTTE: We've always had a stove. They had a stove at the little house.

JOYCE: I remember the pots of cabbage and beans and cornbread that Mother would make on that fire and it was so good.

My husband, Bob, was from this county [Watauga] and he was the oldest of 11 children. He and one brother are deceased. We used to talk about it, because this side of the mountain where he was reared on Highway 194, those people all were interested in literature and history. On our side, we were interested in farming. They were literary. I was very surprised at the people who were so intelligent down in that section. They really were.

CHARLOTTE: One story that they always told was how the Tennessee line comes up. You come up through Sutherland and there's this little piece that juts out. They said the reason it was like that, our grandfather owned the land up to that line and owned that land around there and he didn't want to own any land in Watauga County. So they drew the map so his line would always be in Ashe County. I said, "It wasn't very smart because the Watauga land was worth more than Ashe County." Now Ashe County land is really coming to the front and people are developing it over there.

JOYCE: My husband, Bob Davis, was in service for four years. He was the service manager with Chevrolet for 20 years and then he taught 20 years at Watauga High.

CHARLOTTE: I have one daughter and one son. My daughter married Michael Latta. Then he went to Duke and got his doctor's degree in education. He taught and then he worked for the state and they are both retired. She taught library science. She got her degree at Appalachian State University and she got her master's at Carolina.

JOYCE: I have one daughter, Cathy, and she married an Italian and lived in South America. I think they were there 12 years. Then it didn't work out. She has her three children and she has built a house next to me.

CHARLOTTE: I'll be 90 on my birthday in March.

JOYCE: I'll be 80. We're 10 years apart.

CHARLOTTE: I've been doing most of the work on my flower garden. About a month ago, it was absolutely beautiful. The lupine was in bloom. My husband was the flower man. He would have at least seven baskets across the patio every year. He loved potted plants.

IRENE MORPHEW, 89

November 7, 2000

At her home in Jefferson. Her sister-in-law, Iris Morphew,
whose husband was Paul Morphew, is present.

I was born September 8, 1911. One of my first memories that comes to mind right now is that it was about 1918. I remember my folks seemed so concerned about World War I. I said to them, "Is it as close as Conley Greene's?," which was approximately a mile away. I must have been about seven years old then.

This brings to mind, too, in approximately 1918, we had a real cold winter, sub-zero, I guess, and I can remember walking on the ice across the river to school. My brother, who was about six years older than I, took an axe and cut through the river and through the ice and it was way thick. The way I recall it, people would even go on wagons or anything they needed to do, to go to the mill or something, they could go on the river. It was a real cold winter, and the river was really frozen over.

At that time we lived at what we called Riverside, N.C., which was not quite a mile below Brownwood. Riverside was our post office. The Tatums lived across the river. I guess Mrs. Tatum was the postmistress. That's in Ashe County. It was quite a ways down below Todd.

The Norfolk and Western train still came up there to Todd. It did for years, but later it was taken off to West Jefferson and later was taken off completely. When they were building the railroad, they had convicts that were working on the railroad. My two older brothers would play and they got hold of a root and were imitating them getting after the convicts with this root. It turned out to be poison ivy and their eyes swelled shut. This was before my time, but I've heard of it over and over. Mother and Dad had to feed them.

Once there was some kind of a severe storm that washed out a trestle.

Ruth Mae Goodman Morphew and her children: Irene Isabel ("Dolly") on her mother's lap and brothers, left to right: Howard, John, and Glenn, about 1914 (courtesy of Irene Morphew).

I've often wondered since how they did it, but the neighbors across the river managed to flag down the train. Of course, if they hadn't flagged it down, it would have been disastrous.

Glenn Morphew was my older brother and Howard was the next one, then John was two years older than I, and William was about three years younger than I. Paul was not born until we came to live near West Jefferson. There were five boys and one girl.

One time, I guess when John was the baby, my mother climbed a tree on the river bank and was picking Balm of Gilead buds to sell. The baby crawled into the river. She jumped out of that tree to get him and apparently she didn't get hurt.

I want to show you a picture of the home and particularly the meadow. It is still there. All but the house and 13 acres, I think, has been sold into a development. Up on the ridge beyond the beginning of that picture, you can look down on the bend of the river in Brownwood. It's a beautiful view. The reason I'm showing you this, I think the flood was probably 1916, and I can remember very vividly that the river was up so much. I would say it was approximately half way up through that meadow. It was a pretty big meadow and I can remember us sitting on the front porch watching. We didn't think it was going to get to our house, but we were very concerned. Big houses went down that river, I don't know how many, but several. One or two were store houses and it was really awesome to see that and to see those houses float down that river.

I can remember Grandmother Morphew, Mrs. Silas Morphew or Louisa Morphew; I can remember her sitting on the porch. I can just barely remember, because I don't know when she died. She was smoking a pipe. That's uncommon now, to see an old woman smoking a pipe. I think that my dad had this house built. Silas Morphew's house where Dad lived when he was a young man was way down in the lower meadow, much closer to the river. That house or any signs of it are all gone. It was after he married Mother that he had that house built. My father's name was James MacDonald Morphew and my mother was Ruth Goodman Morphew.

I don't know nationwide what the situation was, but I knew nothing of cars at that time. So far as I know, I had never heard of an automobile. I think that when we moved to Watauga, which is still on the New River, we probably rode the train up to Brownwood although it was very short. I remember some of the neighbors gave me a little decorated coin purse and I was so proud of that. I thought we rode the train, but then we went in a wagon. We moved in a wagon to I guess you would call it Laurel Springs, which is probably about eight miles below Boone.

My brother John and I were in school, I think it was where the Liberty Grove Church is, near Riverside, and the school was there, too. A thunder storm came up and we ran but we were really drowned rats when we got home. Our parents were just scared to death about us. I can't remember riding in a wagon any, going to church or anywhere like that then. We walked everywhere. I don't know how many miles it was to school, but it was at least one mile and it might have been more.

Dad had a wagon built for my three older brothers, and it was not just any little play wagon. They could haul almost anything on it. It was a great big wagon, but still a play wagon. I think they just had to pull it, but it was really a pretty large wagon and they could do some work with it.

I can remember after Christmas was over, I'd feel so let down. We didn't get much, but after Christmas was over, I'd think, oh, well, there's Easter coming. At Easter Mother would color eggs, and to me those were the most beautifully colored eggs. I don't think they had dyes back then, so I don't know how she managed. I would look forward to Easter. One year the old fairy rabbit was supposed to leave a big nest of colored eggs, and we couldn't find it. We were supposed to hunt it and find it. Away down in that meadow about two-thirds down there was a hole

Irene Morphew, age 10 (courtesy of Irene Morphew).

where they used to put some trash in. That's where it was. They said Mother had to give us a tip about it.

Uncle Arthur Morphew, my dad's brother, came over on the train from Robbinsville, N.C., and he caught the typhoid fever. Now, that would be unheard of. When he came to our house, he was down some time with the typhoid fever. Mother had such a time. She had to scald everything and it was just terrible how hard it made it. I think that was supposed to have been right before I was born. He lived, but he went back and one of the other children took the typhoid and didn't survive. To me, it's kind of interesting that we had no hospitals. Apparently, the closest hospital was Bristol, Tennessee. One of our neighbors, Cecil Miller, took appendicitis, and they loaded him on the train to send him to Bristol. It's just unbelievable the difference in this day and age and back then.

Times were so different. There probably was a hotel in West Jefferson, I'm not sure, but up in that area there was no place to stay. My dad was part owner in a union store. That meant he had at least one if not more partners. It was probably about a mile or two miles away, he ran the union store. Of course, people stopped there when they came through. A U. S. Senator, Senator Simmons, came through the country and Dad brought him home to spend the night, I suppose because it would have been hard for him to get anywhere where he could get lodging. Mother would tell that I was always afraid of people when I was a baby. She said she put me on a nice dress. She sat me down on Dad's lap and said, "Now, Jim, this is one time you're going to baby-sit, you're going to take care of this child while I cook." She said Mrs. Simmons had on a white dress and I sat there just charmed.

When the following Christmas came there were presents from Senator and Mrs. Simmons. I remember mine. It was a doll with a white, knitted suit, and it had those little jingle bells all over it. I had it for a long, long time.

I can remember fishing at Riverside where I was born. They wouldn't let me fish except with a bent pin. All I could catch was minnows. We had no ice back then, but we had a real cold spring and springhouse and it was not right in the house. Of course, we had running water. It was real cold, that water was. That's how they kept the milk and everything cold.

Then we moved by wagon to Watauga County and our post office was Rutherwood, N.C.. That was where my grandfather, Silas Morphew, was postmaster. When the Civil War was over he was disfranchised, because he was postmaster during the Civil War. Our house was not quite a mile from the Laurel Springs Church; that's the only big church you see after you get to Deep Gap. It was maybe a mile down below that right on the river.

The river bottom meadow, I heard somehow through the family, that that river bottom there was as rich as any garden that you would find. It was just real rich. That's where my brother John, the brother next to me, and I were when it came a real hard rain. The river backed up into the creek. I don't know how come he did this, but I was with him and helped him. He had a fishing pole for me and one for himself and we caught about a dish-pan full of fish. I think they called them horneyheads. One wouldn't much more than pull a fish out till another one would jiggle. I suppose we ate them, I don't know.

When my brother William was five years old he took sick, and Mother kept him home from church on Friday night. He had to go to the toilet a lot, so she kept him home. On Saturday he was worse. My brother rode on a horse back to Ashe County to get a doctor, and he had no luck on Saturday. On Sunday he went to Boone and he got back sometime in the afternoon, maybe two o'clock, but it was too late, my brother was dying. They suspected something was wrong with his kidneys.

There was a ford in the river where you could go across with a wagon.

I don't remember going across there, but on up the meadow was a place that must have been more shallow. John and I were trying to stilt across the river and go over in the woods about a fourth of mile or less to the mailbox. I suppose my father made the stilts. We got wet and we didn't want to tell our parents. There was a new highway being built they called the Boone Trail. So we went over on the Boone Trail and loafed and played until we got dry. The only time back then that I ever remember a car, there was some family came in with an automobile. I'm pretty sure they had a colored chauffeur. They came by, and that's the first time I had ever seen a car. It would probably have been 1919, because my brother died in 1919.

Dad had a new house built, I presume on the same property. It was in the woods. We must not have lived there long. I remember one thing particularly. The woods caught on fire. Of course, that was before fire departments. The neighbors really rallied and came to help us. I'm pretty sure there must have been a creek as well as the spring. The spring was several yards from the house. I'm pretty sure it was a woodshed. They poured water on the woodshed and kept it just as wet as they could and backfired on the woods and that saved our house.

My brothers would trap for rabbits. They had what they called the rabbit gums. I don't know how they worked, but they triggered somehow. I know they'd go pretty often and check their rabbit gums. I think they were in kind of a pine grove. I don't think we sold the fur, but I'm pretty sure we ate the rabbits.

I was postmaster here [in Jefferson] a long time, so that ran in my family. When I was at the dedication of the post office at Boone [it was mentioned on the program that] Marion F. Morphew was the first postmaster at Boone. It would have been my Uncle Frank.

My dad was 18 years older than my mother and some of the first years we were in Jefferson, I would visit this Mrs. Logan and she was telling me about my two uncles. So far as I know, my dad had never mentioned them. Uncle Ellis Morphew and Uncle John Morphew were lawyers in Jefferson, but they both passed away before they were 30 years old. Strange to say, Dad just hadn't talked about it. Uncle Arthur was a lawyer and Uncle Frank was a doctor. I think Uncle Frank lived at Marion, N.C. His folks lived over about Bristol. I think it was Uncle Arthur went somewhere in Maryland and studied law some.

I was postmaster for 38 years, but it seems like a dream now. I retired in 1972. Dad had the farm at Beaver Creek and then he came here and had this house. The Morphew house nearby burned November 15 of last year. He had this house built, so the way that it seemed to be handed down was so he could send the boys to school. He didn't send me off to school anywhere. Glenn, the oldest one, stayed in a dormitory and boarded here. The

Irene Morphew at her home on November 7, 2000.

Jefferson School was first a Methodist school. Mr. Bill Scott was once head of it. He was a minister. I know he would come back and they even visited us some.

Uncle Jim Goodman was superintendent of schools here in Ashe County at one time. Uncle Charlie Goodman and he were both teachers in the county and I think Uncle Hayden taught some.

My dad bought a store here in Jefferson and he had right much land. His store was a general store, but it is no longer in existence. It was next to the courthouse. People would come there to court and there were no motels in town. There was the Mountain Inn. I think we ate there one time when we came to Jefferson. A lot of the people came to that store and they would eat sardines or cheese and crackers and whatever he had in the store. A lot of people ate there. I know a lot of times he would bring some of the former neighbors up to our house for lunch because they enjoyed seeing their neighbors back then. He built a big white house right next door [to my house here].

The schools back then were country schools and they were from the primer to the seventh grade, one teacher. When I first started to school I could say the primer by heart. Of course, the teacher didn't have much time to pay attention to each student. Mother was concerned. She'd say, "What does c-a-t spell?" I'd say "dog" or something like that. She took me out of school and put me in the blue back spelling book, which had pronunciation. I think I still have it here somewhere. The teacher said, "You don't need to worry about her," because I could say the whole primer. I could say it by heart, but I couldn't read a word. I believe the teacher's name was Keller, the one that said that.

At Beaver Creek, I can remember walking through pretty deep snow to school. That 1918 winter must have been a terrible winter. Now, 1960 that terrible storm was here. I waded through snow almost waist deep for a short distance then to the post office. When that 1960 snow came I moved out and I lived with a cousin of ours that was just a short distance from the post office. My mother had passed away in September. They scraped the highway to the jail. I went through it and it was almost waist deep. One day when it had drifted so terribly, one mail carrier got in about four o'clock and I think that was the day I sold less than a dollar's worth of stamps. They called in the National Guard.

At present these are not normal times [for the river]. The river is terribly low now. They say that you can just walk across it and not get much wet at all. It's been so dry.

Essentially my father didn't do a lot of farming on the river, but he knew that there were very rich places there. I think he had corn and stuff like that. Father didn't do the work, my brothers did. This was when I was a baby. They left me with Grandmother Morphew and the barn was pretty far from the house. Once when they left me with her I crawled about half way to the barn.

My parents both lived to be 77 and my brother lived to be 77. We went to see my great-uncle and his son, who lived a fourth of a mile from the house where the woods burned. That's close to 421 now. The house still stands. It has several gables on it. My uncle, Riley Greer, grandmother's brother, came in from hoeing corn and he was 99 years old and he lived to be 102. He'd been doing that all his life and didn't quit for old age. They worked hard back then.

Nellie Mae Edmisten, 87

March 14, 2000

At her home on the east side of Boone.
Her oldest son David is present.
(David died on August 6, 2000.)
Mrs. Edmisten is the widow of Walter Edmisten.

I'm 87 years old. I'll be 88 the 18th of April. I was born April 18, 1912.

I went to school down on the river. I've forgotten what the name of the school was—New River Academy, I think it was. Mrs. Sally Ray taught me. All of us kids went. I know along the way my brother, the third one, he didn't like to go to school. He didn't get much of an education. He'd stop and fish till we came back and he'd join us and come back home.

I was a Hollars before I married. Lige and Ethel Hollars were my parents. I lived near here, where I'm living now. All Walter, my husband, had to do was go across the river and go to my house to do his courting. We met at the church, Three Forks Baptist Church. From then on he courted me. We got married when I was 17 years old. How we met down at the church, him and his mother was sitting behind us and he was a-picking at me. You know, we wore hats a long time ago with streamers on the back of them and he pulled that hat off. I turned around and smacked him in the face. That didn't stop him; he kept coming. My mother got onto me for not paying more attention to the sermon. I guess he got punished when he got home.

My husband Walter died on February 21, 1995. Over his lifetime, he was a farmer, a professional meat cutter, rural mail carrier, for 32 years a state wildlife officer, and a member of the Watauga County School Board. We were married for 66 years. He was a good husband and father.

Going back, I joined the church down there when I was 12 years old. The whole family joined. I was baptized in the New River. We used to go to church at Brushy Fork Baptist Church before we moved over here. We lived on Brushy Fork, the Hollars family did. So I was baptized down there in the river when I was 12 years old. It was cold. The river is cold till it gets real hot in the summer. From then on we went to church. Every Sunday we'd go; we was faithful. Of course, we met friends up and down the river in that vicinity.

Boone was a center of trade that we came to then. It was the only place we had to come to.

I had to help my mother in the house all she could get me to help. I wanted to be out after the cattle and horses and on the farm. I'd rather be with the cattle and outside than to help in the house. Of course, I had to go in when she said so. I helped my mother in the kitchen and with the washing and ironing and house cleaning. We had to iron then, iron everything that we wore nearly. We didn't have electricity then. We had to heat the flatirons on the cook stove.

Nellie Mae Hollars, age 16 (courtesy Nellie Mae Edmisten).

We had a wood stove that we cooked on. I learned to cook pretty well before I got married. We had running water in the house. It came from a spring pumped in the house. It was gravity flow.

DAVID: As a matter of fact, the spring was located some 300–400 yards away, a tremendous distance away, all the way across a traveled road. It was high on a mountain, and it came under that road and into the house. We had a big spring race where the milk and the butter and all that kind of stuff was kept. The springhouse was attached to the main house. We entered from the kitchen of the main house and that's where we churned and kept the butter and made homemade mayonnaise.

NELLIE: My mother done her own churning and we had our own butter. But we graduated from that and went to an icebox. We bought ice and had an icebox in the house. That didn't keep the milk cool enough for my daddy and we went over to the old spring and took our night's milk over there to have to drink. I took it over there and went after it a lot of times. We kept it in a metal bucket that had a lid to it. We had crocks that set in the spring race. The churns could be either wood or crockery. My mother's

Nellie Mae Hollars at Grandfather Mountain before her marriage (courtesy of Nellie Mae Edmisten).

was wood. It was an up and down churn. I had one of those that turned over and this is what happened one time. We had the butter about done and ready to take out and David came along and he thought he'd churn some. He unhooked it and the lid was off and it just went all over the place, all over the wall, ceiling, and everywhere. The old churn is sitting on the front porch yet with flowers in it. I had the wooden churn, but I've got my old dasher out there hanging up, but the wood part came apart.

I had one sister and three brothers. My daddy was a farmer and he bought and sold cattle, too. He ran a slaughter pen over there for years. In Boone, there was the City Meat Market. He owned that. Then he sold out and went out of business.

If one of us got sick, the doctor would come around to our house. One of them was Dr. H. B. Perry. Our children were born at home. The doctor would come to the house. My husband Walter's mother was a midwife. She went all around through the country tending to ladies that was having babies. She delivered about all of Hill Bumgarner's children. I think they lived way up here on the bottom of Rich Mountain or Howard's Knob, one of those places.

I went to the New River Academy. It was down there right about where Brown's used car place is. After that, I went to high school in Boone. My husband was three years older than me. When I married, we lived right up above here in an old house. It was a log house then. We lived there for a while, lived with his folks. His father said, "Two families can't live together in one house. I'm going to buy them a place to live, give them a place." So they gave us the place out in Perkinsville. The house is still there but I don't know who lives there now. It's behind the Wilco service station.

DAVID: As a matter of fact, the property that the Wilco service station owns was part of the property that belonged to that house.

NELLIE: In the meantime, Walter's daddy died, and his mother got a lady to stay with her in the wintertime. We moved out like a bunch of gypsies to that house for the summer. We moved out of there in the winter so our children could go to school. They'd catch a bus out there. Then we'd come back down here of a summer to farm and live down here. So we went back and forth like that for several years. We decided to sell that house out there and build one down here, and this is the one we built. David was in his teens by then. The house is still on the original property. He bought out all the other children's share on out through here to the river.

At flood time on my parents' farm, we were not affected very much. We were right much up the hill on a kind of high knoll. There are all those trailers over there now. We owned all that where the trailer park is now. Then they built Raven's Ridge up on the mountain; we owned that, too. All of that was the Hollars property when I was growing up and over on the other side of the road, too. I don't know how many acres there were, probably 120 or so.

DAVID: It was bounded on one side by the river. Now the properties here and there did not exactly abut the river at the same place. There was another farm sort of in between where the water plant is now for the Town of Boone. That farm there was in between this farm and theirs, but the river was a common boundary.

NELLIE: There was a little creek that went down through there called Mutton Creek. When the flood of 1940 came it didn't get to our house. It was up high, but there used to be an old bridge down there and it took it out, down between the new bridge and where the old church used to stand. The abutment to the bridge is still there. It's where you go across to the dog pound over here. The old abutment would have been between the current bridge and there. They didn't used to have that low water bridge there; there wasn't anything over there. We crossed the river in a canoe. Anywhere between here and that bridge, you crossed the river either in a rowboat or a canoe.

You know where the old Three Forks Baptist Church was. It was right beside the river down there, right down this road. We went there a little bit to the old church before the other one was built. When the other one was built we went over there. I don't know how many years it was before that was built. It wasn't too many because I don't remember going to that old place very much.

DAVID: What was the relationship between you and John and Jones and Craig and Margaret as you were growing up? Tell us something about that.

NELLIE: Well, we done things together and played together. There wasn't much to do back that day and time. We played checkers in the winter time. We didn't know nothing about skiing. We rode on what they called sleds back then. We rode down off the mountains on a sled. They made them first, old wooden sleds. They didn't have nothing on them to guide them, no steel runners either. We played ball. Mostly though we were in the fields and the garden. We didn't have much time to play ball; we were working. Our social life was mostly at the church. Our school didn't have any parties back then, or I don't remember it if they did. We studied there about all the time. We had some kind of old wooden desks. One would have a back to it and the seat had the desk part to the one behind. That's how it was.

I was the oldest one in my family, so I had a lot to do back then. I helped with the younger ones. David here, he had to help with the younger ones when they came along in my family.

We grew on the farm most of what we ate. Our major crops were corn and beans and potatoes, just all kinds of vegetables, potatoes mostly. Then we grew buckwheat. We had that ground and had buckwheat flour. We took it over to Winebarger's mill to be ground. It's been there many a year.

DAVID: Back when I was growing up, and it might have transpired into that, he [my father] had more livestock than he had actual vegetable farming. Was this the case then, or did this transform into that later?

NELLIE: It was into that later. We had a big potato patch, I know that. We didn't have any extra to sell. Mostly, the family ate what we grew. We'd save some for seed for another year.

DAVID: When I was young and going over there on my grandparents' farm, they raised cattle and sheep and that perhaps is the way that the creek got its name, Mutton Creek, because he grew so many sheep.

NELLIE: It was mostly cattle, though. I remember my mother helping shear the sheep and she'd use some of the wool, but not all of it, for the padding of quilts. They'd sell some wool. She'd make thread for knitting. She had cards and my aunt had one of these spinning wheels. I think it was a big one. They'd make thread for knitting. My mother sewed our clothes. She was a real good seamstress. We would get the cloth from a store. She made the boys' clothes as well as the girls'. She even made the pants for them. She'd sit up of a night and get up early. She was one of these people that was wanting to do something all of the time. She couldn't sleep for thinking about what she's going to do the next day. She wanted to be busy all the time. I

Winebarger's Mill still stands just off Meat Camp Road in Watauga County. Built in 1840, it is still operated occasionally by the fourth generation of Winebargers, though it is now powered by a tractor instead of the water wheel.

used to be one like that and I wore myself out. I've had one of my shoulders done and I need the other one. They're just worn out, I think. I guess it is arthritis.

I've been busy here this morning. I had some apples I had cooked and they needed to be worked up and I decided I'd make some pies out of them. I've made a lot of that stuff all my life. My children come back here to do their canning and freezing. I've got a good place downstairs to work. I give advice on how to do it.

DAVID: What did your dad think when you and my dad got married?

NELLIE: Well, Walter asked for me. But my dad didn't approve of it, thought I was too young. But we got married anyway, without his approval. No, we didn't elope. We got married at Blowing Rock Road by Rev. Bob Shores. He's not living now. It's been a long time. He was a minister. We didn't go on a honeymoon. We came back and got to work. We lived with his family for a while until his daddy decided we needed a place of our own. We have six children. First, David was born. There was just 17 months between David and Paul. He was born the next year on September 10. Then Joe. It was a little longer between them two. Then Betty, then Rufus, and

Baker. Baker's the baby. I think they've all done well. We always taught them to work and then tried to help them with an education all we could. Of course, we couldn't help the first ones. We didn't have enough to help them with. Rufus is a lawyer. Betty, she's a garage woman. She's a-working up in the garage. She helped Dick [her husband, Dick Church]. She's in there now after he passed away. Prior to that though she taught out at Hardin Park Elementary School. Now she's the administrator of the garage. She's got some retirement and social security.

DAVID: There's three of us graduated from ASU [Appalachian State University]. I did, and Paul did, and Baker did. Now I am a Trustee of ASU. Joe got his undergraduate degree up here, so that's four of us. Then he got his doctorate from the University of Florida. Rufus graduated from Carolina [UNC] but he got his law degree at George Washington University up in D.C. [Rufus has served as Attorney General and Secretary of State for the State of North Carolina.] Baker is U. S. Marshal for the western district of North Carolina.

NELLIE: Yes, I am proud of all my children. Paul is retired from Philip Morris. He is down there in Concord. I have 18 grandchildren and 20 great-grandchildren. They don't all come to visit at once, but this is a big house. There's plenty of rooms down here.

DAVID: We've had as many as 20 people here at one time, quite often.

NELLIE: David's got six grandchildren. He has two daughters. His son passed away when he was 19. He was in a wreck.

It was good land down there along the river bottom on my parents' farm. I know we grew a lot of corn down there. I remember hoeing in the corn field. Yes, I remember the river flooding.

DAVID: As the river would flood and bring the land from upstream, it would really deposit the topsoil on their land and would make it better land than it was before. It's sort of like the Mississippi Delta. What little it would flood over into their land, the current was not swift so it would deposit.

NELLIE: The biggest part of our property was flat. It was two fields down here.

DAVID: There wasn't over 12–15 acres actually on the river.

NELLIE: Out there where all those houses are now, those business places, is one of them. Another one is down here where that rock crusher is, out that way where all that mess is, that was all in the flatland.

They always said my folks came from Holland. I was Dutch. Walter's folks said they were English.

DAVID: I've always heard that the Edmistens were a mixture of Scotch-Irish and Norwegian.

NELLIE: As to changes that have taken place since I was growing up, yes, I've seen a lot of them. Television, transportation are two of them. When I was growing up, my dad had about one of the first Ford cars that were put out. We had the first telephone over on Brushy Fork, one of these kind that you have a phone and you ring up somebody. Everybody could listen to one another. I was just a young child then. I was young and I remembered all that. Isn't that something, I can remember back then and now I can't remember things.

We didn't have electricity up there when I married in the family. My mother and daddy had it and I moved out of a house that had all that stuff.

Walter and Nellie Mae Edmisten at their first house (log house covered with siding for warmth), in the 1930's (courtesy of Nellie Mae Edmisten).

We had outside toilets up there, his mother and daddy did. We had to carry water from a spring. After we were married awhile, he worked on the old house and put electricity in and put water in the house and put a bathroom in, and made the house warmer, put siding on the house.

That house burned down when Joe and Margaret lived in it. They were gone that night.

DAVID: It was a log structure, the basic house was, with a basic structure, an upstairs and downstairs. I guess the logs were that thick, but the chinking had, over the years, sort of eroded. They put siding on it.

NELLIE: It had been storming and they think the electric storm caught it on fire. The wiring was bad in it. That first electricity we had was the New River Light and Power, the one the college started.

DAVID: As a matter of fact, the old original dam was just upriver right over here. My grandfather helped build it with horses and a slip pan. It had a couple of handles behind it and you'd tilt it up and let the horse dig in it, with a mighty strong man behind it. It was scooping up dirt so that you'd put it into the dam structure.

NELLIE: I am now 87 years old. I think I would retire to some degree. I enjoy reading, watching some television, going to church when I can, visiting on the telephone, and sending cards and letters once in a while. Of course, I am looking forward to visits from my children, grandchildren, and great-grandchildren. I don't know whether I will make another garden or not, but if I keep my health, I bet I will.

DEAN COLVARD, 86

February 5, 2000

Interviewed by Annabel Colvard Hunter Harrill
at his home in Charlotte.

My father and mother developed the farm where I grew up by putting together some property that my mother's father, John C. Shepherd, had given her and some property that my father sold in Wilkes County. The new Ashe County farm had two log houses on it and my parents moved into the better one of those houses. My oldest sister, Ruby, was born in this log house. By the time I came along, they had sawed timber from the property and built a new house. I was born in the new two-story house.

I did all my growing up there until I graduated in 1930 from Virginia-Carolina High School located astride the North Carolina/Virginia state line at Grassy Creek. About one mile south of the Virginia line on old Highway 16 is an intersection of a state road numbered 1551. That road extends for two miles to Weaver's Ford and New River. Our farm was about one mile from the river on #1551.

Between our house and the river were the New River Baptist Church and the Brown Corn Mill where we had our corn ground into meal for home consumption. The mill was located between the church and the river. We frequently rode a horse to the mill with shelled corn in a long cotton bag draped across the saddle either in front of or behind us. The hammer mill was driven by a water-cooled gasoline engine. The miller measured out a portion of the shelled corn as his payment for the grinding. Just below the mill toward the river was a road leading to the New River Church cemetery where both of my parents were buried.

At Weaver's Ford there were two stores. One was owned by Mrs. Debord and contained a small store and the Weaver's Ford Post Office. Nearby on the bank of the river was another store owned by Roby Walker, a nephew of

73

my father. Between the two stores a bridge was built across the river at a later date. This riverside location at Weaver's Ford also served as the place for immersion of the new members of the church. All of the children except me were baptized in the river at that location. For reasons unclear to me at that time I did not respond well to the revival meetings that were held about once a year for conversion of new members. Although I was never a member of that church, I attended Sunday School and monthly church services and frequently attended the revivals which were held about once a year.

New River near Weaver's Ford also provided a location for fishing and swimming. The fish we caught were a mixture of whatever would bite a red worm on a hook. There was not a very good supply of trout. There were crappies and occasional catfish. We didn't know what we caught. We just caught fish. Sometimes they were big enough to fry and sometimes they weren't. We never kept the catfish. There was a swimming hole down the river from the stores and the baptismal site where we could go swimming in the summertime. The bushes were grown up thick enough that we could strip off our clothes and go skinny dip. There was a rock from which we could jump. We didn't do any great diving. Our fishing and swimming had to be worked into our busy program of farming.

Uncle Dollie Brown and Mother's sister, Aunt Lelia, had a home just below the swimming hole overlooking the river, a beautiful view of the river. There was a road parallel to the river. Between the road and the river was a very fertile strip of land next to their barn where they grew excellent crops. That was a part of the property where Mother's father was reared. Aunt Lelia received a tract of that land about equivalent to what Mother received for our farm at a separate location.

The third one of those Shepherd girls that my father was told about when he went prospecting was Aunt Swan. She married a produce dealer, Preston McMillan, who lived in Marion, Virginia. We went to see her in Marion off and on. We sometimes rode the train across the mountain from Troutdale to Marion. I've forgotten what they called the train, but I do remember that it had to back up and go and that some people got out and walked when it would back up.

Troutdale and West Jefferson were the two railroad stations nearest our home. We got our fertilizer and did some marketing at both locations, probably more at Troutdale than at West Jefferson. It was a little bit closer than the North Carolina railroad station which was in West Jefferson. There was good campground over at Volney, Virginia, where we would camp overnight with the wagon and cook our breakfast. We had a feedbox for the horses. We could go on to Troutdale and get a load of fertilizer on the wagon and get back before dark. Our turkeys and livestock were sometimes marketed through the railroad station at Troutdale.

Before we had paved roads across the Blue Ridge Mountains from North Wilkesboro to West Jefferson, the Virginia markets were sometimes more accessible because of the location of Troutdale in the south end of the valley of Virginia. This provided access to Baltimore markets. We sometimes shipped dressed turkeys to Baltimore.

The cattle buyers would ride through the country on their horses. They had good judgment on how much an animal would weigh. They would offer a specific price and if we agreed to sell they would accumulate those animals near their scales and drive them by road to Troutdale where they were put on railroad cars and shipped to markets in Baltimore or elsewhere. I was told that at about this time some people had driven turkeys on the road to the Troutdale railroad station. I never did participate in turkey driving nor did I see others drive a flock of turkeys along a road.

Dean W. Colvard, Chancellor Emeritus, UNC-Charlotte, Charlotte, N.C. (courtesy Dean W. Colvard).

There was a lot of sawmilling of timber in our area. Our home was built from lumber sawed on the property that my mother inherited. We sometimes sold timber just as we sold calves, chickens, and other things. If we had some good logs, we could take them to the sawmill. Usually there was a sawmill somewhere that would buy the logs. Most of the land my father started developing into a farm had been in timber. I can remember working with some other people, both black and white, who helped grub the bushes off the land and get it ready for planting. I can remember cultivating that land the first year when we had all those stumps. That's the farm that my father and mother developed and where I grew up. We had 70 acres.

We had very little machinery. My father was sort of a daring innovator, in a way. He had very little money but he was looking for ways to get machinery to do some of the work rather than to have to do it by hand. I can remember harvesting our grain first with a hand swung cradle, then with a reaper and a binder. We never had a combine during my boyhood. The grain was bound and shocked until it dried and then it was stacked until the thrashing crew showed up. My mother tells the story of the thrashing crew. (See Mary Colvard, p. 84–85.)

My mother told the story of a very severe winter. It was rare for New River to freeze over. Mother spoke about having ice 18 inches thick. That is a lot of ice! There were just a few times when you could go across the river all on the ice. I can remember doing that once or twice down near those stores. They usually had little boats tied up along the river that could be used with hand oars to paddle to the other side. In some places small ferry boats provided a way to take a wagon or several people and miscellaneous products across the river on the ferry. They usually charged a fee for this kind of service.

I can remember skating on the frozen river. You had to be pretty careful because it was not frozen uniformly and it did not melt uniformly.

We never owned metal skates. Any skating we did was in our winter shoes. We made sleds to ride on the hillsides, but those were homemade sleds. I never had a steel sled. We made wooden sleds with a lever on the side which could be used as a brake and as a guide to make the sled turn one way or the other. Usually it turned over and we rolled down the hill or on the ice. When the ice began to thaw and float down the river it would sometimes clog in the river bends and the water would behave like putting down a water gate in the Panama Canal. It just shut everything off. It was an exciting time in that isolated area. The water would flow around the ice and over it and back up. When it backed up it created enough pressure that it broke loose and flooded the area below. It did this on its own. Nobody manipulated the dam or water gate.

The river did play a role in agriculture at that time. I mentioned that the bottom land and the meadow land along the river was the most fertile area because erosion had brought the fertile soil out of the woods and from the newly cultivated hillsides. The loamy soil tended to be washed down by the rain and to lodge in flatter areas along the river. That's where the most lasting soil fertility existed.

The two most fertile fields would be either the strip along the river or along a small stream or a new ground that had just been cleared and still retained a lot of organic matter. As the cultivated land on the hillsides began to lose its fertility, we started adding commercial fertilizer. We added it in such limited quantities that it didn't have a big impact. If I were managing the farm where I grew up now, the first thing I would do would be to spend as much money as I could on fertility. The land in Ashe County grows beautiful grass if the fertility is there. Sometimes the addition of limestone is necessary. The Ashe County area was one part of the country that had not always been in forest. There were many hillsides covered with native grass. That is an important characteristic of Ashe County. I do not know the full history of the cultivation of the land, and I'm not absolutely sure that it was never in forest.

When the young men in Ashe County finished high school or attained the age of 18 or 19 years, they usually left the farm to seek employment elsewhere. A few farms were large enough to provide a livelihood for them to stay on the farm. It would not have been possible for the seven children in my family to have subdivided the farm or shared its management and attained an income competitive with other employment opportunities. Most of the young men tended either to go to Detroit to work for the automobile industry, to West Virginia to work in the coal mines, or to Maryland to work on large farms.

When I grew up I wanted to go to college at Virginia Polytechnical Institute (VPI) or to North Carolina State College and become a vocational agriculture teacher. My father did not have the financial resources to support his entire family to go to college. I had my best look at the outside world through my vocational agriculture teachers. They took students to Elkin to see the Klondike Dairy, to Catawba County to see a number of Jersey dairy farms, and to livestock and seed judging contests at various places. I won first place in judging beef cattle at VPI as a high school Future Farmer of America. I saw my first talking movie in Salisbury on one of these trips.

Virginia-Carolina High School was unique in several ways. It had been built by volunteers from Grayson County, Virginia, and Ashe County, North Carolina. It was supported by both states. Virginia supported the lower grades and the vocational agriculture department. North Carolina supported the department of home economics and the high school and a department of auto mechanics. It was a 12-teacher school in a multi-building campus at a time and in an area where the one-teacher schools still existed. When we played baseball the pitcher's box was in Virginia and the home plate in North Carolina.

My older sister took the three years of Latin that were available and I opted for all of the vocational agriculture that was taught. At a later time I regretted not having had the Latin; however, the vocational agriculture teachers gave me my first real view of the outside world and of the options that more education might open up. That was a very significant motivating factor in my intense desire to find a way to go to college. One of the professors of vocational agricultural education, Dr. Walter S. Newman at VPI, whom I came to know from attendance at Future Farmers of America meetings on that campus, later became president of that institution. He was sort of an idol or mentor to me, although my contact with him was very limited. In my mind he was a guiding star. I went to VPI two or three times for the annual Future Farmer meetings. My vocational agriculture teacher, William C. LaRue, was an important mentor.

When I graduated from high school and had no money to go to college I did what other young men in the area had been doing. I decided to go to West Virginia and seek my fortune. A cousin who was working in Welch, West Virginia, as a carpenter took me with him to that small town. He was not in the mines but I rode with him and got a job on a highway construction project. I was too lightweight for most of the jobs they had, but they assigned me as a water carrier. I took a bucket and went up to a sulfur spring and got a bucket of water and brought it back to the workmen who drank it out of a common dipper. I was somewhat shocked to learn that people drank water with such an offensive sulfur odor, as it came right off the vein of coal. I was accustomed to Ashe County fresh spring water. I soon learned that if you're thirsty enough, you'll drink the water that's available.

After working for about two weeks, my cousin was making a trip back to Grassy Creek and I decided to come with him. Another cousin was going to Maryland, so I went with him to seek my fortune on farms in Maryland. I got a job at $45 a month with board and room working on the farm. I was husking corn, picking apples, and doing other chores on a good farm owned by a member of the Maryland legislature. His name was David Garfield Harry and he had a good Jersey cattle dairy farm. But I didn't get a chance to work with his Jersey herd. I was sent to the fields with other assignments. I worked on different farms in that area until near Halloween when my source of transportation was heading back toward home. We spent the night in Winchester, Virginia, on Halloween night on the way home. Things seemed pretty tame because I had been used to seeing wagon wheels that had been hung on telephone poles at Grassy Creek.

My good fortune came when another cousin, Evan Colvard, told me about Berea College where I could major in agriculture and work my way through college. Evan was an uncle of Frank Colvard who now (2000) lives in West Jefferson. I applied immediately.

My application to Berea College was rejected because I did not have a required course in geometry. Although school had started in September, I immediately went out to Virginia-Carolina High School to see if I could enroll for a course in geometry. I went to school one year taking one course to get qualified for admission. I passed that one course and got admitted to Berea at the end of my first year out of high school.

My dad took me to West Jefferson in our Model-T Ford to catch a bus. The bus carried the mail and any passengers that wanted to go to Knoxville through Boone. When we got up to Boone the bus broke down. It took four hours to get it running. I read all of Daniel Boone's signs up and down the street. I had never heard much about him, but I was learning in a hurry.

That delay changed my plans and took some of my money. When we got to Knoxville that night I had missed my connecting bus and had to stay over to catch a bus the next morning. My dad had given me $100. I had to spend some of that $100, probably $1.50, for a room in Knoxville. Then I caught a Greyhound bus the next morning for Berea.

That was 1931. At the Berea bus station some of the seniors were there to meet the incoming freshmen. They took me across the campus and the first thing I saw was the Daniel Boone Hotel and other Daniel Boone markers. I felt as if I was right on his trail. After one day of orientation, I thought we were wasting time. That wasn't what I had come for. So I got a job and went to work before orientation was over at 11 cents an hour in the college creamery.

During my four years at Berea College and two years of employment as a teacher and farm manager at Brevard College in the beautiful valley of the French Broad River, I came home to the New River area as often as I could.

An opportunity for graduate study at the University of Missouri in 1937-38 led me to a master's degree and a job at the Mountain Agricultural Research Station at Swannanoa, North Carolina. My original plan was to pursue a Ph.D. degree in animal physiology at the University of Missouri. After a few months devoted largely to laboratory studies, I concluded that I should seek a job and reexamine the direction of my career.

A very important part of the Missouri experience was the renewed contact with Martha Lampkin, who was working as a medical technologist in Kansas City. We were good friends at Berea College but never dated each other. I declared my interest in keeping in touch with Martha and we were married on July 7, 1939.

Dr. E. J. Coltrane, President of Brevard College, had become a highly respected mentor. He told me about an opportunity for employment as assistant director in charge of the Mountain Agricultural Research Station at Swannanoa, North Carolina. This led to an interview and employment by the recently elected Commissioner of Agriculture, W. Kerr Scott. That job and World War II led me to an important challenge near the north fork of New River in my home county.

Soon after the Pearl Harbor attack by the Japanese, the U. S. Army chose the Mountain Research Station as a site for a 1,500 bed casualty hospital to treat wounded U. S. soldiers from the European military activity. The North Carolina Department of Agriculture and North Carolina State College agreed to vacate this location and find two new sites in different parts of western North Carolina for new research stations. It became an important part of my duty to help find and develop these two new stations.

When I brought the site selection committee to Ashe County we drove down Highway #16 from Glendale Springs along the south fork of New River to the junction of Highway #88 and thence to Transou farm at Laurel Springs.

The committee had a very favorable impression of the river in the mountains and of the 425-acre Transou farm. They recommended unanimously that it be purchased for the upper mountain research station at a price of $56 per acre. They authorized attorney W. B. Austin of Jefferson to handle the transaction. Mr. Austin asked my father, W. P. Colvard, who was then county surveyor, to make a survey of the property lines and the purchase was concluded.

It was my duty as assistant director in charge of the Swannanoa station, which was being dismantled, to manage the relocation process, including the location of another research station in Waynesville. For more than a year I made the trip from Swannanoa or Waynesville to Laurel Springs about once each week.

The development of the Laurel Springs station, about five miles from the south fork of the New River, and my boyhood experiences one mile from the north fork, were enough to give me lasting nostalgic memories of several communities bordering on this beautiful north-bound freshwater river. My successor as assistant director in charge of the Laurel Springs station was James A. Graham, who later served with distinction as North Carolina Commissioner of Agriculture.

The research connection with North Carolina State University led me back to graduate school and a Ph.D. degree from Purdue University and employment as a professor and dean of agriculture at North Carolina State University. The direction of my career had been determined for me.

After serving as president of Mississippi State University and as the first chancellor of the University of North Carolina at Charlotte, I retired in Charlotte with my wife of more than 60 years and returned to New River country as often as I could for vacations and to visit with my cousins, Frank Colvard and Wayne Shepherd of West Jefferson and two daughters of Fred Colvard, Edith Crutcher and Annabel Harrill, who shared their beautiful homes on the former Fred Colvard farm which was bisected by the south fork of New River. The Fred Colvard farm also provided the location for the beautiful golf course and clubhouse designated as Jefferson Landing.

Mary Elizabeth Shepherd (Mrs. W. P.) Colvard

November-December 1972

Some personal observations by Mary Colvard.
Excerpts from an interview recorded
by her son, Dean W. Colvard.

I went to school for the first 10 or 12 years of my life at a little one-room log school building that was called the Brown Schoolhouse. The building was donated by my great, great uncle, Uncle Harrison Brown. It was built on his property. In later years, about the time I was 10 or 12 years old the community got together and hauled in saw logs to a sawmill which was on my father's place at that time and had timber sawed to build a new school house. It was a one-teacher school at that time. It eventually became a two-teacher school and became known as the Fairview Schoolhouse. It was close to Grassy Creek, near the Hurley place up on a mountain, and we walked through the woods about two miles to get there. There must have been about 50 students in this new school, but in the old school I don't guess there were over 25. In later years they added more to the building, and I guess there were around 75 to 100 children by the time I graduated from seventh grade. They went through the seventh grade. I was 16 years old when I finished the seventh grade, but I went back to school after I finished as long as they would teach anything. They kept adding on, getting higher grade teachers and adding on a few more grades like geography and advanced spelling and things like that, so I guess I really finished about the eighth grade.

The year of 1909 was the first time I ever saw your father. His niece brought him to our house. He was looking for a wife. She had told him about the Shepherd girls, and he said he would like to meet them. So his niece brought him to our house to meet the Shepherd girls. He came all the way

The Wiley P. Colvard and Mary E. Shepherd Colvard family in 1949. Left to right, sitting: Audrey, Wiley P., Mary, Carol Wade. Standing: Charles Deward, Ruby, Arleine, Mabel, Dean (courtesy Dean W. Colvard).

over on a horse or in the buggy all the time he was courting me. It took him about half a day to come from Wilkes County over there. He had to travel through some pretty rough weather, on horseback about 50 miles with the temperature around 12 to 14 above zero. I remember one Christmas he came over and he got to his sister's and that night the river [New River] froze over, and he couldn't cross. We lived on the other side of the river, so the next morning he and his nephew, Roby Walker, who was about 18 years old, got out and chopped a channel for the boat and they crossed in the boat and came over for Christmas and left his horse on the other side.

I was married about the time I was 18. We lived at Wilbar, North Carolina, which was in Wilkes County. He had a small farm there when we were married. We lived there several months and then we sold that and moved back to Ashe County, Grassy Creek, where we lived for about 42 years, I guess. We moved into this small log house while we were building this two-story, six-room house. My husband logged the lumber, sawed it, and had a carpenter to build it.

My husband was the magistrate over there, and he married a lot of people. I remember some very exciting weddings that he performed. He met people in the road sometimes who were looking for him, and they were wanting to get married and sometimes they wouldn't even give him time to come home and change his clothes. He married them on horseback and in buggies. I remember a young couple that drove up one Sunday morning in the buggy. We were dressing getting ready to go to church, and they wanted to get married. He said, "Why don't you come on in the house and give us a little time to get ready?" and they said, "No, we don't have time; we want to get married right here in the buggy." So we all walked out and he married them. Your Uncle Harrison and Aunt Sibbie Shepherd were visiting us for the weekend, and we all witnessed the marriage.

He married Wiley Taylor and rented him a house. Wiley stole his girl. She was about 17 years old, and they ran away and one of the neighbors, an elderly couple, hid them in their house till her father passed by. He came to our house because he knew that my husband was a magistrate, and he thought they might be down there, but they hadn't ever gotten to our house. After he went back home they came on to our house and got married and stayed there that night. Her father never did find her, and they left the next day. Later her father thought more of this girl and her husband than he did of anybody in the family. He lived with them until he died and made his home with them. Sometimes people would give my husband a dollar or two for marrying them. He never did charge anything. He just let them give what they wanted to.

He did all sorts of legal work. He was considered a very good magistrate. People came to him for advice and different things all over the county. When they'd get in trouble they'd come to see Squire Colvard to see what he thought about it. He was known as Squire Colvard. Later he got to be county surveyor and worked as county surveyor for a good many years until his health got so bad he couldn't travel around over the county. He was a county commissioner, and he was on the board of education. He was always interested in politics and the building up of the community. He helped build the Virginia-Carolina School where you children, most of you, got your education. He used to go with the children to ball games and kindly chaperone because there were times when it wasn't safe for a group of children to go without some elderly person on the bus with them.

Before buses, we had school wagons for a while. At first children had to walk to school. It was about two and a half miles from where we lived and a lot farther for a number of the other children, so you children rode horseback, two and three to the horse, for several years. Then the community decided they would put a wagon on the route by our place. Jim Garvey and your daddy and several other men went in together and paid Mr. Garvey a small salary to get him to take his team and haul the school children in that section of the community to school. From where Mr. Garvey lived it was about five miles and the roads were very bad and muddy and sometimes the mud was so deep and the roads were so bad that your father would take our team and hitch it in front of Mr. Garvey's team because it took four horses to pull that school wagon with right many children on it.

We had to get up about four o'clock to get our work all done and get your lunches packed and get you off to school in time to walk two miles and a half to school. Lots of times there was big snow and bad weather and sometimes you would spend the night out there with some of our friends. I know especially Dr. Waddell and his wife would take you children in sometimes of a night when it would be a-raining and take care of you over the night and help you with your homework and send you back to school next day.

Dr. Waddell brought most of you into the world, not all of you. We had other doctors in the community when we first moved there. He lived over about Cranberry when we moved over there, but he later moved out there close to the school building and he attended the birth of the last three or four children. Dr. Wagg from Grassy Creek attended the birth of the first of you children.

We used to have a switchboard in our house where we could connect to different lines, and I spent many a night staying on the phone getting Dr. Waddell traced down for somebody that was real sick. He would just go night and day, ride either on his horse or buggy, for years until the cars first came around. All the roads weren't good enough for a car to go on. Sometimes he'd go part of the way in his car and walk in to people's houses. He was a wonderful doctor. He kept different horses, and he always kept men to take care of his horses and take care of his wife. He didn't have any children. He always kept a lot of help around. He was a wonderful man. I guess he did more for the Grassy Creek community and I'd say for Ashe County and part of Alleghany County than any man I can remember.

The switchboard had two telephones hooked up with different lines. We had to have a switch to connect them. We could connect the two lines, but they had to call me to get me to connect them or find the doctor. That was during a terrible flu epidemic when so many people died of flu and pneumonia. I spent many a night, sometimes half the night, tracing Dr. Waddell. He was a very good family friend.

My grandfather, my mother's father, was killed during the Civil War when she was a girl. His name was Houston Hash and they lived at Fox Creek. Her name was Ludema Hash. He was wounded and came home and died during the Civil War. That was hard times. It took people a long time to get over that Civil War.

I can tell you a lot about the threshing crew coming. My husband raised a lot of grain and sometimes about the time the threshing machine would get there it would start raining. They stacked it in big stacks in big rakes kindly and they'd get the grain wet and they'd be there maybe half a week. I remember all those days I cooked for a crowd of threshers. They'd thresh a little while and then they'd break down. They'd get the machine repaired and then it would start raining. A lot of them were a good ways from home, and they couldn't go back home every night so I had those threshers to cook for day and night, to wash for sometimes three or four days at the time; but it wasn't always that way. Sometimes they'd come in and the grain was good and dry and they'd thresh out a couple of hundred bushels of grain in a few hours and go on to the next farm. We raised most of our food, and we'd go to the gardens and bring in corn and potatoes and apples and kill chickens and fry ham. My husband always had a lot of honey. We had bees. We canned fruit, and we always had plenty to eat, plenty of milk and butter. It was kindly a get-together day. The farmers all went in and helped each other thresh and the women helped each other cook and wash dishes.

They pulled the threshing machines with horses and steers. We always had those to take care of and feed. They were always looking for a better pasture, and they would break through the fence and get in the grain fields and corn fields. We had quite a time way back then. People nowadays don't realize what farming people went through way back 50 years ago. Way back I can remember when they had to cradle all the grain by hand. I remember having as many as 10 men in the harvest field to cook for. Later we got the binders. We never did have what they call combines today. The first machine we ever got just cut the grain down. That was a reaper. It had rakes on it. Next we tied it up and dropped the bundles. That was the binder. I guess that was about all we had on the farm, but about the time we left the farm they got the combine.

I used to be able to take the rifle and shoot a snake or a hawk or most anything. I didn't have any trouble killing anything that got in my way if I needed to shoot, but I guess most farm women had to learn to shoot those days. There were a lot of wild animals and things around. I never did do very much shooting, just when it was necessary to kill a weasel that got after my chickens or hawk that caught my baby chickens or something like that.

For years about all the mail we got was carried by horseback. They'd have big mailbags, one on each side across the horse, and they carried those mailbags for miles and miles from one office to the next. Later we got the rural delivery mail.

The Virginia-Carolina High School was a boarding school for a while. They took boarding students for several years before people got cars that they could take their children. It was the only high school in the community when you children were growing up. There were a good many boarding students, and there were a good many children that rode horseback a good long ways out there to school. Many a night we had children in our home that would be stranded by hard rains or deep snows and would come and spend the night because it was far to their own home. All the people were good to take in the students that lived a long way from home.

In the summertime you children went to a subscription school. It was just a little one-room school over near Ed Phipps, our good neighbor. We paid so much to hire a teacher to get our children a few extra months of schooling because our school months were short. We didn't have many months of school because of the shortage of money. During the summer when the children were small a good many of the community people hired a teacher and you paid so much a month for each child.

We had different grocery stores. There was one at Grassy Creek that we traded a lot at, and there was a small grocery store at Weaver's Ford. You children used to go down there and get groceries when we needed little things. We didn't buy much other than coffee and sugar and rice, not like people do today. Of course, we didn't have any electricity back then so we had to have more lamp oil than anything else to keep our lights burning. We had to buy dry goods to make your clothes. I made most all the clothes all you children wore up until you were eight or ten years old. We used to grow turkeys. We'd sell turkeys and order a lot of things from Sears-Roebuck and Montgomery Ward. Your daddy used to load up the wagon with apples and take a load to North Wilkesboro or Marion, Virginia, and later on to Trout-dale, Virginia, and bring back a load of fertilizer and 100 pounds of sugar and a good many yards of muslin to make sheets and pillow cases and a lot of the clothes that you wore.

You used to go down to Mr. Brown's corn mill toward Weaver's Ford. Your daddy always loaded up a wagonload of wheat and took it to the rolling mill. That was over at Wilson, Virginia. There were two rolling mills not too far away, and he'd take a wagonload of wheat, enough to do us all winter. We always had plenty to eat. We didn't go hungry. We had a lot of canned foods and at one time we had the cream separator. We separated our milk and churned the cream and sold the butter. I even shipped butter sometimes. I don't remember us ever selling any milk to the little cheese factory at Grassy Creek, but in later years we sold milk to the cheese factory at West Jefferson.

Your dad was always very much interested in fruits of all kinds. As I remember, he sold Stark trees for a while and he bought a lot for himself and he sold a lot to the community and got a lot of orchards started that way. One time we had the best orchard around there anywhere. We had more fruit than they could do anything with, and there wasn't much market for it.

Your father was very good with figures and he always helped to hold elections and anything that required a lot of mathematics. He was a very good pensman. He helped build the voting house out there where they used to hold elections. It was built by the community. It's still there now. They still vote there. I was up there this fall at Dewey Cox's, and he said they still voted there.

The people have all moved off of that river down there now where it was sold out to the dam company and there aren't many people down there to attend church anymore so that community has gone down a lot in the last ten years.

We had colored people that lived close by that did a lot of our work and our washing and did a lot of the farm work. There was an old family that we thought an awful lot of. His name was Simon McMillan, Uncle Sime and Aunt Hettie. Then there was a family of Andersons that lived close by. Lee Maxwell lived close by. There were right many colored people in that section. We never had any problem in getting help when we needed it, because they were all needy and were willing to work for most anything we had to pay them. Lee Maxwell did some of the clearing of the land around there.

Wiley Arnold did most of the clearing up on our farm. He and his wife Ann did a lot of work for us when we lived on the farm. They were white people, but they had a large family of children.

Your dad got crippled rather badly by a fall from an apple tree and was on crutches for quite a while. The neighbors were good to help out, though, and we got along. One spring when all of our crops were just getting planted everybody in the family came down at one time with the measles. The neighbors came in and cultivated our crops till we got able to do them ourselves.

I remember about some of the floods that we had on the New River when we had ice or other kinds of floods. I saw what they call the ice freshet. That was quite a sight when the ice broke loose after it had been frozen all winter, that cold winter. I believe that must have been about 1918. They measured some of the ice after it broke up and it was 18 inches thick, and when it started going out it was quite a show. The ice clogged up down the bend of the river where it was cold and shady, and it just threw the ice up along the banks as high as a good-sized building.

Carol Wade Colvard Noronowicz, 62

September 8, 1999

By e-mail from her home in Delaware.
Carol grew up near the New River at
Weaver's Ford in the Grassy Creek area.
She is a sister of Dean Colvard.

When I was growing up, the river served as a focal point for recreation — swimming, wading, skipping rocks, fishing, or just strolling down to the river to stand on the bridge, listen to the sounds of the river, and enjoy its beauty, mystery, majesty, and surroundings. The river provided a romantic atmosphere for Sunday afternoon courting. Young boys might even go "skinny dipping" on a hot summer afternoon or after a hard day's work in the fields. When my older sisters who had married and were living in other states came home to visit, the river just seemed to call. While there were good spots for recreation and approved "swimming holes," the river could also be treacherous with unexpected drop-offs and surprising currents that could swallow a naive swimmer, and this tragedy occurred all too often.

I was baptized by the New River bridge at Weaver's Ford and joined the New River Baptist Church. Baptisms were social as well as spiritual events, usually attracting large crowds and inspiring family gatherings. On Sundays after church, families usually had dinner and visited in each other's homes. I remember pleasant Sunday afternoons sitting in the porch swing or rocking chairs on Aunt Lelia Brown's wrap-around porch overlooking the river.

Ownership of river bottom land was coveted for the fertile soil; however, the river could flood and wipe out entire crops. Homes along the river

Carol Wade Colvard (right) around 1950, about age 13, and her sister Ruby's daughter, Coleen Warren (now Coleen Mister), who was visiting from Baltimore (courtesy of Carol Wade Colvard Noronowicz).

were always susceptible to floods, and many homes were flooded repeatedly. Residents along the river had to be survivors.

There weren't many bridges, and I remember my mother, Mary Shepherd Colvard, who was born near the river in 1892 in what was known as the Fairview area and lived to be 102, telling about fording the swollen river on horseback when she was only 12 years old and the river was so deep that the horse had to swim. Knowing the danger of the swift current, her mother was furious with her father, John Shepherd, for allowing her to do that.

Then there were the times the river froze over in winter. A deep freeze followed by a thaw could cause an "ice freshet," when the ice would break into large chunks and rush down the river with great force, slicing trees in two and damaging everything in the path. Mother talked about a time when word spread by the limited telephone network that the ice was breaking, and people rushed to the high ground to watch.

The river served as a point of reference when giving directions—"up the river," "down the river," "across the river." An errand for me was to ride horseback to the mill "near the river" with a sack of corn, which my dad and I had shelled, slung behind the saddle. While the corn was being ground into

Carol Wade Colvard and nephew, Jimmy Barnes, playing in the New River, in the early 1950's (courtesy of Carol Wade Colvard Noronowicz).

cornmeal, I would ride "down the river" to visit Aunt Lelia and Uncle "Dollie" Brown, who lived on high ground overlooking the river. Then I would pick up the cornmeal on my return ride. This errand was one of my favorite things to do, and I can remember how happy and free I felt riding the horse. Sometimes I would spend the night at Aunt Lelia's house, and I remember going to sleep to the peaceful sound of the water gently flowing over the rocks.

I think we pretty much took the river for granted — its danger and its joy. It was a hard life but a good life, and it's only when you have left the river that you fully appreciate what you left behind.

RUBY TRIVETTE, 85

February 22, 2000

At her home in Todd.

I live about a hundred yards from the Ashe County line in Watauga. I have lived in this same place for about 80 years. My folks moved here from Ashe County, just across the line, when I was five years old. I started school at five the fall that my folks moved into this area.

At that time everything was a lot more primitive than it is today. My paternal grandmother was reared and lived much of her life on the New River, going up what we call the Big Hill Road, turning off below the store, going to the right and going up to what was the Tatum farm. The old line of Tatums lived forever. My paternal grandmother lacked six days of being 104 when she died. She resided here with us; my father was her son. She resided with us a little time after he had passed away and she had her 100th birthday here with us. She had a daughter who lived near Damascus in Virginia with whom she spent the rest of her life. When she died she was brought back here and is buried on the family farm in the Howell Cemetery, which was part of my mother's inheritance. My mother was the daughter of Thomas and Sarah Howell Adams.

There are some myths and legends concerning the first Adams who came to America from England. Of course, it's hard to separate the actual truth from what we've heard all our lives. Some of it I know was an exaggeration. The original Adams came from England and we were told there was a vast estate. My grandfather descended from the youngest son of whoever Adams it was at that time. In those days the oldest son was the inheritor, and the youngest son did the best he could. So, we're told that he stowed away in a sugar barrel on board ship and came to the New World. Of course, in modern days we always embellish it and say he stowed away on the *Mayflower*, something that I seriously doubt.

Marshall and Celia Trivette and children, 1919. From oldest to youngest, Blanche, Paige, Ruby, Joseph, Thomas. On porch of same house where Ruby Trivette still lives (courtesy of Ruby Trivette).

There's another story concerning that. It's being researched by my first cousin, who is pretty sure that the first of the Adams line came over with Lafayette and was a bugler, I believe, in the early days. Whether that's so or not, again, I have no way of knowing. On my grandmother Trivette's side of the family, she and all of her brothers lived to be very old. On my grandmother Adams's side, they died with heart trouble very young, and that has been quite true as far as my family is concerned. There were eight of us children and except for the last child, who was a blue baby, those who lived at least a few years have had heart ailment and all of them have died with heart trouble. A couple had heart trouble and cancer. At the present time, I and my brother Tom, who is a few years younger than I, are the only two living. So I think we've inherited the Adams gene of heart trouble all the way around. He has some, and in September I was diagnosed with heart trouble.

I have lived here for about 80 years. My family farmed for a living. We raised on the farm just about all the food that we consumed. We grew our own wheat and corn, buckwheat and some rye, which we used for bread. We had a few cattle and a team of horses that we had to feed and look after. Most of the produce we bought from Cook's Store, which eventually has become Todd General Store. Cook's Store was founded or came to this area in 1914, the same year I was born. I guess I was probably close to five years of age when I remember my father bringing me to the store, the first time I recall being in the local store. It was a new world to me. When I stood on Fifth Avenue and looked into the shops of New York City, all that was not as interesting to me nor as wonderful as walking into Cook's Store for the first time and seeing all the things. I especially remember Mr. Cook's daughter, Jenny, who was just about my age, got us a bar of candy out of the store. I'll never forget it. I think it was the first I'd ever had. I'm not sure why I would remember it that way, but I remember it was a small bar and Bit o' Honey was the name of it.

The store in those days carried just about everything you could think of, from horses' harness and plow equipment, and just about anything and everything you needed: nails and staples and axes and hammers and washtubs. By the way, I guess it was a great number of years that we had our baths in a washtub and we didn't have a bath every day either. We washed feet and hands and so on every day, but about Saturday night we had the weekly bath. The creek runs right back of the house and we children used that to wash our feet in the summer time, and we did go barefoot all summer. We worked out in the fields and the garden and many times we'd have chapped feet.

Mr. Cook, at his store, also bought all sorts of herbs and leaves and things that were sold later on to go into medication. He would buy such things as catnip and life everlasting, lobelia, pennyroyal. All these things were used in medication and made up a great deal of our homemade medication. I

Todd General Store, Todd, N.C. The store was built in 1914 by Walter and Monroe Cook and has been operated continuously since then. It was long known as W. G. Cook's Store. The house to the left of the store is the original Cook dwelling. Both the store and the house are listed on the National Register of Historic Places. They are now owned by Joe Morgan.

remember catnip tea was a wonderful thing for children with colic. Peppermint and pennyroyal steeped and made into a tea were also used, and the best I remember it was probably used to stimulate and sweat out — they used to think you could sweat out — the cold.

In the early days, Todd had Cook's Store, John Cox's Store, Nimrod Dobbins's Store, Graham's Store. It also had a bank and a drugstore and a big lumberyard. It was in the '20's when the Norfolk and Western had a train coming into Todd. It was a railhead and that certainly helped the situation financially. The chestnut timber, which formed the basis of a great deal of the commercial value, was cut and most of it went into crossties and other building material. The best I remember, they saved the tan bark and shipped it out, I guess, for tanning purposes. Then the blight overtook the chestnut groves and trees and when they were decimated, it wasn't long after that until the train was taken out of this area.

We grew our own corn and cornbread was a great deal of our bread. We carried that down to a mill that was situated just below where the country store is now and we had what was called a meal sack. It was a narrow sack but it seemed like it was three feet long, and I can well remember my brothers and I picking up a meal sack full of chestnuts. You could also sell chestnuts. We liked to dry them. I don't know why they didn't get wormy in those days as they do now. We'd dry them and use them in the wintertime as nuts. The best I remember we scalded them in salty water and, of course, they got hard as bricks but we didn't care.

This is as close to the river as I was. As a young child, I don't know that I had any direct contact with the river. In later years, the river was used as recreation, some swimming, not much boating until recent years, with tubing and canoeing and things of that sort. But I'm sure it played a great role in the life of the early settlers in this area. I can remember hearing my father talk about the winters being so cold that the river would freeze over. With a yoke of oxen, the men cutting the timber could log the timber on the ice. The young people in Todd were a little closer to the river and a good deal older than I was, and they'd have their skating parties at night.

The river was a source of food for people. Many people fished and bullfrogged, gigged. I think the railroad sort of followed the river. Much of the land adjoining the river was very rich, because it was alluvial soil. It had been brought in during flood time over the years. But as far as I'm personally concerned, the river didn't have a great deal of influence on me. I remember sneaking off from Sunday School — the church was on up the river from Todd — a couple of friends and I slipped off from church one day. I guess we left probably before services, after Sunday School, and went up the river. We thought we were going swimming, and none of us could swim, I'm sure. But we did, what we called, "go in swimming."

I'm sure the river also had some effect during the Civil War days because I've heard my grandmother tell that even after the war was over that a lot of the damn Yankees came through raiding everything they could get their hands on. Somehow or other, I don't know their area of communication, don't know how they passed on a lot of this information, but probably through the grapevine. They got word that the raiders were coming, and her folks had one Negro slave. I've actually seen pictures of him. His name was Pete and he was always called Uncle Pete Tatum. No matter what the family might have, if they got word of raiders coming, they'd have the cattle and hogs and everything possible driven off into the swamp around the river. It didn't make any difference if they had family silver or whatnot. Her father — I guess it was homemade whiskey, if it was I don't know whether he made it or not — always had his toddy every night. We were told that her father would always insist that the Negro take his whiskey keg out and place it in a hollow tree somewhere not far from the house. He took care of that whether anything else was taken care of or not. I don't know that it was ever mentioned, but I'm sure that they had a time chasing down the cattle when it was safe to get them back in. I can just imagine them trying to get the hogs back in. Of course, in those days they let their hogs run wild and they fattened on chestnuts and hickory nuts.

I have heard it mentioned very briefly that there was a mode of taking care of runaway slaves through here and I don't know whether it was up the river or how they managed it.

My grandmother, as I said, was quite old. What form of education she ever had I don't know, but she read and, in fact, she taught me to read, taught me my letters, and I learned to read before I ever went to school. I learned the letters from bags of sugar, match boxes, and things of that sort. Then when I went to college I didn't know that the English she spoke, many of the words were pure Elizabethan English. I thought she was just old-fashioned and strange. She had many beliefs in things that we no longer accept. One was, she believed in witches. She could recount so and so, some old crone that if you crossed her, your cows would give bloody milk or go dry and all such things. I do remember that when my father died, we had some bee hives out along the back of the yard out there. I can see her now putting on her black bonnet and black cape with a black ribbon tied around her arm going out there and bending down and telling the bees that the master of the house was gone. She believed that if she didn't tell them, the bees would leave. Then I learned later that that was a tradition that had been handed down for years.

The first schoolhouse that I can recall in this area was a little school just on up the road a little ways and it was called Laurel Ford, 'cause I think the little school was built in an area where there were plenty of laurels around. My mother and her brothers and sisters, I'm sure, attended that school, and it must have been a very short school term. One gentleman that died within the last 10 years or so remembered going to that school, and he remembered one lady's name that taught at the school. I can remember his mentioning Kate Crosswhite as one of the teachers. I think in those days that they used some physical discipline, because he told about the boys being sent out to cut their own switches. They learned when they did, to take the knife and sort of ring it around so when they got hit pretty good, the switch would break into pieces. I am not sure, but I guess they had to pay a subscription to go to that school.

In the interview that I did with the *National Geographic* [June 1999], they kept wanting to know about the barter system, if we used the barter system in the early days. I said, "Yes," that I could remember taking many a chicken by the leg, carrying them down to the store and trading them for sugar and matches and things we didn't raise here on the farm. It wound up that when they were checking before publication, they called me several times and they would read me what they had. They had me carrying chickens by the *neck*, which I assured them that if I'd carried them by the neck I didn't think that they'd take them at the store.

Up above our barn in the field there was such a growth of mayapple and life everlasting. There was rabbit tobacco that grew back of the cemetery and my brothers and I gathered that and rolled it up in brown paper and smoked it. Oh, yes, it made us sick. Catnip was one of the things that we did gather. We gathered that, dried it, and we'd take it down to the store and we would buy school supplies and some of our clothes, I guess, I don't remember too much about it.

We had our school clothes, which we pulled off when we came home, because we all had chores to do, and we tried to save them to wear the next day. They weren't always washed every day, either. The little girls wore dresses. I can well remember even at the time I was in high school there was no gymnasium, but we played a little basketball on an outside basketball court. We girls had our own suits. They were homemade, big, old, wide bloomers. I guess we thought we were really going to town when we got our basketball suits. They came down to our knees, below our knees.

Before the highway system came through here, we walked to school on the old dirt road that went along the base of the field. About where the firehouse is down here, there was a field and it always blew full of snow in winter. It was waist high to us. As children I guess it was just about over our heads, but we thought it was awfully deep. In those days we didn't stop school for a little snow. Everybody walked. Later on, there was a gentleman who lived down the river, a Mr. Roby Seatz who took one of his wagons and put seats along the sides of the wagon and hauled the children to school from down the river. Later on we had school buses, but that was the primitive school bus in this area.

Here on the farm we grew corn for our meal to make cornbread which we used for dinner and supper. I can remember having cornbread for breakfast. It was called egg cornbread, used egg in it and a little shortening and I guess a little flour. Once in a while we'd have egg cornbread for breakfast and have our own meat. We always killed hogs and usually in the fall we'd kill a beef. We had our own chickens and eggs. We also grew buckwheat. I remember during the war years taking buckwheat up to Meat Camp to the Winebarger mill. They still grind a little there. We also grew some rye and had it ground into rye flour. I've never been able to make rye bread like my mother and grandmother did. I just don't remember if they used yeast or exactly how my mother did the pancakes, the buckwheat cakes. She'd mix it up and I think she put maybe some cornmeal in it. I'm not sure whether she used potatoes to make the yeast or not, but she'd mix up a big pitcher full at night and set it before the fireplace, in which we kept a little fire all night, and kept it warm. I can remember she'd always set the pitcher that she mixed it up in a pan because during the night it would get warm and it would rise up and sometimes run over. It had just a little bit of a sour, almost a sour dough, taste to it. We thought pancakes with butter and molasses and meat and gravy was the most wonderful thing we had.

We made our own molasses. We boiled the cane juice down and would make as much as 100 gallons every fall and sell it for 25 cents a gallon. Of course, a lot of people made their own and what we didn't eat ourselves was used in feeding the hogs; it helped to fatten them up. I don't think we ever made any maple syrup here, but my grandmother Adams, who lived in the next house up here, always made some. In fact, she caught cold boiling down the maple sap and got pneumonia at a time when they didn't know how to treat it and it killed her. Across from her house up there were numerous maple trees up on the bank above the creek. They always tapped them and had the spills and the buckets set down under them and they'd carry the sap out and boil it down. I can remember her making a little sugar; of course, that took a lot more boiling than the syrup.

We were, I would say, about three-quarters of a mile from the river. It's still rich ground. Our farm is in the fertile valley. I don't know the names of the creeks down here. One goes straight on to the South Fork of the New River. I guess one is called the Long Hope Creek. I've been on Long Hope and the stream up there is much smaller than either one of these, but there's some sort of metal in it. There's almost a rust-colored deposit on the rocks. It's been years since I've been up there on the Bald Mountain and on the Long Hope side. We used to walk up there. In those days we didn't have much to ride on. It was horseback or buggy or something like that. I can well remember when the first automobiles came to this area. It was such a novelty. We could hear them way over here on the hill chugging along on the old dirt road. The young'uns who lived in Todd would run to see them and they'd follow them on up here, and then we'd all follow them and maybe push them out of the mud holes for a ways. That was up in the 20's but I'm not sure just what year it was.

About my school days and my teaching days at Elkland, I went to school over in Ashe where Tom and Martha now own the building [Elkland Art School]. In those days it was just a plain wooden building. In the early days before the government began to help any on it, children took their lunch, or those nearby as we were here, would go home for lunch anyway, because Mother always cooked dinner. I can well remember my younger brothers, after the Esso service station was put up, they'd go into the henhouse and gather an egg or two and go by the store and get an egg's worth of candy, and I guess they'd get a handful.

The schoolhouse as it was in the earlier days had classrooms on either side and in the center was a stage and on either side there were long folding doors for purposes of entertainment or whatever we needed for a group gathering. Those were pushed back and big classrooms on either side then were opened up to the public. It might have been the first year I was in school, but I was still just a brat. Somehow or other I could remember pretty well. So in some of the entertainment that was put on at the school, somebody got the bright idea for me to give a little recitation. My mother had made me what I thought was a beautiful dress, sort of an organdy or voile and it had little pink roses on it. In those days we wore our dresses way down long. I don't remember this myself but I've been told so much and teased so much about it. I came out on the stage to say, "Star light, star bright, first star I see tonight, I wish I may, I wish I might, have the wish I wish tonight." I was told that when I started I got hold of the hem of my dress and kept winding it around my fingers until when I got through I had my dress tail swung around my hips. I was teased about that for years.

We had such things as fiddlers' conventions and box suppers in which the ladies gussied up a box, usually with crepe paper, all fixed up, and packed a box lunch. Then it was put up for sale. All the girls and women who had husbands or boy friends, other men in the group when they started bidding on their wives' or girlfriends' boxes especially, they'd keep running the price up. What money was made was for school use, books or whatever, because school supplies in those days were very, very inadequate, but we got by with it. We had cake walks and things of that sort. We didn't know but what we were living the high life in those days.

When I started teaching, my first teaching year, I had graduated from college with a B.S. degree in 1940 from Appalachian. I graduated from high school at Boone in 1932, but my father was ill and I was needed at home and I didn't start to college until 1936 or '37. At that late date I decided I was going to get a whole four years in by going year round. I finished up in three years, and I went to Wilkes County for my first year of teaching. I went down there in a strange place, teaching in high school, and at that time I weighed less than 90 pounds. The high school students, especially the boys, were almost grown men. I was new to the area and they were new to me, and I think they were determined they would run me off the first go-round. I went from lunch one day to my classroom and opened up the desk drawer and there was a red fence lizard about this long in the desk drawer. I knew if I did what they wanted me to, I'd scream and carry on, and I knew if I did that I need never go back in the classroom. So, I "retched in," as my grandmother would say, I "retched in" and got him by the tail and carried him over to the window and dumped him down in the shrubbery. From that time on they were pretty careful not to bother me, but I know that they intended to get rid of me.

The man who taught economics, Tom Hayes, who was a native of

Wilkesboro, quit about Christmas time to go into a hardware store. We switched classes around. I was certified in English, French, and social studies, so I picked up his economics class. In my eagerness to be sure that the children understood what I was talking about, the difference between natural resources and man-made resources, I was just running on at full speed and said, "Things like land and water are natural resources, and man couldn't make them." So I went on with, "Man cannot make land, man cannot make water." About that time the roof went off with laughter.

Another time I was teaching colonial history and we talked about the fashions and the way they dressed. Trying to make them realize that men wore short breeches and women's skirts were dragging the ground and how they eventually changed, I used the term, "As the men's pants went down, the women's dresses came up." Again, I just ruined the whole thing.

I had only one year in Wilkes County because my mother, having inherited the Adams heart trouble, was ill, and I needed to come closer home. There was an opening here at Elkland School and I came home.

Elkland was an old wooden building. It was all raised somewhat off the ground and over to the side, when the government help became available, they made a lunch room. There was very little money during those Depression years and children would bring in potatoes or canned stuff or whatever they had to pay for their lunches. We got some government cheese and peanut butter and things of that sort.

I can well remember we had school buses at this time, but in the wintertime in bad weather, the buses would just run so far. When they went as far as they thought safe and made their rounds, my sister-in-law, Ruth, and I were probably the only two teachers that could get there. We'd go in and build fires in the old laundry-type stoves.

When I went to school somebody had cut some timber on the ridge above the school building. There were a lot of tree laps and somebody had cut them up in cord wood, the length to go in the old laundry-type stove. At recess we were marched up on the hill to get us a load of wood. Of course, the larger children carried two or three sticks and even the little fellows would find them a stick to carry in to heat the building. Ruth and I many times built fires. By that time we'd have the building somewhat warm when the children came in, and we'd just have two or three rooms warm and we'd bring them all together. We'd have classes of sorts and when one of us was holding classes, the other one would go down and cook lunch for them. We'd have lunch and then let them go home. We'd had enough to call it a day.

The children would bring in produce and we'd serve that and the surplus goods from the government at that time. I can well remember a couple of our cooks. I know the children would bring in canned food, not a quart can, but a half gallon can of blackberries, blueberries, wild huckleberries, apples, peaches, and so on. One time those cooks mixed the blackberries and the huckleberries and served cream over them. It wasn't whipped cream and it wasn't whipped topping, it was just cream over that for dessert. That was the best eating I think I've ever had.

We didn't have indoor toilets at that time and the gym wasn't built then, but out on the hill toward the old gym were our outhouses or johnnyhouses. In the wintertime it was a hard matter to walk out there. One day one of the teachers went out on the hill to the outdoor toilet. When she came back in, she took a shortcut and came in the door on the side. I think that was where the lady who taught the little fellows was. She came through that door, through that room, through two or three more rooms to get back to her room. Every room she passed through, the children just died laughing. The teacher in the first room found out what the matter was. In dressing after being at the toilet, she had gathered up her skirt and her petticoat and caught them in her girdle. So there she was traipsing through the school and the little young'uns just screaming in fun.

As to recreation, we didn't have many dances in this area. Baptist was the predominant religion and they didn't believe in dancing. We made our own entertainment. A lot of the kids down in Todd would come on up in this area, and they'd gather here and we'd do everything from fry somebody's chicken, build a fire and roast corn and potatoes, maybe make molasses candy.

Somewhere along the way, before the REA came through here, my oldest brother and a friend of his who lived on up the road and the family who lived below us, went in together, built a water wheel and had a dynamo and made their own electricity. We had a washing machine and with all the boys in the family, that was a blessing. Somehow one of my brothers got hold of a little radio; it was a little bigger than your tape recorder. On Saturday nights, there weren't many radios in the area at the time, and a lot of the young people and some of the elderly would gather in here on Saturday night to listen to old Uncle Dave Macon and Little Jimmy Dickens. There was one song that was not played until after midnight. So we were sitting here after midnight and it went something like this: "Down in the chicken house on my knees, I thought I heard a chicken sneeze..." and that's all I can recall of it. It was so funny that everybody had to hear that before they left to go to bed.

In those days we had revival meetings. We called them protracted meetings and they'd last at least a week or 10 days, maybe two weeks. That was about the only time, outside of school, when the young people could get a little courting in. About the time they'd think about closing the meeting, it was amazing how often some of them got so deeply interested they had to run the meeting on a few days.

Today we no longer have prayer in school. When I went to school and even after I started teaching, we had a little devotion every morning. Even when I was in college in Boone, we went to chapel. Dr. Dougherty was there and Dr. Williams, the geography teacher. Cratis Williams was there. Dr. Eggers, the English teacher, had such a reputation. He didn't believe in having freshmen in his class. He let me know right off that I didn't belong in that class and he gave me a hard time till the first exam we had, and I was the only one that passed his test. From that time on, I got along all right with him. I especially liked Dr. Cratis Williams.

A great many people in this area had musical talent. They could just pick up most any instrument and play it. Some Grogan boys that lived back Three Top way and their sister, who died about a year ago or better, Ethel and Gaither and Thurman, I can remember those three Grogan children. They were all musically inclined. I don't remember what they played, the violin, or the fiddle as we called it, and the guitar and the banjo. Those were the most prominent instruments. People would just get together and play and sing informally. "Cripple Creek" was one of the songs. A little bit later on after the radio became prominent, I remember one of the favorites was "Maple on the Hill" and "The Old Ship of Zion"— that was also quite favored, and many of the old religious hymns.

When I was just a student over here at Elkland, when we did have these protracted meetings around, we were lined up at school and marched to church. They had church in the day time. We were marched to church for the service and we were marched back. Today I guess anybody would be put in the penitentiary if he did that.

There were two doors at the church, one on the left for the men and one on the right for the ladies. Husband and wife did not enter the church together and they didn't sit together. In the middle of the church, there were a few little short benches back this way, to the old stove, with a great long stovepipe going plumb out the back, and all of us young'uns liked to get on those little seats. I guess we were not always as respectful as we ought to have been, but we learned not to do a lot of things we wanted to do then. We didn't have Sunday School rooms. Everything went on in the same building, same place. I think eventually they had some curtains to draw off. We had the beginners and they had little cards with pictures on them and a little writing on the back. I guess then we had the adult class and maybe the teenagers. We didn't have many classes and we didn't have a great many people there, but we managed to get by.

In the beginning, as far back as I can remember, some of our ministers came on the train from Abingdon. Maybe we just had service one Sunday out of the month. A little bit later we went half time, then three-quarter time, and we became full time relatively only a few years ago. We had one minister who lived in this area, and he pastored a little church called Pilot Mountain on down the river. On Saturday he walked down there to the church, had services, and he stayed all night down there. That left his wife up here alone. He and my father were good friends, and inevitably when he went to spend the night, my brother and I had to go up and stay with her.

Ruby Trivette, recent photo by David S. Howell.

In the old church records, there's one instance in which one woman was turned out of the church because she got mad and threw her husband's old hat in the fireplace. You didn't have to do much in those days to get churched. They were very conservative about dancing back then, too.

My grandfather Trivette was a soldier in the Civil War and he didn't come back. That's all so long ago.

I remember hearing about how they hanged a Negro over in Ashe at the courthouse years and years ago. My grandfather, who lived in the next house up here, we're told, rode a horse or a mule into Jefferson for the hanging. In the attic of his old house above the kitchen, hanging up on a peg was a piece of rope. We children were told that that was a piece of the rope that hanged the Negro. That scared the living daylights out of us and we never did like that house. I don't like that house yet. It's still there. It's been remodeled and the attic is gone, but I still don't like the house. I don't remember why they hanged him. I don't know that I ever had the initiative to ask why. I was just so concerned that they did. We were also told, and I don't know how much truth it is, that there was a Negro, I guess it was during the Civil War days, that escaped and went back here on the Bald Mountain somewhere in the wintertime and froze to death.

There is this tale about the man that saw something in the spring up on Bluff Mountain. I've been on the mountain several times years ago. I don't remember the man's name. He bent down to drink out of this spring and he saw something in the spring, some image that frightened him so that he ran off that mountain. In running off the mountain, he crossed a rail fence. Where he'd grasped the fence to leap over it, he left his fingerprints. He came on home and he was very ill. I guess he'd killed himself running. They got the doctor, Dr. Graham, who lived back up the road. He told the doctor that if he lived nine days, he'd tell him what he saw in the spring, but he didn't live his nine days. They always told that he saw the Devil in the spring.

The McGuire house across from the store [in Todd] was once a hotel, the big house, long before the McGuires got it. I don't know who built it. Some people by the name of Hulcher lived there and we were told that his wife poisoned him and that for years you could hear him moaning and groaning in the room he died in. That was just a tale. I don't believe there's anybody lives there all the time now. Uncle Tom McGuire, who was not my uncle, that was a term we applied to elderly people, lived there. His wife died and his son who owned the garage building there in Todd was moving to Winston. It looked as if Uncle Tom was going to have to go down there and live with them. I'd been away for a few days and came back and learned that Uncle Tom had gone out into the barn and shot himself. He killed himself, I think, out of grief and the idea of having to leave home.

At one time we had several doctors in this community. This was once a really thriving community. Todd, and I think West Jefferson, too, were suggested for the site of Appalachian State University. I've heard that Boone offered more benefits, I don't know if it's true or not, but this big field above the highway over here was considered as a site for the college at one time.

The chestnut blight ruined the timber and the economy just went down. Following that was the Depression.

As to the future of this area, we're having quite a few people move in and build homes. Then down on the river there's also some development taking place. The fact that N.C. 194 has been turned into a scenic highway brings people in, too. More tourists come through here since that.

Then there's the availability of an airport in both counties. Ashe is bringing in some industry from time to time which will increase the population. The trouble, I think, has been that we educate our young people and yet there are no jobs here for them. They have to move out to make a living. There have been doctors and lawyers, all kinds of professional people who had to leave.

I have done some gardening in the past. I've developed a little of the genetic heart trouble and I don't do nearly what I did. I had a hip replacement two years ago and until then I did my own lawn mowing. Last year I had just a little bit of it plowed up and I had a row of potatoes, a row of beans, and three or four rows of corn. I had some lettuce and mustard and an onion or two. I like my home-grown tomatoes. I have a few flowers. I usually have a row of gladiolas in the garden and I have an area around the pear tree out there that I put into flowers in the spring. I don't know whether I'll try a garden this spring or not. It depends on what my heart trouble amounts to. The danger is the blood clotting. I've been on all sorts of heart medication, which I guess I'll probably take the rest of my life. I can look after myself and that's the main thing.

Beulah Blevins, 84

March 25, 1999

Interviewed at her home on Deep Ford Road near Lansing by her granddaughter, Pamela Blevins.

I was born December 23, 1914, in Staggs Creek. My mother said I was a Christmas baby. My father's and mother's names was James Church and Effie Brooks Church. My grandpa and grandma Brooks's name was John and Jane. They lived in Warrensville. My grandpa and grandma Church's names was Alex and Oma Church. They lived on Staggs Creek. I remember going to my grandma's, made me happy to see them and be with them. They was lovely people.

The first school I went to was a little log house. Staggs Creek, a little log house school. It had one room. Me and my brother went one morning. It come a little snow; we had to walk for miles. Got on top of the hill and the sun was shining. My brother said, "Let's rabbit hunt." We stayed out all day rabbit hunting; eat our lunch. My parents never did find out but what we went to school.

I remember my first day in school, but I didn't remember any more. I had fun going to school, enjoyed it till one day I had to 'cite a poem. I started Lansing School, and my teacher made me stay in for lunch and recess. That was the last of my schooling. I went out and got a job. I hadn't been to school the day before, and I didn't know I had to say a poem. That was when I quit school. I regretted not going on, but I went out and found a job in a sewing factory in Lansing. We made many things: quilts, overalls, shirts, and night-gowns. That's where I learned to make quilts, and I've made many quilts for my children and grandchildren and people I gave to.

Seemed like, at that time, my calling was to help people in sickness. I'd go stay with them. I stayed where they had babies and people was sick; I took care of them. I still, at 84, hope to do some more. The places I stayed was in

Beulah Blevins shows her quilt in the late 1980's (courtesy of Beulah Blevins).

Marion; over in Chilhowie, Virginia; Elizabethton, Tennessee; Kannapolis and places where my uncle's wife would have a new baby, and I would go take care of the children and the baby.

When I's young, me and my friends would visit this old lady. We loved to go see her, talk to her. She got very sick one day, and they had to sit up with her day and night. Me and my girlfriend went to see her one night, and the family was very tired. We told them we'd sit up with her that night. Well, up in the night she got worser, and got the family up and she passed away. There wasn't nobody to dress her. Back then they dressed them at home. They asked us if we could. I thought my girlfriend was stronger than me, so we did. I started to wash her. I looked around and my girlfriend was passed out, so I had to dress her by myself. Back then they was a man where we lived made coffins. Back then they dressed them at home; put them in the coffin. They wasn't any funeral homes that I remember of back then. I've sat up with many people. I sat up with my grandma Church. She had cancer. I was with her the night she died. I've sat up with many people of the night when I was young. Back then after they passed away, people would come in and sit up with the family.

We didn't want to dip snuff, and some girls carried in their pocket a pack of Golden Grain. Had cigarette paper and rolled their own. They said,

"Now puff it." I did and they said, "Now inhale it." I did and it about killed me. That was the last of the cigarettes.

I dipped snuff all my life. My grandma Church would come visiting on Sundays to my home, and my parents didn't allow us to smoke or dip snuff. She'd slip me a little in her hand, and I would go out and dip it. She was the one that learnt me to dip snuff.

When I was at home, my dad and me went to church every Saturday and Saturday night. They had a revival, and I got saved. My aunt, who had been dead for a while, I seen her with what looked like a crown on her head. She was such a sweet person. I joined Low Gap Church, Christian Union Baptist. Me and my grandpa Church would walk for miles when they's a communion to take communion and wash feet. Back then they had no cars. You could look out, the church house was full, horses tied, buggies. They'd come on horseback.

I met my husband, Paul Blevins, at a carnival, and we got to going together. One night he wanted to take me to a box supper at Landmark Church. My name was second on the board. And so, I won a cake for being the prettiest girl. They put up a can of pickles, and they all bid on my husband being the ugliest man. So, I got the cake, and he got the can of pickles. We had a laugh, but he was a very handsome man. We had fun.

My husband and I got married in 1936 on my birthday. We lived in Crumpler on the New River. I don't remember when we lived at the river whether the road had a name back then. Now they call it the Aubrey Turner Road. To us was born five children. My husband was a carpenter. He built many houses and some church houses. And he was a census taker, a judge at the election, justice of the peace. My chores was to stay at home and take care of the children. I hoed tobacco. We planted beans, we had fields, we sold beans. Had two gardens. I canned a lot. Sometimes I canned a hundred cans of peaches and vegetables. My husband and our neighbor would go to South Carolina and bring back bushels of peaches, tomatoes. We killed hogs; we had two or three. I canned sausage, meat. We raised corn, rye, wheat, and even buckwheat. We'd go to the rolling mill with a wagon and a team of horses to get our flour and meal ground. Where we took our meal and flour to be ground was called the Helton rolling mill.

It was hard back then to make a living. We had wood stoves. We'd iron for a half a day with irons. We didn't have washing machines back then; we had a tub we washed in, a washboard, and the hide would come off of our hands. We would make our lye soap, and our hands would be blistered when we got done. We had a springhouse. We'd keep our milk and butter in it. We churned; I had a churn. We milked about three or four cows. We sold milk, and I'd churn to pay the bills. We'd sell chickens to buy coffee, sugar, things we didn't raise.

We would make apple butter. We peeled all day. Had a big black pot on the outside; put a fire under it, and we'd stir about all day. Law, did we have a canning when we got done. We did. We growed cane. We made molasses, build a furnace, we'd skim, make molasses. Grind it with a horse, go around with a horse. It would go around to grind the cane and run it off in a tub, and then we had a boiler on. We'd skim till the molasses.... Then we had wooden paddles, all of us around the boiler to sop the boiler. That's when they came off. My kids done that, neighbors' kids. Law, big crowd come for molassey making. We had fun back then, but it was hard times.

If we had a corn shucking, we hauled the corn into the barn, and the neighbors would come in and help shuck corn. If we had a bean stringing, they was there to help. We'd peel apples, dry them to make dried apple pies. Neighbors then, we holped one another. We enjoyed getting together, their company; we laughed, talked on the Bible back then.

We had a lot of get-togethers. Our families would all come together (about 35, 40) and have dinner. We had reunions, get togethers, and sometimes we'd all get together and go out on the Scenic [Parkway] and have lunch. It took a lot of cooking. I'd cook chicken, make dumplings, bake about seven pies, two cakes, with the beans and the vegetables and the preserves we canned (we'd pick wild strawberries, canned dozens of cans of them to make preserves) and biscuits, ham. We'd have homecomings at church, and I'd bake apple pies, about seven, stack them on top of one another, and chicken. Pie and chicken and beef, we'd take to the homecoming. We had stuff to eat, but it was hard. We worked for it. Every day we was in the fields or in the garden, canning, topping tobacco.

A lot of joy when I'd go a-fishing with my mother. She was in her seventies; she'd come and say, "Let's go a fishing." Boy, I was ready. We'd sit all day and fish, and I'm glad I went with her. She loved to fish. I fished down where I lived. We lived right on the river. Law, I used to catch suckers, have a bucketful. Did we have fish back then! We fried them and eat them. Oh, my husband loved fish, but he didn't like to go a-fishing. I was the fisherman. He didn't have no patience. My mother had more patience than Job. She'd sit there in the hot sun if we couldn't find a shady place. "Now they're going to bite in a few minutes," and we'd sit with her until she gave out and wanted to come home.

When I was young, they wasn't any cars, and we walked for miles. My uncle lived across the river, and my mother said we're going to see him, her brother, that day. I didn't know we had to cross the swinging bridge. We got to the river; she said we got to cross that bridge. I said, "No"; I pulled back. I feared it; I was scared to the inch of my life. She got me by the hand and led me across it, swung. "Boy," I said when I got to my uncle's, "I ain't crossing that bridge again." That was my day; I couldn't think of nothing else but getting on that swinging bridge. Well, come time to go home, my mother grabbed me again, took me across. Was I frightened. The bridge was about three to four feet wide. Had a little wire on each side, and, boy, did it swing. I never went back. I said, "Mom, that was my last time." I didn't go back to see my uncle again. Has times changed since back then. They had wooden bridges to cross on, and now they have concrete. Times has really changed since I was growing up.

Back then us girls got a job. Two or three of my friends, we'd walk for miles to go to our job. It snowed big snows, and we'd wade it up to our knees, no galoshers. One day we decided to hire a little man to take us to work. He had a T-model Ford. Well, were we happy. Started out that morning, it stopped at the foot of the hill. We'd get out and push it over and then we would ride down the hill. It was the truth.

The first house we moved into after we got married was a wood house. It had wood all over; it wasn't painted, but we were happy there. But I think the house was haunted. We didn't have locks on the doors back then like we do now. We had little wooden latches. One night I heard something coming through the kitchen, and I woke my husband up. He ran in there. There stood a cow in our dining room. He got the cow out.

Sometimes the door, for no reason, would open. One night, my son was about six months old and he was a-crawling and I was afraid he'd get up out of bed and go in the front room. I laid a chair in the door. I heard the chair move. Got up; they wasn't no chair there. One night the rocker went to rocking. Went in the front room; there wasn't nobody in it. I kindly got scared, but we lived there for several years till the flood come, the 1940 flood.

It was terrible. We had tobacco out; it was white with bloom. Gardens, apple trees full of apples, and the flood took everything. I know the night it came, it was about dark, and I noticed haystacks going down, trees with green leaves. The river was full of pumpkins, apples, and my husband said we'd better move. They's a house up on a hill. We got above the house; there's a barbwire fence. We wrapped two of our children up in a quilt, and my husband said, "Don't wear your shoes or you'll lose them." Took our shoes off. Trees, logs a-going down. We got up to this house. Looked down; our feet was bleeding where we'd waded. They took care of us for a night or two. It was something I'll never forget. It was just like a ocean. We brought our two children by our house; we didn't have any clothes, nothing to eat. Oil pumps were turned over, the river was full of oil; couldn't eat apples. Nothing. We had a bunch of chickens. They all drowned, about ten. We had two hogs. My husband knocked the end out of the hog pen, and they went to the woods. Saved them.

We went home in about two days. We didn't have anything. The water come up to the mantle. It ruined everything: furniture, our pictures (old

Beulah and Paul Blevins in center and their five children, left to right: Wanda (Pam's mother), Jack, Joe, Dorothy, and Marcella (in front in white dress, near Marcella's playhouse), in the 1950's (courtesy of Beulah Blevins).

pictures); we didn't save them. My two children asked for something to eat, but we didn't have nothing to give them. My aunt and uncle come and picked us up, took us home with them. They was larger people than we were. We wore their clothes. They was big and baggy, but we was tickled to have them. They took us to my mother's and she took care of us for days and days. We started over. We didn't have much, but we started over.

My husband cleaned. He dipped the water from the river back in the house to get the mud and sand out. The wallpaper was hanging. Things were rusted. People brought us in things. Our neighbors come and washed the quilts and things and feather beds and dried them. We had good neighbors back then. They helped us till we got on our feet.

In about a year, we decided to move off the river. We were scared of the water getting up again. We built out near to the highway. We had no money back then. Me and my husband got out and sawed logs, timber, to build our house and stuff to casing it out with. I know one day we was up on the hill, and my son (we had three children at that time), I laid him on a quilt. Cut a tree; come the wrong way; just missed him. I know I didn't want to saw timber no more.

Then along came Appalachian [Power] Company gonna build a dam through there. Said it would come up to our upper windows. We had an upstairs in our house. Scared our family. We sold out to 'em, and they never did build it. Then we moved out on Deep Ford Road in the 1970's. We have lived here ever since.

My kids' names are Rev. Joe Riley Blevins and my other son, James Jackson Blevins, and my daughter, Dorothy Lyalls, and my other daughter, Wanda Blevins, and my baby daughter is Marcella Doby. My grandchildren … I've got eight grandchildren. I have seven great-grandchildren, and they're very precious in my life — my grandchildren and great-grandchildren. I have a grandson who works for IBM. He lives in Raleigh; him and his wife and two kids. They sent him to Scotland, and he went to England to find out where the Blevinses came from. He thinks they came from England or Ireland. They live in a castle over there. It is very beautiful. They will move back very soon. They went for two years.

My husband and I was married about 52 years before he died in 1988, October the 19th. We had a happy family; we was close knit. On Christmas, they would all come home for Christmas. I'd prepare their dinner with a lot of help. My daughters and daughter-in-laws, they would help. We enjoyed Christmas together and my grandchildren and great-grandchildren, but it's never been the same since he left us.

Pamela Blevins is a writer and a columnist for The Jefferson Post *and the Ashe* Mountain Times. *Although she has been handicapped by cerebral palsy since birth, she is adept in using her computers; "I don't have enough dexterity in my hands to control a mouse, but I'm able to manipulate the computer arrow with a joystick. I have another special computer program that puts a keyboard on the screen. I still type with my nose at times because it's faster."*

Marye Gambill Lineback, 83

July 18, 2000

At her home in Sparta.

In elementary school we went to Gambill's school, which was close by. I used to walk behind my brothers. I think I started school when I was about five years old. Since I had older brothers, I could go along pretty good. I will talk about the time we walked from our home, my two older brothers and I, to catch the bus to go to high school. We would come down to the New River and my brothers would pole the boat and cross over and then we'd walk, it was about a mile to the river, and then we walked two miles on up to Elk Creek Church and that's where we'd catch the bus to go to Piney Creek School.

I had two older brothers, one was four years older and the other was two years older. The older one was tall, six feet, and he could walk faster than we could, so we usually left him eating his breakfast when we started for the river. He caught us by the time we got down to the boat. We crossed the river. I've seen it when it had mush ice on the side of the river, and we'd have to push the boat through that to get to the landing. This neighbor and friend that lived there on the river, Earl Farmer, would come when we felt like we couldn't pole the boat or didn't trust ourselves to pole it. He'd come over and get us and set us across. That's how my brothers and I got our education. They graduated in 1932 and I graduated in '33 from Piney Creek. I had some good teachers. I especially liked the one that taught English and French. She was my first cousin's wife and he was a judge finally. They were Gambills.

My mother had two sisters that married Gambills who were not close kin. Then my grandmother married a Gambill the second time. Her first husband died when my mother was four. My maiden name was Marye Madeline Gambill.

The way I met my husband, a lot of people came to Farmer's Fishing Camp to camp and to stay there. They had cabins. The Linebacks came up there and he said he saw me when I crossed the river. We met sometime after that, but not there. I don't know exactly what year it was but I went to Winston-Salem and stayed with his people. He had a brother that stayed at Earl Farmer's and he'd come over and visit. I went down there and took a business course in Winston-Salem. Then I went to work and I finally married my husband and lived down there for forty-some years. Before that, I have some more stories about the New River.

Before the bridge was built, we had a ferry. I can remember it had a cable, but they had to pole it across, too. They put horses or a car or whatever on it. They had old cars then. Our first car was an old Star car, and Mother used to ford the river up at Horse Ford, which is a little further up the river from the low water bridge now. She took cream and cheese and eggs to the market in Sparta. She'd come back there and cross the river and ford it with the old Star car. One time she got stuck in the mud coming out. She also took cream, so she had a milk can in the car. She didn't know what to do, so she got out and she got the lid off the milk can and got some sand and put it under the wheels so she could get out. It worked. She had a lot of narrow escapes.

My mother's mother lived up there at Crumpler. One time Mother was going to take the buggy. This is when we were all little and she left us with Dad when she wanted to go home to see her mother. So she started with the buggy and old Dan. He was sort of a high-stepping little sorrel that they liked to drive. She got up to the South Fork of the river and it was really deep. She thought, "I don't know if I can cross this river." But she wanted to go home so bad that she thought she'd just try it. They got in there and it was so swift that it washed them down the river and the horse didn't get out at the landing and there she was in that buggy. She thought she could make it if she'd hold onto the lines and get out. She kept talking to old Dan. They were right against the bank and he clambered around and finally came out at the landing and got them out. It was really a bad situation. I guess she waited until the river went down some before she started back.

I remember Dad talking about when the river would freeze over, they'd drive cattle across it on top of the ice. I remember my younger brother talking about driving the cattle across and riding a horse. One of the Farmer boys decided he'd help. He went and got his old horse and he was going to help Tam and he was sort of talking rough. Tam likes to tell this and laugh. He and Tom were about the same age. Tom got on the horse and he kept beating him and getting him after the cattle. The horse fell down right in the water. He got out without any problem, but Tam got a good laugh out of that because Tom was going to show them how to get the cattle driven across.

Dog Sterling on the Riding Rock in New River, May, 2000 (courtesy of Marye Lineback).

Another time my cousin wanted to get across the river and it was sort of deep, but they had a riding rock, they called it. If the water was over that riding rock, it was not safe to go across. Maybe it wasn't quite over it, but the river was really deep. They were in a surrey and my cousin and my oldest brother were in the surrey on the back seat. They were driving across and Dad was sitting in the front driving the horses. He had someone in with him but I don't remember who that was. They got out in the river and the water started coming through the surrey, through the door. A surrey is more like a carriage. This was a two-seater. Anyway, the water started coming through it on their feet, so they sat up on the back side of the seats. They decided they weren't going to get through so Earl Farmer came with his boat and got Arthur and Farrye out and then got them on out with the horses. That was a sort of scary time.

One time we saw the bridge covered with ice. The river had frozen over, especially up at the dam at Mouth of Wilson. All the ice came out and came down and covered up the bridge. You couldn't even see it and we were so afraid that the bridge would be gone. The bridge was built after I moved to Winston-Salem. I'm not sure what year it was built, so I can't give you any dates on that. Several times the water would get over it. When Hurricane Hugo came it washed logs and trees and everything on top of the bridge and we couldn't get across. It washed out another bridge further up, across the creek. We walked across under the timbers and got across and went up there to see that. That was some storm. It might have been '89.

That was a terrible thing. It bothered a lot of people because the power was off. One of my brothers was living over here at Elk Creek Church then. He had to get back over there to help with the dairy and the cattle. He took his chain saw and he had to saw trees out of the road to get there.

My husband Hiatt had several jobs. At the time of the war, he was 4F because of his hand. He had lost these two fingers in a shooting accident; a gun exploded in his hand. They denied him going into the service. During the war we came up to the mountains. Mother and Dad wanted us to move up here. We came and stayed about six months and decided it wasn't for us. We had Neal, he was four then, so we moved back down. We lived there and added on to our house and then Steve was born. My sons were in Boy Scouts and I worked with them, 4H and stuff. The bookmobile came to our house, so they could always get plenty of books. We all liked to read. We lived two miles from the city limits of Winston-Salem out toward Muddy Creek on West Robin Hood Road.

Neal grew up to be a college professor. He first went to Western Carolina. He wanted to go up there, but he only stayed there a quarter. He decided that wasn't the place he wanted to be. He came back and went to work at R. J. Reynolds and worked there for a year or so. Then he decided he needed to go back to school. He went to East Carolina and did his undergraduate work there. Then he met Katie and they got married and he decided to go on. They went to the University of Tennessee and lived there. Then they moved to Alabama and finally returned to Appalachian State University in Boone.

Steve went to N.C. State and got his degree in civil engineering.

My husband's name was Hyatt, but he spelled it Hiatt a lot of times. I think on his birth certificate it was Hyatt. Both Steve and Neal worked with their uncle. They'd go with him to work surveying during the summer months. He kept them out of a lot of mischief and it helped me out.

I still go to the Primitive Baptist Church. My husband loved to come up here. Well, we all did. We'd bring the boys and come to the mountains and stay. Then after we bought an old house, we'd all stay over there.

The house I would like to take you to see is my parents' old home place. I guess if we go up on top of the hill and look down over the hill we could see it, or maybe we could drive down in there. I haven't driven in there 'cause they have cattle in there now. The old house has just about fallen down. My mother and dad built a new house then over across the hill from it in 1957. All this on the north side of the New River is Gambill country. When you drive down to the low water bridge, you come to a dairy farm. It's my brother Tam's. Just one brother and his son own the farm now. My other brother that lives over at Elk Creek Church isn't a partner with them any more. They divided the partnership. I lived on the farm my parents farmed when I was growing up. That's just across the hill from the river.

I was chief cook back in those days. I had one sister who was four years younger and she was such a tomboy. She wanted to go ride the horses and do everything like that. Mother liked to work outside, too. So if there was anything to do in the garden or the field, she had me stay in the house cooking or whatever. I know my oldest brother liked butterscotch pie. It was my job to fix him some butterscotch pies.

Dad had beef cattle and milk cows, too, for our own use. Mother would save the cream. She skimmed off the cream and they had a milk separator that got the cream out. Before we had running water, we had a spring. We did our washing down there at the spring house, heated the water, and boiled the clothes. I can't remember the date, but my husband and I came up and he knew how to do plumbing.

Cleve and Maude Gambill (parents of Marye Lineback) and dog in front of their first home (courtesy of Marye Lineback).

He knew about the pump, and so we went to Wytheville, where he bought a pump and put it in at Mother's on the back porch of the house.

We grew the feed for the cattle. Dad always planted corn. I remember he'd kill a beef and hang it up. We had a woodhouse and had an area above the woodhouse to put the meat in the meat box. They'd leave it there all winter. The winters were cold then. Mother would go up there and cut steaks out of that hindquarter. It was cold enough to keep it, I reckon. Dad had a man come and build a root cellar. This old cellar is still above the house. They still use that to store potatoes and things. We were very pleased to have that. I remember Mother fixed apples in a barrel and they'd use sulphur down in a pan underneath and burnt the sulphur to preserve those apples in the top of the barrel. Of course, they always had the garden.

Dad always had honey bees, and my husband worked with those, too.

Neal even got into it. He'll have to tell you some bee stories. We always had honey. Dad took corn and wheat and had it ground into meal and flour over toward Brushy Creek. We had plenty to eat. We raised it every bit ourselves. Mother would go and trade things for the coffee or staples. She was the only one that drank coffee. The rest of us drank milk.

Marye Lineback in July, 2000, near her childhood home.

As to our clothes, I had an aunt that was a real good seamstress, and she'd come over and stay with Mother a week or so and help her sew. Mother couldn't sew very well, but she'd like for Aunt Minnie to come. It was her oldest sister. Mother was the youngest. Aunt Minnie could just lay down a newspaper and cut out a pattern. Then I took home ec in high school and learned to sew a little myself. My sister turned out to be a good seamstress. She finally took home ec at Appalachian and went to finish up her last year over in Virginia and got her degree. Then she taught home ec when she moved to Maryland. She went during the war, she and a cousin, and worked there in an airplane factory in Maryland. She married and stayed there and is still there.

My mother was from Crumpler. Her father died when she was four years old, so I never knew him, but I knew her mother. Grandmother came to live her last years with Mother and Mother took care of her. My other grandmother's old house is still there. When Mother and Dad were married, they had a couple of rooms of the old house and lived there until two of the older boys were born. Then they built the house there where I was born. My grandfather, Dad's father, died when Dad was 21, so I never knew him either. Grandmother lived there until about 1930 when she passed away. That was my dad's mother, Mattie Halsey Gambill.

I didn't do any fishing in the river. I guess we had such a hard time crossing that river, I didn't want to play in it or anything else. I didn't learn to fish until I got married. They were all fishermen, the Lineback boys were, and so I guess it rubbed off on my two boys, because they like fishing, too. We would go down to Cape Hatteras every summer. I would get to fish a little, too.

I had pneumonia and pleurisy when I was seven. We had this old Dr. Smith that lived at Independence, Virginia. He said I needed to come, I needed to have surgery. They didn't have any kind of antibiotics or anything like that. I had an uncle living over there, so Mother and I went over and he took us in. I remember sitting up in the bed while they ran a needle in. They didn't think I'd live, but I managed to get through it. It was touch and go there for a while.

We didn't use the old homemade remedies, herbs, and things, but my mother-in-law did. She believed in it. She had 11 children and they all lived to see her pass away. I remember Mother Lineback coming up one time and Dad was having some kind of arthritis or bursitis and she wanted to put on a poultice. She got a mustard poultice lined up. Mother never did do much of that, but she thought that would be a good thing to use on him. I guess it helped, I don't know. This old Dr. Smith delivered the rest of the children. I guess he delivered all of us. I know Billie, my sister, fell off a horse and broke her arm when she was about eight or nine. They had Dr. Thompson come over from Sparta and set her arm.

The only car we had back then was that old Star car and we didn't get that till we were in high school. I remember brother Arthur driving it and we were coming down that long holler as you're getting down to that old house and it was slick. It had just sleeted or snow was on the ground and he put on the brakes too much. We just slid around and headed back up the other way. He learned to drive and we didn't have any paved roads in there and we'd get stuck in the mud. I remember my husband had a Ford Roadster. One time, up there about Rose Gambill's, the road was different then than it is now. They've straightened it out a lot. We got stuck and he got out and had his boots on, so he carried some of us out. I remember him carrying me out. The road was really muddy. When we were teenagers, we'd go out and I'd go with my brothers and we'd go to square dances. We started out in the old car and got out there past Rose Gambill's out there on the ridge. We had this neighbor boy with us. We had the chains on it so it'd be sure to get out of the mud. We lost a chain in the mud and they had on their good clothes. They had to get out and scrape along in that mud to find the chain. We'd pulled off our shoes when going home. We'd come back to the top of the hill and had to park the car up there. We couldn't get down after a hard rain. We'd walk to the house barefoot. I remember one time we were crossing the creek and I was wondering how I was going to get across. Of course, we had skirts then and I had my shoes off, and this neighbor boy said, "I'll get you across." He grabs me up and says, "We'll just step through." The creek was deep, you know.

I thought for a long time I was born in the log house. There's an old log house there. When Mother and Dad decided to move over there with my two brothers, before they got the new house built, I thought I was born in that old log cabin. They said, "No, you were born in the new house."

I remember one time when we crossed the river we picked blackberries, then canned them and made jam. We always had plenty to eat. We crossed the river. We decided that we'd wade the river there at the lower part of the meadow. Dad had land right next to the river. They'd always plant things that would grow down there. Near the river it did better. We waded the river where it was a little more shallow down there. We'd take our buckets and pick blackberries and wade back.

My father's and mother's names were Cleve Gambill and Maude McMillan. Her mother came to live with them; she was a Dixon. She married again after all of her children were married and gone. She decided to marry Press Gambill from West Jefferson. I remember going to their house. They had a spring house and that was interesting to me. We had a springhouse, too. We had to keep the milk there before we got a refrigerator. We had carbide lights. We had lamps for all those years to study by. Then we got a carbide outfit that was a little better. We kept that until electricity came. I really don't know how the carbide was operated. I suppose it had to have something installed somewhere.

Before we had electric lights, my brother-in-law wanted us to have some electricity there. So he and my older brother went somewhere and they bought a water wheel and put that in. Three families used that. Earl would turn it off and on. At ten o'clock at night he'd turn it off, whether everybody else was ready or not. One night my brother Dale was having his birthday and he'd gone to Galax to get his girlfriend and brought her back. We were having a birthday party for him. Several of the neighbors were there, teenagers, and the lights went out about ten o'clock. Well, we weren't quite ready. So Dale got on a horse and went over there and turned the lights back on. Earl had already gone to bed.

The water wheel was operated on Rock Creek up there that runs in right beside of the low water bridge. That was quite an interesting thing. We were so pleased to get that. That was before electricity came to the county.

We had the springhouse, and when it'd come a hard rain, it was sort of down under and we had to go set everything up or get it out because the water would come right through. It's a wonder we didn't all die with disease of some kind because the barn was further up and all that would wash down. The spring was cemented but after a while we'd have to go out and dip the mud out and then the water would come back up in the spring clear. It was quite a struggle to keep everything working. It was hard work back then. When Mother got that pump on the back porch, she thought she was

Marye Lineback's grandchildren boating on the New River near the Mouth of Rock Creek (courtesy of Marye Lineback).

something. She could get a washing machine then. She would still heat her water on the wood stove. Then she got an electric stove, too.

They got telephones well after I left there. I remember the old telephones that everybody listened in on. It was a neighborhood telephone. Everybody knew everybody's business because it was a party line.

Dad always had hogs. He had sheep and he killed mutton. When we'd have the meeting at the church once a year and have the communion meeting, all the distant churches would come and he'd kill a mutton. Then later on he acquired this land across the river, which was called a cove. He had goats over there. Once in a while he'd kill a goat. Of course, that's not as good as the mutton. Dad would sell the wool. They'd have sheep shearings and they'd have the wheat threshers. All those events came. They would come around with threshing machines and we had to cook for them, and that would be a big meal. Some of them would stay in the house. I had to cook back in those days.

If you walked out on top of the hill there, you could see the Manbone Rock. They claimed that they had found the bones of a salesman there on top of this rock, and that was always the name of it. The boys would go across the river there to go to the cove where Dad had the land. He just grazed it, put the cattle over there, and that's why he had to bring the cattle back across the river in the winter time.

There's a cave up toward Cox's Chapel and my sister-in-law took us to that. It wasn't too far from her house. I think there were bats in there and they had all sorts of scary tales to tell about that cave. I didn't want to go in it, but we got to look in. It was beside the river up there toward Penitentiary Ford. You go over toward Virginia. One night we wanted to go to a square dance up toward Cox's Chapel and we had to cross the river at Penitentiary Ford. It was a rainy night and we had to go on horseback. My friend came on his horse and my brothers got their horses and here we went. It was at night and we were going to cross on the ferry there. All we had was a lantern at the ferry. I was really sort of scared of that trip. We put those horses on that ferry and went across. We spent the night, though, we didn't come back that night.

Nell Graybeal Sutherland, 83

September 29, 1998

*At her home near the old Riverview School
on the North Fork of the New River
in Ashe County, North Carolina.*

My mother and father were borned here in Ashe County. My grandfather on my mother's side was Elihu Graybeal (1848–1932), who married Mary Graybeal (1851–1947) on August 8, 1868. My grandfather on my father's side was Henderson Graybeal (1846–1923). He married Mary Osborn (1846–1927) on June 2, 1866. He fought in the Civil War.

My father's name was Reuben Colombus Graybeal (1871–1928) and my mother's name was Rebecca Cornelia Graybeal. They, too, were both Graybeals. I've heard it said that Graybeals married Graybeals to keep their riches in the family! But it's just an old saying.

After they were married they lived here in Ashe County for several years and had four boys. Then they bought a farm near Jonesboro, Tennessee. It was a beautiful farm. My brother Cicero, my sister Pearl, and myself were borned in Tennessee. My father and mother had a dairy farm and made butter and delivered it to Johnson City, Tennessee, to certain customers there. The paper they wrapped the butter in had their name and address on it. They had things going pretty well, and, of course, they farmed on the side.

At that time, we didn't have ice cream in the store. My older brother would visit us on Sunday and bring chunks of ice. Well, mother didn't save out enough milk to make ice cream; they used a separator. So, we'd have to go to the field and milk a cow. I don't know what the cow thought being milked at two o'clock in the afternoon, but we all enjoyed the ice cream!

When we were growing up together, Cicero, Pearl and myself were the only children at home. We enjoyed our childhood life. We grew up with horses, ponies, and a pony wagon, as well as a T Model Ford. Once I entered my pony in the County Fair and she won third prize in a race. I think if I had ridden her in that race she would have won first prize because we understood each other so well. Our neighbors used to say I could ride like an Indian. I guess that was about right, too. Not having any sense, I've been through some pretty dangerous situations! Once I rode across a creek when it was swollen from a flood. I thought my pony was swimming! I think of that today and how dangerous it was. Did I tell my parents? No!

In my youth most all my relatives were here in North Carolina, so I would come over here and visit. That's how I met my husband, Paul Sutherland. I had a favorite uncle here named Tom Graybeal. His full name was Thomas Jefferson Graybeal and he was married to Lula Belle Graybeal. Their home would remind you of the Waltons on TV. I always loved to visit in this home and I had several cousins in this family.

Paul and I were married on March 16, 1935, and I've now come to North Carolina to live. To this union was borned one daughter, Davia Carolyn. She is married to Bryce Cook and teaches at Blue Ridge School here in Ashe County. Bryce owns the Cook Cafeteria in Mountain City, Tennessee. They have a daughter named Maria who is married to Craig Pinto, a pilot for US Air. Maria is a social worker with the Carolinas Medical Center in Charlotte. They have one daughter named Mary Catherine, which makes me a great-grandmaw! This family is my pride and joy.

Paul and I had 56 years and four months together. We lived with Paul's mother, Bina Sutherland, in this very house until she passed away at the age of 92 years and five months. This house is pretty close to a hundred years old. We worked on our house a little bit at a time down through the years. We began putting down hardwood floors in it and back then a room would cost about $13.00. As money was made, we kept doing a little at a time and got it looking a little better and feeling more comfortable. At that time in my life, I didn't see the beauty of the mountains, nor did I hear the rippling of the water. I reckon I didn't take time to see the beauty of the earth as I do now. How can some believe there's not a God when only God can make a tree?

Paul never gave up farming altogether. He served for several years as Deputy Sheriff and owned a bloodhound, which helped him in many ways. People would come after Paul in the early morning to take his dog and try to find their chickens that had been stolen during the night. Paul even captured convicts that had escaped from prison in the Buffalo community. He also worked for a time bringing out steel from the mountains. People survived in many ways. In his time of service, Paul made no enemies.

In 1953 Sprague Electric came to Ashe County. We both worked there

Nell Sutherland's home by the North Fork of the New River at Riverview Community Center in 1998.

for several years and retired from there. Sprague Electric was a Godsend to our area. Soon you began to see new brick homes going up all over Ashe County. Sprague Electric is now United Chemi-Con. I worked several years in the Riverview School lunch room before working at Sprague.

I have been asked if we are related to the Sutherlands over near the Sutherland Church, and, yes, my husband was. They are fine people. They were all well-to-do and owned acres and acres of good land. Paul would take me up highway 88 and point out to me where so and so owned all this through here. But people do pass away and land gets divided and scattered.

Paul's mother was Bina Graybeal Sutherland who married Emmett Sutherland. She was Postmaster at two different times at Fig. Yes, Fig was right here in this community, but the address extended far out. Back in the twenties and thirties peoples' politics was a very dear thing to them. They were faithful to their party and every time the Presidents, from Democrats to Republicans, changed, the post office was sure to be moved. Some folks, hard up for money, would sometimes wait till the last minute on voting day to see who would pay the most for their vote. They was many fights about politics.

I've thought also about how the New River contributed to our lives. Of course, it runs right behind the house here. It sure furnished us fish! Mrs. Sutherland and I loved to fish. I guess that was our hobby.

One time I was fishing at a low bridge here almost in the yard. The bridge took you over to the house across the river where Mr. Brown lived. I began catching fish so fast I ran to the house and got a washing tub. I put water in the tub to keep the fish alive, at least for a while. Other people saw me and ran and got their poles, but by that time I guess I had caught most of them. A man came from West Jefferson to deliver some furniture to Mr. Brown and he wanted to buy some of my fish. I didn't sell any. Well, a few years later I had bought some furniture and the same man was delivering my furniture. When he saw the bridge he began telling me the fish

Paul Grant Sutherland when he was deputy sheriff and his dog (courtesy of Nell Sutherland).

story. When he said the lady wouldn't sell him a one, I began laughing. It was too good not to let him know I was the lady fishing!

The river would freeze over in the winter. Back then we had such cold winters, down in the zeros. Mrs. Sutherland spoke about the ice when it started breaking up. You could hear it cracking and popping. It would float down and pile up and that ice would last until about April. I think the winters were worse then. They were so cold when you hung your clothes out to dry they would freeze to your hands! We didn't have electric dryers back then.

But the weather was good for preserving food. Oh, it was wonderful to cure meat, hams, fat back, and beef. That was the best eating that I've ever eaten, when we could cure it. We used salt cure. We had a smokehouse, a special place to hang our meat. We had hogs, too. We would kill at least two to three hogs every winter. Back then we didn't hear about cholesterol. You could enjoy your food! Mrs. Sutherland and I would can meat from daylight till dark.

There was no spinning or weaving in my day here, but I sewed a lot and pieced quilt tops. Once I carded some wool and padded a quilt and quilted it. When I washed it, it drawed up, so I had a crib quilt — which I didn't need! From then on I padded my quilts with a cotton batting. I'm still piecing and quilting. My favorite pattern is the Wedding Ring.

I wanted to tell a little about the flood of 1940. I remember for several days there was a good, steady rain. At that time my garden was in and the corn was ready to eat. I got my umbrella and went to gather us some corn. And the river was rising fast. The rain didn't let up and we began seeing logs, bushes, and haystacks swirling around in the muddy water. Our tobacco crop was covered with water. Our daughter Davia was one year and one month old. I packed some of her things I thought I would need for a few days. I was ready to move to higher ground, if necessary. My brother-in-law was home from college during the time and they kept measuring the water and they'd come in and tell us how it was doing. Finally, the news was it was decreasing, and we began to relax some. Overall, there was several lost their lives and somewhere around 30 homes were washed away. In this community we were more fortunate than others. I think the estimate for the county was near two million dollars. The flood was the big story for several weeks to come.

There's a lot changed since I was young and we did live quite differently back then. Today we have motor equipment and electric to help do the jobs — such as power saws, washing machines, stoves — most anything you need to save our energy. Cars to drive, instead of horse and buggy days. Neighbors don't visit like they used to do — now we are invited instead of dropping in.

The recreational activities were mostly around the church. Some of the time the neighbors would get together in the homes and sing. Mrs. Sutherland was the organist. She played for revivals and also in the homes. They would sing the old hymns, such as *There is Power in the Blood*. Our neighbor, Mr. Brown, that lived across the river, at the close of the day would come out on his porch and pick the banjo. We would be on our porch facing his home and the river, listening to the little creatures that performed at night, while listening to him, too. Too soon the sandman would come and we retired to our bedrooms. The day was over.

We would have camp meetings, too. I've got a picture of the camp meeting grounds that was in our community. About a mile up highway 88 was a great large tabernacle. Cabins were built and a kitchen and dining room. The finest of preachers would hold the meetings. Children would come and stay during the whole time. Vernon Lewis was a great leader and a great singer. He lived in this community. We would hear him singing by the time we were in sight of the campground. People gathered there for their reunions and

Campground for religious meetings at Riverview, destroyed by flood in 1940 (courtesy of Nell Sutherland).

worshipped. The camp was a loss to the community when it washed away in the 1940 flood.

The next loss to our community was the closing of our school. In 1994 the doors were closed for students. Paul and I would sit on our porch and listen to the children and watch them play. Sometimes we would hear the principal speaking on the intercom. We missed all that after the school closed.

The same year, people from this end of the county from the Tennessee line, up the creeks, over the mountains, and in the valleys came together and began the groundwork to make the school into a community center. There was lots to be done to repair the building and grounds. We began having fundraisers. All our effort to see it develop into a good thing for this part of the county never seemed a burden to the people. They worked with harmony, along with donations and volunteers. It is now a great place to serve the people.

Through Wilkes Community College, the Center has opened up the opportunity for anyone to finish their high school education, along with offering computer classes. Several have taken advantage of the service.

The restaurant is greatly appreciated by the people in this end of the county. It provides us with good food and an atmosphere to feel free to socialize with friends and read your paper while enjoying a good cup of coffee.

Nell Sutherland celebrates her 85th birthday (courtesy of Nell Sutherland).

The community serves a luncheon every Thursday in the banquet room. Everyone that can brings a covered dish. Meat is furnished from the donation box at the luncheon. After lunch there is a Bible study. Everyone that attends thoroughly enjoys it. The Center also has a department store to fit the needs of the families. It is a great service. The community has organized a Lions Club with 50 some members. The Club meets at the Center. They have contributed a lot of volunteer hours and donations to the Center.

I want to express my appreciation to the ones that have moved back to the mountains and the ones that have recently moved here and found this part of Ashe County a beautiful place to live, and who have been so constructive in the projects of the western end of Ashe County on Highway 88.

My life has not been a bed of roses. I have learned that mistakes are not a sign of failure. They lead you to a better way of life. I have been blessed with good health and blessed with strength to see my immediate family to their destination. I leave you with this thought: Please, down through your life, take time to smell the roses!

GWYN HARTSOE, 83

June 16, 1999

At his home on Peak Road in Creston.
His wife Mae and son Robert are present.

I can remember back to my great-grandparents a little, and I can remember my grandparents well. My grandpa Hartsoe, he lived on Mill Creek there, and he come from Rowan County. The Hartsoes came from Germany to Pennsylvania; that's where they first settled. And these come down to Rowan County and then three brothers come from Rowan County into Ashe County. One of them settled at Idlewild, one settled at Mill Creek, and one on Horse Creek. That's where the generation started up here. Then on my grandpa Miller's side, I believe he come from Germany; I believe that is right. He lived on Staggs Creek. His name was Jonathan Miller. I was 15 year old, I believe, when he died. When my grandpa Hartsoe died, I'd been married for years.

I can remember when I was seven years old when I went with a wagon to Bristol. I'd been begging my daddy to go on trips with him and he finally said he'd let me go. It was November and he had a wagon and a big team of horses. He had a wagon and he had 50 bushels of apples in it and he took them to Bristol. We started and we'd go about 20 to 25 miles a day. It took a little over three days to go from here to Bristol and then coming back it took several hours less 'cause you come right on, you wasn't loaded. We's camped along the road and we got into what they call Bartese just out of Bristol. That's where people camped with wagons and they'd be sometimes 12 to 15 wagons camping there at once when you'd get there. We pulled in there and it was November. It was cool, not cold, just cold enough for it to snow. It was cloudy and we got ready to go to bed. We'd been sleeping on the ground, just had a big tarp of a thing he laid out on the ground, then most of the time laid hay or something on it, and then put a quilt over that, and

129

then lay on that and then put quilts over the top of you. That night, he said, "We'd better sleep under the wagon. It's going to snow tonight." Well, I never thought nothing about it snowing. We crawled under the wagon and made our bed in under the wagon and we slept. The next morning we got up, I waked up and was wiggling around. It was after daylight. My daddy said, "Lay right still, it come a big snow last night. Don't bother it, it sets on the edges of the quilt." We was just as warm as we could be. I had an uncle along with a wagon. He said he couldn't lay in the bed, he'd get up in a minute. He said he'd get up and clean off a place and build a fire and then we'd get up and get our breakfast. Sure enough, he got up in a few minutes and built a fire up. People got to crawling out after he got the fire built. There was 10 or 12 people around there in wagons. Most of them had eggs and stuff that they fried for breakfast and meat and one thing and another cooked over the fire.

We went out and we sold the load of apples out that day. They was two of my uncles was along and then a fellow by the name of Milt Roark had a wagon. They was four wagons in that group that come from here over there. They all sold out, but I believe it was Milt Roark's wagon had seven or eight bushels of apples the next morning. So they didn't leave him, they just went ahead and took that one wagon and all of them went with him and they got out and sold them apples, and then they started home. We's gone eight days from the time we left here till the time we got back home. We had a team of two horses pulling the wagon.

As we went over there, we got to what they call Iron Mountain. I was just seven years old, but I could drive the horses. They was gentle and Dad let me drive the horses. We started up the Iron Mountain, him and his two brothers and this Roark fellow — two of them had boys with them — and they's driving a team and I's driving a team. These fellows got out and was walking behind the wagons. I laid down on the wagon seat and went to sleep. Dad said when they's behind, they happened to look down. I had dropped the lines down and they's dragging under the wagon, the ends of them was, and they happened to see the lines. He come around up there. They said I was the back wagon and when they'd stop to rest, then my horses would stop and when the others would start, they'd start. They said they noticed that the wagon would run back just a little when they'd stop before the horses got stopped where they could hold it. They wasn't nobody to pull the brake stick. I was sound asleep. Course, we hardly ever met a car. They just wasn't no cars much on the road back them days.

We got a pretty good price for our apples, I think $1.50 a bushel, the best I remember. It was a big price at that time. It was worth the trip. We raised our own apples. We had a variety of different kinds. Now Virginia Beauty was the best one to sell. I know around us there people had Virginia

Beauty trees, and they'd sell them to you for 25 cents a bushel. We raised some ourselves and bought them up from our neighbors to make this trip. Didn't spray the trees or anything back then. It wasn't necessary.

When I was 17 year old, I went to CCC [Civilian Conservation Corps] camp. You remember them. I didn't have nothing to do much around home and I went to town one day and they was a woman working in the office up there. I knowed her because her father was a doctor from Warrensville and we used to know them well. Her name was Ruth Tugman. I said, "Ruth, I want to go to CCC camp." She said, "Well, I can't send you, your father's not on welfare or anything." I said, "Well, I want to go anyway." She studied a while and she said, "I'll tell you what I'll do, I'll let you go down there as a substitute. In other words, send a number and you can go extra. You'll get to ride down there and back. They'll furnish you a ride and a place to sleep that night and then bring you back. I don't guess you'll get to stay." I got on the bus that was taking me; the bus come to West Jefferson and picked up 15 or 20, I guess. I was talking to a boy as we went down. I told him I didn't guess I'd get to stay. He said, "I'll tell you what you do, when you get down there you get in the front of that line, as close to the front as you can get and go through there to be examined." He said, "You'll get to stay, they won't send you back." So I did and I never heard nothing about me being a substitute. I went on through and two or three days after that, getting all them shots, I was sick. I'd of give anything to be back home. But I stayed in there 18 months.

I went to High Point, N.C., first and then from High Point, they built a camp over at Winston-Salem. They picked so many from the High Point camp and trained them to go over there. I went over there as a leader and helped build that camp. They done away with that camp at Winston and then I went to Yanceyville, then to about 12 miles out of Danville, Virginia, and I stayed up there until I left and come home.

I guess it was the next year after that that I went to Pennsylvania. I went up there and worked in a cannery at 25 cents an hour. I worked there about two months and then they was building a flood wall at the Holtwood Dam. We went up there then and went to work there, and we worked a while there.

Then I come back home and stayed about two months. They started electrifying that railroad then from down Fort Deposit to Philadelphia. I went down there then and worked on that 17 or 18 months on it. Then I come back home and I farmed some, messed around, first one thing and another for two or three years. Then when war was about to break out in '41 I went down to Holly Ridge, N.C., to help build that army camp. Come back from down there and they was building a bagging plant to bag powder over here at Dublin, Virginia, and I went over there and got a job.

I rented an acre of land for $10 a month. I had an old house trailer I'd

Left to right: Gwyn Hartsoe, his daughter Joanne Hartsoe, and Wally (last name not known), outside Baltimore, while Gwyn was working in the shipyard, 1942 or 1943 (courtesy of Gina McCoy-Hopper).

made. We moved it over there. My wife and me had one young'un. We got over there and they was so many people coming in and hunting for a place to stay and something to eat. I run up on a fellow sawing over there from this section over here and he said they had a bunch of cull lumber. I asked him what they wanted for it. He said, "They'll give it to you if you want to haul it." I said, "What would you haul me a couple of loads over here for?" He said, "$15 a load." I told him to just bring it on. He brought it over there and I built a building 14 feet long and 10 feet wide. I put me in a drink stand and sold drinks and stuff in it. Then I decided that I'd fix to feed boarders and went and built another section down the side of it. But I went and checked on it and I couldn't sell a plate lunch. I couldn't sell it that way. They said I could have a table and let them sit down at the table and eat. I could furnish it thataway. So I done that. I had to haul my water. I'd haul a pickup full of 10-gallon cans of water every day, and I had barrels on the outside. I made outside toilets. I worked there until the plant was done. We were through with that the week after the war broke out. We left over there and come back home.

I was married while I was in the CCC camp, just a little while before I left the CCC camp. I was married on the 6th day of July and then I left the next spring. We were both 19. After I come back from there, I went to Baltimore and worked in a shipyard a while, down the other side of Baltimore. Then I come back home and I bought me a sawmill and went into business for myself.

I had a sawmill for 20 years. It was located here. I bought timber down in the east part of Virginia once and over in Virginia and Tennessee and everywhere, just wherever. I would move the sawmill. It was portable. I'd move it from one place to another. You had to take it apart. Then at the last, I put it on steel tracks and put a trailer-type wheel under it and fixed it so I could hook it behind a truck. I had a complete mill. We sawed to beat everything. Nowadays, they got them big mills. I pulled a lever on it; when you sawed, you pulled a lever to pull up to the next board. Now you sit there and push buttons like a typewriter. It looks right funny to see a sawmill running and nobody driving the carriage or anything, a man sitting off near the door, up kindly over looking down at it, operating it. But that's the way they're run now.

I farmed some while I was sawmilling. Through the war, I hauled produce and stuff. I raised beans and stuff and hauled them to the market. There was a big market for beans back then through the war. I made three round trips to Baltimore and back one week and never went to bed. I hauled 1,500 bushel of beans up there that week, 500 bushels a load. I made the three trips and my brother was with me. He was just 15 years old, but he went with me half the time; he wanted to go with me. He'd help keep me awake. I never did go in the Army. They never did call me. I worked in the shipyard. I left from up there while the war was going on to come home. They told me there at the office, "You better not leave; they'll put you in the Army." I said, "They can just put me in, I'm going home." I come down here, and I went to farming and bought this sawmill and went to work and I deferred all the way through it. I didn't have to go. At the shipyard, we were building ships. We built cargo ships. On the last six months I's there, I welded gun foundations mostly and freshwater tanks. When you was welding a fresh water tank, you had to get them right. That was important.

We opened our country store after the war. It was about 1948 and we had the store open about 15 years. My wife got to where she wasn't hardly able to look after it. It didn't make enough for me to stay and fool with it. I had other work and we just closed it up. By that time supermarkets were beginning to come in. There was no money in it for the small grocery. You take today, these little stores, you can go to the supermarket and buy as cheap as they can get it wholesale. We done all right with the little store while we had it. We didn't make no big money, but it run the family, in other words, bought our groceries and stuff. Then she went to work at the post office. Then she got to where she had to give that up.

My grandfather Miller was a Dunkard preacher. That was back kindly before my days. I can remember when he still yet preached. On the by-pass down here, they's not been no preaching done there in years, that was the Dunkard church. He used to preach there. He lived on the head of Staggs Creek. He'd get on his horse and preach once a month. Twice, he preached on Saturday night and then on Sunday morning at Taylors Valley, Tennessee. He'd ride a horse from right over there plumb into Tennessee to preach once a month at a church over there. He done that for several years.

Before we's married, I bought 30 acres of land over there on Mill Creek. It had a big old log house on it. After we's married, we moved in that log house. It snowed a whole lot that winter and I got up at different times of the morning to build a fire and you could track me on the floor where the snow had blowed in. You'd shake it off your quilts on top of you. It was a big log, two-story house.

MAE HARTSOE: Our daughter would always ask how we met. Gwyn told her that he run me out of a briar patch one time, that he rocked me out. But what it really was, girls back then didn't wear overalls and pants. I had on my brother's old overalls and had a hole in the knee. We was digging potatoes and we saw him a-coming up through there. They was a path that would go around the hill to go down on Mill Creek. I jumped down off the fence after I seen him coming 'cause I didn't want him to see me like that and hid in the corner of the fence. He had this little dog with him, they called him Toby, and Toby treed me. Gwyn didn't know I was in there and he got to throwing rocks in there and I had to crawl out.

GWYN: Our daughter, she's just little and she's asking me how we met. I told her that I run Mae out of the briar patch and caught her. The school young'uns was talking about how their parents met and she said, "Dad run Mom out of a briar patch and caught her."

I can remember Poley Hartsoe that made jars. He was Sylvanus's grandson. Poley's the one that used to come into Ashe County and peddle pottery. He first started coming from Catawba County up there with a wagon and a team and he'd bring a load of them jars and leave them with Cora Roland. She was a Hartsoe before she married Emmet Roland. What he didn't sell, he'd leave there for her to sell for him. Later on he'd come, he had an old T model Ford truck, and he'd bring stuff up here. He made all kinds of them. They say if you can find one of them now, it's worth all kinds of money. I don't have any, but I believe Ivalee Seagraves has some. She was a Hartsoe and she lives down at Warrensville.

When our family first came into this country, the original spelling was Hertzog, and it changed to Hartzog and Hartsog and Hartsoe. Idlewild was the brother to the one that we're from; they was brothers, and he spelled his name Hartzog. There's still some people that spell it Hertzog, but not around here. It means duke or leader of armies. This cemetery over here on my property on Mill Creek, they are spelled three different ways. They's one or two over there: zog and sog and soe. All the same family, you might say. My Grandpaw Hartsoe spelled his sog, and then he had two sons that spelled their name sog, and three sons that spelled it soe. I don't know how come. That was back before my day.

Now down here before you turn off to the river bridge, there where the old store house used to be, they'd

Gwyn and Mae Hartsoe with "Pete" the beagle, 1964 (courtesy of Gina McCoy-Hopper).

hold election there before Creston used to hold election. It was the first time Roosevelt run. Dan Jones come up here and some of them dared anybody to holler for Roosevelt. He hollered for Roosevelt and they jumped on him, two or three of them did, and whipped him. He went down to Clifton, I was about 16 year old, I wasn't old enough to vote, but I'd went over to Clifton and was running around on the outside where they's holding election, and he come down there and he gathered up three carloads, part of them couldn't get in and was hanging on the running boards of them old cars, and they come up and they run everybody out of Creston down there. They had them in the woods running. Doc Robinson told me one day, we's talking, I don't know how it come up, but he was talking to me, that was years and years after that. He said he made the most money a-sewing up heads and stuff that day he ever made in one day in his life. Doc was funny. He was a good old country doctor, they's no doubt about that, but old-fashioned.

I can remember when I was about 16 year old, a fellow lived right up above us. His wife was in the family way and he come down to the house, brought a horse down there one evening about three o'clock and wanted to know if I'd ride up and get Doc Robinson. I told him I'd go. It was pretty

Gwyn Hartsoe in Blue Ridge Wagon Train, 1967 or 1968 (courtesy of Gina McCoy-Hopper).

bad, sleeting a little. I got on that old horse and rode it up here. It was a right smart piece, took about three hours and a half to ride it up here and then back. It was after dark a while and I knocked on the door. Mrs. Robinson come to the door and I told her what it was. She said, "Lord, he can't go, he's out all last night, he just come in a few minutes ago, he's wore completely plumb out, I don't think he can make it." I told her who it was and she said, "Well, I'll tell you what, I'll go in there and ask him about it." She wanted me to come in there, and I went in there and explained to him who it was. He said, "I'll tell you what; we'll try it. You go out there in the barn and get my horse out. I've got two in there; one of them will be wet. It was raining and bad and it was just put in a few minutes ago. It won't be dried off yet. Get the other one that's not been rode. The saddle is hanging up there. Put the saddle on it and I'll be on out there in a few minutes." I got out there and I got the horse out and put the saddle on it and got it ready. In a few minutes he come.

I forget how many fences there was that we had to lay down, gates we went through. Back then, for Doc and all these fellows where they was going from one creek to the other, you didn't follow the road. They'd be trails up on the ridges where they rode horses and people would have gates put in. We came out on Mill Creek at the last gate. That was the last I'd seen of the old man Doc till the next evening about three o'clock. He'd went on up there. My mother was up there at the house where he went to. She come in about 10 or 11 o'clock that night and she said the baby was born about 15 minutes after Doc got there. Doc went to bed then after the baby was born and was all right. He slept till the next evening some time, got up and come on home.

I've heard Mrs. Robinson tell about taking water and thawing his feet loose from the stirrups where the ice on them would freeze his feet to the stirrups and she'd take hot water and pour on his boots. Joe Robinson down here has told me about doing that. He said that he carried hot water out when his dad come home and had to pour hot water to get his feet loose from the stirrups where they'd froze to them.

About my schooling, I went one day for my brother and one for another fellow and then went one for myself. I didn't have much schooling. I got up to seventh grade at Mill Creek. I started in the eighth grade a little. I didn't actually have the seventh grade good enough. I started down here at New River then and I was walking from the head of Mill Creek eight miles down over there to school and then eight miles back. That was 16 miles a day. Now that's not very enticing to get you to go to school. Back then people didn't pay too much attention to whether they went to school or not and that's as far as I got.

MAE HARTSOE, 83

June 16, 1999

At her home on Peak Road in Creston.
Her husband Gwyn and son Robert are present.

My grandfather came from Davie County. My father was born in 1880 and he came up here in 1882. My grandfather's name was George Washington Walker and my father's name was William Wesley Walker. The people down there, so many of them were dying of typhoid fever. My grandmother, who was my grandfather's second wife, died with typhoid fever when Dad was two years old. That was partly why he moved. My grandfather heard that the water in the mountains was pure and he thought the water down there at Mocksville was carrying the typhoid germ, so he decided he'd come to the mountains. He come in a covered wagon pulled by a yoke of oxen when my dad was just two years old, still a baby, you might say. They wound up over on this mountain. Of course, Dad was sick; he hadn't had the proper food probably. This little old widow lady lived up in there and she had two daughters. He went to her house and asked if he could get milk for my father. Since she saw how sick the child was, she wanted to keep the baby a few days and doctor him up and see if he would be all right. He let her keep him and he got better. He thought if he was going to settle over there, he needed somebody to help take care of the baby because he had to build a cabin and till the land and make a crop. He decided he'd ask one of these girls to marry him. The lady had two daughters, so he went up and told the old lady that he would like to marry one of her daughters. She said, "Well, we'll go in this other room and talk it over." They went in the other room and came back out and she said, "This younger daughter will marry you." Her name was Mary Jane Hodgins, but they called it Hudgins at this time. So they got married and raised my father.

My grandfather, George Walker, was a Baptist preacher. That's what they tell me, but I can't remember it. I was just 11 years old when he died, so I really don't know.

In 1899 my father met my mother and he married her. They was over on what they call the Little Buffalo. Her name was Mary Emma Faircloth. She was born in 1882. All I know about that is that they had two children that died. One was a little boy that was three years old which died with diphtheria. Then the other baby just lived a few hours. They're both buried on Copeland. After that, they went to Rich Hill where my dad had bought a farm. There were nine children of us all, living children. I guess the rest was born on Rich Hill. I know five of us was. My daddy just farmed till he got to logging. He always worked with a team of horses and did a lot of logging for people, getting logs out of the woods to the sawmill. He farmed and had a few cattle, a few sheep, and we always raised most of what we eat, from what I can remember. We all worked hard, which all families had to do at that time. We always seemed to have enough to eat, not like people have food nowadays, but plenty of vegetables and things like that. We always canned up a lot of stuff.

My older sister was 13 years older than I was. After she married, I was the next girl in line. I had to work in the house, but I worked outside, too, just the same as the boys did. They did a lot of things I couldn't do. We raised and canned food. I can remember when cherries would get ripe; they was cherry trees down on the creek, but up on the head of the creek where we lived, there wasn't any cherry trees. People would go down there to the cherry orchard and they would buy a cherry tree. You got all the fruit that was on that tree, but you had to pick them yourself. We'd have to take the cherries home and seed them. From what I can remember, we must have seeded them by hand. I know how I hated to have to sit and seed cherries. Everybody had to pitch in and help. That's the way we canned our cherries. Of course, we all pitched in and picked blackberries and canned up all our food. We always raised a big garden.

I don't know how much you had to pay for a cherry tree, but it wasn't very much. We always canned up a lot of vegetables. They always raised an awful lot of sweet potatoes, and they kept their own seed potatoes. We had this big bin down under the floor that had been insulated. It was about five or six feet, something like that. I don't know what it was insulated with, probably sawdust. You raised up a section of the floor and they always kept sand in there. They put a layer of sand down and the following year when they dug the sweet potatoes, they picked out the good ones that didn't have any bad places, broke places in them, and kept them for seed, which, from what I can remember, was about three bushel. They'd place them down in that sand, then they'd put a layer of sand, then they'd put another layer of sweet potatoes till they got the potatoes in there and then they'd put the floor back down over it. They kept good all winter. Then in the spring of the year when it got time for them to plant potatoes, they'd raise the floor up and get all the potatoes out and save the sand, of course, for the next year. Then they bedded the sweet potatoes and raised their own plants. They sold plants. I know how I always hated to have to help plant those sweet potatoes 'cause they was always so many of them. Dad believed in raising plenty.

I don't remember how many acres he had, but it was just a big garden. They dug up big ridges around through the garden and you set them about four inches apart and they was always lots of sweet potatoes. We always raised lots of cabbage. We buried the cabbage underground for the winter time. I can remember, we had cabbage up in the spring of the year. They would get them out and they would make kraut in the spring of the year. Of course, they made kraut in the fall, but it was usually gone by that time. They'd take these extra cabbage in the spring of the year and make kraut and keep it in big jars, big old crocks.

We went to Rich Hill to school, a one-room schoolhouse. I remember the wind would blow and it would just creak and we'd think it was going to blow over. That building is gone. They built a new two-room school after that. Then they consolidated the schools at Riverview. After the seventh grade, I went to Riverview two years.

Our farm was located right on the very head of Rich Hill. If you've ever been up Rich Hill, the Sapp Cemetery is right there in the curve, and then you go up to Walker Mountain, which was named after my father. It's about the highest place up there. It goes around Big Springs. We always called it Big Springs Mountain, but afterwards they got to calling it the Walker Mountain because Dad lived there. After you turn off Rich Hill Road and go left-handed, that's Walker Road. There's not very many people lives on that road now. People have moved away. It's Will Walker Road.

My grandparents and my parents are buried down in the Sapp Cemetery. I believe it's listed in the census as the Samuel Sapp Cemetery.

I think my first teachers were Anna Osborne, Ocie Graybeal, and Chessie Graybeal. They were all neighbors. Millard Eller was one teacher. Maybe one of the teachers would teach two or three years. I just went through the seventh grade. They's a crowd of children there at one time in that one-room school, so one teacher had to keep up with a lot of children. They were different ages, starting at six years old. School was just six months a year at that time. I know I was real small when I started to school. I remember that because when it'd get bad and raining, the big girls would pick me up and carry me.

When we had recess at school, we played games—tag and stink base. That's a game where you had a base and somebody was on that. The others would try to slip around and tag him and get him off. If whoever's there, somebody must have been watching, if they tagged him before they got to tag the one that was on the stink base, they had to go on the stink base. Sometimes they'd be five or six on the stink base. That's the way it went until you got everybody on or everybody off. I don't know how it got named stink base. There was a lot of different games, drop the handkerchief, ring around the roses, and games like that. They played ball. From what I remember, where I went to school, we didn't play ball much. Of course, we didn't have very much of a play yard, just a little place in front of the schoolhouse.

We walked to school. It was a mile and a half or so from our home. If it snowed, we waded the snow. If they's ice on the road, we went just the same and we'd skate along on the ice. Most of the times you could stand up, but sometimes you didn't.

I remember one time Dad sent my brother and me down below where the Big Laurel Church is over there now, to this lady's house where Dad had grazed some yearlings. We was supposed to bring the cattle home. We went down there and we got our yearlings out. I was about 15 at that time, and I guess my brother was about 12. We started up through there with them. We come up the Roaring Fork, and the road don't go now like it did at that time. Anyway, we came up Roaring Fork and we got to this one house and these old dogs run out from under the floor barking and turned the cattle back down the road. We had to go back and round up the cattle and head back up the road. We got up there and here come the dogs and chased our cattle back. We seen the people looking out the windows but they didn't come out and scold their dogs. We got them back up pretty close that time and I said to my brother, "Now wait just a minute and let me get in front." So I got in front of the cattle and I picked up all the rocks I could get. We got up to the house and here come the dogs again. I started throwing rocks, and I rocked them dogs back under that house. Nobody never did come out, but we got our cattle by that time. Of course, I heard about that for an awful long time. We never did hear from those folks.

I can't remember when I really met Gwyn, 'cause back then we didn't have many places to go. On Easter, people would go up on what we called the Dove's Knob, just something to do, and a crowd would go up there. I guess that was the first time I ever saw Gwyn. That's on Rich Hill, too. It's between Rich Hill and Mill Creek. It was a pretty place to go. You just got out and wandered around and made up your own games. Of course, you went to church and boys walked you home. I guess that's the way we mostly met. We'd usually just go up there to walk 'cause you could see almost everyone you knew when you got up there.

We got married when we were 19 and went to housekeeping. I lived on Rich Hill then and he lived on a hill between Rich Hill and Mill Creek, not many miles apart as the crow flies. He made many a trip across that hill over

Left to right: Frances Sapp (who married Mae's brother, Ben Walker), Gwyn Hartsoe, and Mae Hartsoe, 1935 (courtesy of Gina McCoy-Hopper).

to our house. Then we moved up north and our first child [Joanne] was born in Peach Bottom, Pennsylvania. We stayed up there and worked in Pennsylvania, Maryland, and different places. We came back down here and Bob was born while we lived on Mill Creek. Then we sold out and come up here. The last one was born here and Doc Robinson delivered her. We had three children and we now have two living children.

We moved here in 1945. We're just a short distance from the river here, about a quarter of a mile, but when we moved here, there wasn't any road here. It was a gravel road, but I don't know whether you'd call it a gravel road or not. There's never been no gravel on it. It's a mud road. There wasn't any houses up through here at that time. It was a wee bit scary in a way, 'cause I wasn't used to being isolated quite that bad. We were raised on Rich Hill and they's always a lot of young people. Of course, we walked where we wanted to go, and they's always a road full of us. They's 56 acres here.

I've always stayed at home, except I did work over at the post office about four years as a clerk, the Creston Post Office. It was over on 88 then, but it's over on Three Top now.

We've had high water here. There was a big flood in 1940, but we lived on Mill Creek at that time. I don't know how many years ago it's been, but the creek overflowed and come out in the yard. You couldn't get through down here at this knitting mill because the water was so big. One year it washed a two-by-six up against that porch post out there, then it went across the road over yonder. You couldn't ford the road through there. It lasted about three or four hours before it went down. This is Peak Road and the other end is West Peak Road, but the creek doesn't have a name. Down here, it's Three Top Creek as you go up Three Top.

We used to go to church down here when we first moved up here up until maybe 10 years ago. It's a Methodist church. They don't have a very large crowd but it's a real nice church. It's real old. It used to be Worth's Chapel, 18 something it was established. Then we started going

Mae Hartsoe with Mary on Rich Hill, 1946 (courtesy of Gina McCoy-Hopper).

up to Big Laurel Church and we've been going up there now for seven years. It used to be if we went to church we walked. I remember Dad taking us to church on a horse, but I never did ride a horse.

I've always wished I could play music, but I can't. After we got a record player, we always had different records to play, which they wasn't always gospel music — whatever was popular along then, whenever you could get enough money to buy one.

There have been many changes since I was young and growing up. One thing that I really notice is that when couples get married nowadays, they usually have them an apartment or a little place to live, and they've got to have everything furnished and it's all got to match up just exactly. When we went to housekeeping, we used what we could get our hands on. We just mostly had a table and a stove and a bed and some chairs, and, of course, a few other things, a few cookers and a few dishes. We got along just fine, better, I think, than people get along now, because they have it all handed down to them. We worked for what we got. When you do that, I think you appreciate it more.

After we moved over here, we just done the things that most farmers do. We made a garden, we milked the cows, we churned our own butter. We

Mae Hartsoe and her "old-fashioned but-terbeans," about 1980 (courtesy of Robert Hartsoe).

had chickens and had our own eggs. We always had some hogs and killed hogs and worked up our meat. We were taught to do as we's raised. We always had a garden and done a lot of canning. We used glass jars. We canned meat, too, even canned chicken. We canned it and steamed it. Then we didn't have pressure canners. We used a hot water bath to can. You put your jars down in hot water and boiled it so long, two or three hours usually. You sealed your cans before you cooked it. Back then we usually had those zinc lids and jar rings. Food didn't keep good then like it does now, because you couldn't always tell when your cans were sealed up good. We canned all of our corn. When we had beef, we didn't usually eat much beef at that time. For the last 25 years, we've never been out of beef. We've killed a beef nearly every year. We had a freezer then and started freezing beef and stuff, instead of canning so much, which is what we do now. We didn't eat all the eggs. We saved the eggs and took them to the store and traded them for sugar and salt and things you had to have from the store. When we moved up here, there was a store about a mile from here. Then they's another one down here about a mile and a half at the mouth of the Laurel where you turn off 88.

We used to have a little grocery store out here next to the house. I worked in the store. The people who came were just local people that lived all around here. Many people had to walk to go to the store then. We had basic things like sugar, coffee, flour, meal, and canned goods. We had just groceries and kerosene. We always had kerosene 'cause people had to have a lot of kerosene at that time for kerosene lamps.

GWYN: When we first moved up here we were here about two years before we got electric. The electric came in, I guess it was about '46 or '47. Down here at Sharpe's Dam, most of that power went to West Jefferson. When they first come in here, our electricity run about $1.50 a month. Of course, we use a lot more now than we did then, but then it was mostly just your lights and little stuff like the electric iron. Later on we got electric stoves and everything.

MAE: We've been up here 54 years. We have six grandchildren and nine great-grandchildren. Two of them are step-grandchildren. Robert lives right up the road here. Our daughter [Joanne] lives back over at the old homeplace; she built a new home over there. She stays up here part of the time. She lives in Atlanta, Georgia.

One grandson lives in Winston-Salem. One lives in Georgia. The other grandchildren all live in North Carolina. Just one granddaughter lives close. Our grandchildren don't believe that things were like they was when we was growing up. They think we're just getting a little excited when we start telling them about it. They've always had so much. We didn't know we's missing out on all this. But I believe we got along better then than we do today.

GWYN: We lived good, we didn't starve or anything, we just didn't have a lot of money to spend. At that time, in the mountains here when we's growing up, there wasn't any factories or anything to work at, just the farm was all there was.

MAE: Now people come from far off to settle up here, and I can understand why. It's nice and peaceful.

Mrs. Hartsoe died on September 1, 2000.

WILLIAM EARL (BILL) FARRINGTON, 81

October 22, 1998

At his home near Shatley Springs in Ashe County.
His wife Leona is present and participates.

I grew up on the New River. We had about a mile of frontage on the river [near the Sheets Bridge and the site of Zaloo's Canoes]. We did most of our farming along the river. We did a lot of work to clear land. We did all our plowing with oxen because the land was too steep for horses. My dad was away on construction work most of the time and I had to run across the hill to Bare Creek and put the feed out for the cattle there and then run back to the milk gap and milk about a half dozen cows. I had made myself a little wagon. I couldn't carry the five-gallon milk can down there. I was always afraid that I would drop it or something would happen and I would lose it all. I made this little cart. I cut the little thin wheels and I drilled a hole through the middle and then I drilled another hole to hold the wheel on the axle of the little cart. Then I had to get to the house and eat a little breakfast and I had to get that milk down to the road so they would pick it up and take it to the cheese factory. Then I had to run to catch the school bus. They were pretty good about it; they would wait unless they had reason to believe that I wasn't going to come and go to school that day.

A truck would come around and pick up the five-gallon can of milk and put it on the truck and they would take it all into West Jefferson to the cheese factory. We counted quite a bit on getting money to run the farm and do the things that we needed to do. They would bring the can back every day.

There were nine brothers and sisters in my family. I was the oldest. I had to keep my brothers from fighting all the time. It just kept me busy. I guess it was good for me. After I got through doing that, I got to go to college

146

over at Lees-McRae [in Banner Elk]. That got me in the Navy and then they found out that I had done certain things, like doing work on lathes and things like that. I can't remember just what year I went into the Navy, but I was over there for two years. I went in before Pearl Harbor, because I was stationed at Pearl Harbor and was home on leave when they attacked. A lot of my friends were killed then.

My granddaddy lived on the river, too. Marion Bower was his name. He was a great little guy. Most of his sons were bigger than he was, but he kept them in line and got everything done the way it should be. I don't know their background, what country of Europe they might have come from. I could never remember far enough back to know when they had moved onto that farm along the river there. They had about a mile of the river on one side. My granddaddy had horses and I just loved to go out with some of my uncles and be around those horses, because it was a little different than being around steers.

We raised mostly corn and we also raised cane. We would strip the leaves off the cane and make them into bunches and take them and feed them to the cattle. So when the cane got up to a certain height, we'd lop the pod at the top off. My dad had an oxen and a cane press. As the oxen was led around and around, another person was shoving in the cane after the leaves had been stripped off. Then we had to make a furnace; we had it from year to year. You'd build a fire under the pan and the juice would run in there and boil for hours. We had a boiler almost as long as across this room. We'd get a bucketful of juice where the rollers were squeezing the juice out. We all liked molasses. I think we sold some, too, 'cause we weren't too flush on money. We'd sop the paddle that you stir it with and get the white foam that's sweet and eat that.

A lot of the young people would come around and first thing you knew they were over on the other side of the big pile of cane, where the juice had been squeezed out of it. It was all just a nice get together, really. Sometimes we'd get the cane and chew it, strip the outer shell of it — it was too hard to bite — so you would just cut it off at each end where the joints were. You'd have somewhere between a foot and two feet of cane. When the vessel that was catching the squeezin's was full, we'd take it and pour it in the big open pan. It was only about a foot high all the way around, but it was a large pan. The boiler wasn't quite the length of this room here, but there was people feeding the cane into the mill and then pouring it through the strainer. It strained all of the stuff that shouldn't be in the molasses.

We took our corn and wheat to have it ground for the winter to an old mill way down the river. They would crack it and run it through the mill and then it would fall down into the mesh, like you have in a screen door. The flour would go through and the chaff would be thrown away. That was

William Earl (Bill) Farrington at his home in 1998.

our winter flour. Corn meal was the same way. I carried many sacks of corn. This was after the corn had hardened and we'd take it over on Bare Creek about two miles— walked across the hill and then walked a mile up to where the mill was and they would mill the corn, run it through and get the corn meal. There were three brothers who ran the mill. Horton Sheets was the name of one of them.

On Sunday for recreation with the girls, we had what you call a johnboat and we'd all get in the boat and go out on those little islands in the river and eat and build a little fire. Things like that was our main way of having a little fun.

We had a very small house up on the hill. Dad had a lot of lumber down near the river. He was going to build a new house for my mother. The river came up and it all went down the river. This downpour had happened during the night and the river was just swollen and it swept the lumber away. He wanted to build a nicer house in a better place. We were back up in a hollow away from the road. It just broke his heart; he never was the same after that. He didn't get to build the house. I think when he lost all his lumber that he'd worked so hard to get he couldn't get over the disappointment.

He was good at building. He was with a concrete/steel bridge company. He went up in Pennsylvania with them and he was pretty much the boss because he knew how to handle all of that kind of lumber and the different things. He was great at getting just the right quality of mix.

He built a small stone church up on Big Ridge. I don't know quite what happened to him. He seemed to feel that he had kind of gotten off what he had started out to do and when it washed his lumber away, he wanted dearly to build a house for our mother. He ended up going to Ohio. I would go and stay with him for a day or two every once in a while. He had an old house that was in a state of rack and ruin and he locked the doors so nobody could come in on him and he had a hole dug where he could get under the house and come up inside the house then from underneath.

The stone church he built is still there. I think it is still used for a church. We were up there about a year and a half ago. It was locked and you couldn't get in but they had done a lot of work inside. I don't think it's any particular denomination. My father had a yoke of oxen and an old farm wagon, and he quarried the stone and took it all the way up to this Big Ridge church. Dad should have been working at a job of some kind, but he loved to do things like that, quarrying and building. He loved to build things. When he was working for Concrete Steel Bridge Company as one of their foremen, he ran the whole thing up in Pennsylvania. When he started working on the church he wasn't working anywhere else, but he wasn't being paid for working at the church. We had pretty slim pickings for awhile there. That was not my church either, not the one I was a member of or attending. My family were Methodists. This preacher, I've forgotten what his name was, but he kind of got him into wanting to do something, so he didn't do too much for the family when he was doing all this. He had a yoke of oxen and he pulled it all the way from just up toward Glendale Springs from the bridge down there; it turned off to the left to go up Bare Creek.

Before I went to Lees-McRae, I went to school at Jefferson, a public school. For a price, this fellow took about a half dozen of us in his car, Carl somebody was his name, and he took us in the morning and brought us back in the evening. He went out around Glendale Springs, somewhere up that way. I went to the Orion Methodist Church and to Sunday School.

My family home, after everybody sort of scattered and left, the floating poker game in the county moved in and first thing anybody knew, and I don't know if it was late fall, winter, or early spring, but they burnt the house down to keep warm while they were having a poker game. This poker game got out of hand. As I remember it, there was a fight and somebody almost got killed up there. They were all kind of poor people and wanted to make a little extra money at the poker game, have a little good luck, and so everybody was pretty much on edge. If they could get it through their buddies, they would take it.

My father's name was James Walter Farrington. My grandfather and grandmother on my mother's side, were the Bower family. I don't know whether Annabel [Colvard Hunter Harrill] told you or not, but her great-grandmother and my great-grandmother are the same person. Annabel's sister, Edie, works in Indian Affairs in D.C. When we were still in Michigan we were having a seminar on the Native Americans and we needed some material. So she sent us a packet with a lot of information. There was a note in there and she said, "I don't believe you know this, but your great-grandmother and my great-grandmother are the same person." They were a very close family. Her father was very good to me.

The Bowers and the Colvards had ties. There is the Bower/Colvard cemetery. When Jefferson Landing bought that property, the cemetery was there and, of course, they couldn't touch it, they had to leave it. Some of the slaves are buried there, more on the low ground.

I went to that [elementary] school for about four years. It was Big Ridge School and it was a fairly old building, two rooms, two teachers, and they had it pretty tough. There were some kids that their parents didn't do anything for them except give them the back of their hand. Anyway, this one boy was just a holy terror. He was determined not to take anything from anybody and he carried a knife. When this teacher was going to give him a couple of swats with a paddle, he came out with his knife and almost cut a couple of her fingers off. That was real mountain country up there and people did not have very much, didn't have any to spare as far as their food and clothing and everything. That was before the Depression. I was born in 1917.

When I went over to the Jefferson school, once some of us boys skipped the first day of spring and we were just all primed and ready to go here, go there, go everywhere. We weren't at all interested in going to school. Usually they counted heads, to see if everybody was there, but they didn't count heads at this particular time, and we took off and went right up to the top of Mount Jefferson, which was called Nigger Mountain then. We would just pace ourselves so that we would come out over at the Colvard farm and get picked up by the school bus and nobody ever said a word to us. I think we just tried that once each year. We knew we'd be in deep trouble if they thought we were doing this as a routine thing, 'cause they would know that we weren't doing much in school.

I met my wife in Flint, Michigan. That was during the war and I was going to the General Motors Institute. A group of us Navy guys would go to the Flint Athletic Club.

On the New River, it was too rocky to have much more than what you call a johnboat on it. That's a boat as long as from this wall over to that wall, 12 feet long, maybe. I've seen some on the river in the last few years; fishermen use them. They're built up in the back and they're pointed in the front like a canoe. You couldn't put too many people in them for if you rolled a little bit, you'd get a boat full of water. They were used just to transport people and maybe a few goods, not much, just what a person might carry, and

Bill Farrington tries his luck (skill) fishing in the New River in 1993 (courtesy of Leona and Bill Farrington).

for fishing. A lot of people had to have one to get across the river. There were people that lived up about half way to Glendale Springs. There was a fellow named Colvard Miller, and he had his house across the river and he had to either wade or have a boat to pull him back and forth across the river. My granddaddy Bower had to do that. They had a boat to take them over from the farm.

LEONA: Our son and one of his employees, it'll be two years the end of this month, got in at Sheets Bridge down there and went for 211 miles to West Virginia. It's the New River in West Virginia, it dumps into the Ohio River and then into the Mississippi River. They left here with two canoes, each one had one canoe. They had all their supplies and the telephone company loaned our a son a wireless telephone. He used to call us about once every other night. He called Mr. Davison, who is the chairperson of the National Committee for the New River, so we would know where they were. They were supposed to call and let us know when they were going to be picked up, how far they got. He didn't call me for a couple of nights and Mr. Davison called and said they hadn't called him, so we began to worry because they were getting into rough water up there. They didn't call and didn't call and what happened is they couldn't get their telephone to go over that far. The two boys knew they had to be picked up the next day, they were going to be at the end of their destination, and they had their tents up and they were sleeping. About four o'clock in the morning my son heard a truck coming and he said, "I didn't even stop to get dressed, all I had on was a pair of underwear." He said, "I ran out and stopped that truck driver." It's a wonder they didn't shoot him. He said, "I begged him to call. I gave him the number of Mr. Davison to call and they kind of said, 'No, no, no.'" So I finally had to give them some money. He said, "I didn't know if they would take the money and call or what." But they came back and they said they got him. Mr. Davison called us right away and said, "Well, we've located them." Otherwise, we didn't know where they were or what had happened to them. Mr. Davison tried to keep me calm and I think I was trying to keep him calm. It was a scary time, because we didn't know where they were. There were some dams that they had to deal with. There was kind of a nice writeup in the New River pamphlet about the trip they took.

We still do canoeing on occasion. Do you know about the race on the first Saturday of every June? That Saturday our son closes his business [Zaloo's Canoes]; he saves canoes for the 4-H and they have what they call the 4-H Race, canoe race, and they give prizes. They canoe five miles, divided up into different groups, of course, and Bill and our son, I think for three years won some awards. They both go canoeing with Scouts and church groups. But the last two or three years Bill hasn't done that. Our son's name is Newton.

In spite of the river being so low this year and the weather so hot, business has not been too bad. It's been much, much worse other years. The one year it was so low, 1987, it was very low and it was a hot summer. A lot of people would come up and we would tell them the river was too low. But they said they didn't care if they had to pull their canoe, it was so hot in Winston and Charlotte, just to get away. But it does cut back some.

Bill stayed with Ford Motor Company until he retired on January 1, 1980, after 33 years. We moved down here [near Shatley Springs] five years ago, but we had bought the house in 1977. We bought it then for us to use and the children to use.

RUSSELL COLVARD, 81

February 25, 2000

*At his home on Nathan's Creek School Road.
His wife Peggy is present for part of the interview.*

Life on the New River was hard in the early 1900's. I was born in 1918. When I was three and one-half years old my mother died, just days after giving birth to my youngest brother, leaving my father to raise seven children by himself. The oldest girl was only 12 years old and the next oldest girl was 10. When the baby was only a few weeks old the family came down with the flu. My dad's sister came to see what she could do to help. She took the baby home with her to keep until the family got well. He never came back. He lived with Aunt Alva Jane until she passed away, and he was a grown man by then.

My grandfather was Thomas Farrow Colvard. He was born over in Wilkes County on October 12, 1835. He was a surveyor, a carpenter, a blacksmith, just a jack of all trades. The Colvards came from Wilkes County to Ashe County. Before that, I think they came from Maryland. I think that it was Calvert first and somehow it got changed. All the Colvards in this county are related and they all came across the mountain from Wilkes County. The first ones that came landed up at Buffalo Creek near Warrensville. Some lived up at Grassy Creek, not too far away.

My grandmother's name was Luticia Cornelia Reeves. My wife Peggy always said that if we had a granddaughter, she wanted to name her Luticia Cornelia, but we didn't insist on it.

Two of my grandfather's sisters married and migrated to Texas. I've got two cousins that live in Texas. I had an uncle also that migrated to Texas. When we were in Texas three years ago we went to visit the cemetery in the town of Gordon, about 50 miles west of Fort Worth. There were a lot of relatives buried there, some I'd never heard of.

153

The Thomas Farrow and Luticia Cornelia Colvard home in the 1920's (courtesy of Molly Gambill).

My father's name was Jesse Reeves Colvard. My mother was a Dickson, Molly Dickson. Now they just spell it Dixon, the same Dicksons that used to spell it that way spell it Dixon now. Jesse Reeves Colvard and Molly Dickson were married July 12, 1903. Molly died February 15, 1922. The children from this marriage were:

Howard Marshall, born December 4, 1904
Thomas Charles, born March 5, 1907
Lena May, born November 7, 1909
Lilah Ray, born June 13, 1912
Ara Blanche, born March 18, 1916
William Russell, born October 24, 1918
Neal Dickson, born January 23, 1922

When gardening time came each spring my Aunt Alice Sheets would come to help my sisters Lena and Lilah plant a garden. I can remember seeing her coming down the road. She would always be carrying a big walking stick and she would have a sack over her shoulder. She would have seeds in this sack she had saved to plant. She would walk through the peak, which was several miles. She lived at Wagoner.

The River [the New] is nice if you live on the right side of it. Our farm was on the wrong side of the river. So, we had to cross the river in a boat, or ride a horse, or use the horses and wagon. We were on the opposite side from everything. We also lived a long way from the store, the school, the town.

My two sisters, Lena and Lilah, finished grade school at Dog Creek School, which was approximately three miles away. The high school was in West Jefferson. There was no transportation to the high school in West Jefferson from Dog Creek. My sisters boarded with relatives near the school. They took turns going one year. One went to school and the other one would stay home to help my dad with the chores and care for me. They did this for two years. An enterprising neighbor built a school bus out of plywood on the back of a Model T Ford truck, which he ran to West Jefferson School. I can remember times when my sisters would leave home before daylight to catch the bus, which was about three miles away. They graduated the same year.

When my sister Blanche and I were ready for high school we were able to attend Nathan's Creek. Sometimes, instead of walking a mile and a half to catch the bus, I would just walk directly to school. It was farther but I didn't care. Sometimes the ice would be in the river and this would keep us from getting across at all. When the weather was really cold for a long period of time this would cause the ice to become very thick and when it would warm up and rain the river would rise and cause the ice to break up in large chunks. These chunks would come down the river pushing and shoving large pieces on the banks that would maybe weigh a ton.

Then there is what we call mush ice. This is when the ice begins to freeze. It's not a solid piece. This is when the ice starts to form but keeps floating down the river. When this gets real thick it is almost impossible to push a boat through it. I've had it to catch me out in the river while crossing in a boat, and I would have to let the boat drift down the river to where it widened out. Therefore, it would let the ice spread out so that I could push the boat to the bank.

My dad was a farmer. Before the Ashe County Cheese plant came to West Jefferson, there just weren't many families with jobs that furnished a regular pay check. Selling milk furnished us a little money. Before that, all we had would be a few calves and chickens to sell. There just weren't any jobs to be had. The way we got the milk to the cheese factory was by taking it across the river to meet the milk truck. We hauled it across the river on a buggy like the Amish have in Pennsylvania.

When I was growing up on the farm we grew a lot of corn. We always thought we had to have a good corn crop. That was our mainstay. This fed the animals—horses, cows, chickens, and hogs. It fed us, too, cornbread. We

Russell Colvard points to ford once used to get from the "wrong side" to the "right side" of the river. Crossing is now forbidden by current owners (year 2000).

always had turkeys which we could sell for extra cash. We grew our own vegetables. We had bees for honey. We made molasses and had our own orchard. We were almost self-sufficient back then. All we had to buy was coffee, sugar, and kerosene for the oil lamps. We brought our corn up the river to have it ground at Cockerham's Mill, which was located where Dog Creek goes into the river. The old millhouse is still standing.

We had to furnish our own recreation in those days. When I was a boy one big thing was baseball. The boys in the neighborhood would just gather and choose up and play ball. We fished and hunted. We'd hunt rabbits, squirrels, quail, and grouse. There were several quail in this area at that time. I loved to hunt for Bob Whites. There were no turkeys then, except domestic turkeys, and no deer.

Often there were dances over the area. They've had dances at my dad's house when I was small. My sisters were grown up by then. People would organize dances in homes by getting the local musicians to come and make music. My oldest brother played the banjo.

I remember it very distinctly when they were talking about flooding this area for a dam. It was in the Seventies. I really wasn't looking forward to the dam, but I never figured there would be any stopping it. I figured it was a sure thing. People finally got together and a fellow that lived farther down the river here in the Chestnut Hill area, Sidney Gambill, had a lot of know-how. He was a prominent lawyer and he used to work up in Washington. They were going to take some of his property for a park, and that didn't suit him. He was the leader and they finally got it stopped. Our farm was still intact. I sold it a few years back, but not at that time.

Back several years, I had a heart attack and eventually had bypass surgery. It was a good bit of work farming down there, mowing, putting up hay, hauling the hay out up here to feed it, so I just decided to set the place in white pines. At that time, I never thought about ever selling. Then the Park Service wanted to buy it and I just let them have it. Now it's part of the New River State Park.

About the changes in my lifetime, probably the economics would be number one. There's no comparison. When I was growing up there was nothing for the men to do to make any money. There were a few jobs at sawmills, sawing, cutting timber, something of that type. Several Ashe County men went to West Virginia to work in the coal mines. Some went to earn money to get a start to help pay for a house or a farm. If you could get a job, it only paid 10 cents an hour around here. The coal mines paid more. I had an uncle who went to West Virginia. He worked as a carpenter for 75 cents an hour.

I have always worked and lived in Ashe County except for about three years that I spent in the Army in World War II. I was in the Air Force. I was a mechanic. I didn't know a thing in the world about an airplane when I went in the Army, but they gave us an exam, and I reckon they thought I could do a little mechanic work. That's where I ended up.

After I came home from the Army, I started out farming. I tried to make a go of it for about eight years and I just starved out. I started out working for Monroe Taylor as a carpenter. He was working at Phoenix Chair when I started work for him and I just ended up staying there working for Russell Barr. When Russell Barr left the chair factory he wanted me to go with him to his new plant. I worked there for several years and left to work for the Ashe County School System in the Maintenance Department.

I retired about 16 years ago from the Ashe County School System where I worked on building maintenance. I continue to farm on a small scale. I keep a few cows and grow enough hay to feed them.

Peggy and I were married in 1952. We have two sons, two grandsons, and one granddaughter. Our older son Leslie lives and works in Gaffney, South Carolina. He has two sons, Bryan and Jason, who are presently attending North Carolina State University. Our second son Malcolm lives and works in the Charleston, West Virginia, area. He has a little daughter named Kelsey Paige who is now five years old.

We did not want our sons to farm. We encouraged them to get a better education so they could get better wages for their work. Farmers have to do a lot of work that doesn't pay anything.

BEN HARRISON, 78

February 5, 1999

At his home on Buckeye Lane,
off Highway 16, east side of Jefferson.

My father worked for the International Harvester Company and he traveled all over. I was born in Tennessee and we lived in several states: West Virginia, Virginia, and South Carolina, before we finally came to North Wilkesboro. That's where I went to school. Then we moved over here in Ashe County in 1940 and ran a restaurant and boarding house in Lansing. I went in the army in 1940, so I didn't stay in Lansing much of the time. It was home. Of course, nobody in the army knew where Lansing was. When they asked me where I lived I said Winston-Salem.

I was in the African invasion in 1942 and then I went to Sicily and up into Italy. We invaded Sicily; I went in at Licata. Then I got a break. I got hepatitis and they sent me back to North Africa to a hospital. I stayed there about six weeks and I caught up with my outfit at Palermo. We stayed there a while and went on to Italy. But I wasn't in the Italian invasion. We rode trucks right up across the straits and up the boot to Naples. That's about it. I finally made it up to the north Apennines and that's where I was wounded.

I was in engineers, best outfit in the army. I was in corp troops regiment and we were attached to the Third Division in Africa. When we got to Tunisia we were attached to the British Eighth Army. They didn't want us and all they'd let us do was take out land mines and stuff like that. We were attached to them for duty and rations. That's where I learned to eat kidney and cauliflower. I didn't particularly care for them, but we had tea every meal and I still drink hot tea a lot of the time. Then we got into Sicily and we were attached to the First Division for a while. When we got up in Italy we were attached to the Free French army and they pulled them out and sent them to southern France when they were invading Europe there. We figured,

Ben Harrison at Memorial Day service, Ashe Lawn, 1998 (courtesy of Ben Harrison).

well, we'd get back with an American outfit now for sure, and they attached us to the Brazilian Expeditionary Force. That was who I was with when I got hurt. I lost a leg.

They put me in the hospital. I was in Walter Reed Hospital for quite a while when I came back to the states. My wife-to-be, Iris Hamby, was in the WAVES in Washington and we got reacquainted. I knew Iris before the war and we married in June 1945 and raised three kids. She was in the communication section of the WAVES. We have three children and they're doing well. I have a son, Robert, who is in the school system over at Oak Ridge, Tennessee. He lives in Knoxville. My oldest daughter, Sarah, teaches school in Charleston, South Carolina. My youngest daughter, Barbara, works for the Board of Education in Wilkes County.

I helped build this "shack" here. You couldn't get dressed lumber or anything then. These rafters and everything are made out of oak right out of a sawmill. I sawed them with a handsaw. The other guy told me where to saw, but I did the grunt work. They didn't have table saws, I guess, back then. We didn't have one anyway. We moved in and I worked for a bottling plant up here in town for a while, in '48 that was. I started working for [Fred] Colvard in '49. He had a pretty good operation for this little county, for a hillside farm.

At one time, his operation varied, but we usually grew about 500 acres of row crops. Then he had 500 breeding sheep, ewes. He ran some cattle, too, about 300 head. He sold the first Christmas trees that ever went out of here, absolutely. Sold them to Kroger's store in Roanoke, Virginia. That's where we delivered them to. I wish I could remember when that was. I have a picture of Avery Starling in here, standing in Fred's Christmas trees in 1962 and they were up pretty high then. So I'd say it was along about that time that the first load of trees went out. On my 25th anniversary of working for him, he gave me a little album with pictures and a $50 bill, two dollars for each year. That was quite a bit of money to me.

I worked in the office. I did the payrolls and I was on the phone a lot. We sold tractors and farm implements. It was a dealership for tractors and we had a parts department and I was the parts man. When you worked 10 hours a day for six days a week, you had to have something to keep you busy.

Colvard Farms was about the biggest business around here back then. When we'd start digging potatoes, we had a one-row digger and a two-row digger that would go underneath the potato rows and pick the dirt and everything up and shake the dirt out and leave the potatoes on top of the ground. We let kids pick them up, I mean youngsters 10 and 12 years and older. Our foreman would just step them off what he thought they could handle according to age. My son, Bob, started working there when he was 12 years old, hoeing cabbage. He got a Ph.D. in education eventually. He's prouder of that work he did on Colvard Farms at 50 cents an hour than anything he's done since. But now a youngster can't get a job any more. That's something that gripes me.

When the word got out that we were going to dig potatoes, that packing house yard would be full. There'd be 150 kids out there wanting to work and we could only use about 70. Fred Colvard would hide; he'd let the foreman and the timekeeper pick them out. Some of the little kids, I felt sorry for them, they'd cry and they'd go to the field anyway. And they'd have to get them by the arm and lead them out of the field. They were all school kids, of course, and when they finished high school, there wasn't that much work in the county for them and they were heading out to these furniture places around the foot of the mountain, Statesville and Lenoir. I was on a first-name basis with the personnel managers of these places and they'd call me and say, "We have a fellow here by the name of so and so and he says his last place of employment was Colvard Farms." It was because he was straight out of high school. After three or four years, these guys knew me and they'd call me and they would say, "I've got a fellow here by the name of so and so that says he worked on Colvard Farms, did he?" And I said, "Yeah, he worked for us." They'd say, "I'm not going to ask you if he was a good worker, because we've never got a bad worker from Colvard Farms." I can understand why. They were leaving here at 50 cents an hour, 60 hours a week, and going down there and getting $1 minimum wage for eight hours a day. Man, they couldn't afford not to be a good worker.

At one time Fred Colvard and Loma Woolfolk had about 10 acres of cut flowers, sold them all up and down the east coast, from Florida up to Norfolk. I think we sold some up above there in Baltimore maybe, but I don't remember. We grew beans, potatoes, cabbage, strawberries, and tomatoes. We grew some crookneck squash one year.

We had three tractor-trailer rigs, one that had an ice bunker on it. It kept stuff pretty cool going into Raleigh and South Carolina. We grew lettuce, the prettiest lettuce you ever saw. Some people down on the coast that Fred knew grew lettuce. He had about 30 acres down below the packing

Fred and Ralph Colvard in commercial tomato field at Colvard Farm in the 1960's (courtesy of Ben Harrison).

house down there. I can't think of these people's names, down close to Wilmington, and he told them he needed some lettuce packers, the lettuce was about ready to ship. They said, "How much lettuce you got?" Fred told them about 30 acres. "Ah, you don't need but one packer." I never saw anything like it. His name was Perez or something like that and he had his wife and two kids with him. We had a big wheel, it must have been 20 feet across, that they dumped the lettuce on and that wheel went around all the time. We had an ice crusher there and we'd crush the ice and had a man with a shovel and we had two racks and the packer would stand in between them and they'd lay a lettuce box on this one and one on that one. He'd turn around and he'd pack a layer and while they were putting the ice on it, he'd turn around and pack another layer and he'd do it just as fast as they could shovel that ice. He was the one packer. We sold five or six trailer loads and they told us that was the finest lettuce that they'd had.

The [New] River runs through the farm, part of the farm. But he [Fred] rented a lot of land. He rented the land on both sides of the river down in the Nathan's Creek area. I know there was 30 acres on one side and 20 on the other. We had 60 acres rented out at Laurel Springs. He rented a lot of land. Up at town here where you turn right to go out toward Bristol on the left, he had about 40 acres in cabbage there. I've got a picture of that that they had in the paper. Now it's covered up with houses. He was a man of nature, Fred was. He'd buy these old farms, hire a bunch of fellows, and they'd clean them up during the winter time and make nice places out of them.

He had some folks come up from North Carolina State. They did experiments for the college. Chuck Gardner was the county agent. His father, Dr. Gardner, was the head of the horticulture department at State College. Chuck used to come up from State and stay here during the summer time. They were testing seeds and things, potatoes and corn and different things. They paid rent to Fred because he had the machinery and men, if they needed the help, and that's the reason they used him. That Sequoia potato was developed there and Fred named it. It's a round, white potato.

He had sheep. He was a good animal husbandman. He had 500 ewes and he averaged 150 percent of lambs, one and one-half to each female. A couple of fellows from the IRS came down one time to check his books for him. Well-educated guys. One of them was sitting there and Fred came in and the man said, "Mr. Colvard, what's an 'e-wee'?" Fred said, "A what?" That guy said, "It says here you bought 100 e-wees." It tickled Fred. We called them e-wees from then on. Most of the old mountain people called them "yous."

Once he bought 47 goats and turned them loose up here on Mount Jefferson. He owned several acres up there. He built a seven-strand fence around that whole place and turned 47 goats loose there. And dogs killed them. And he killed 47 dogs. People would watch from town, it was cleared then; it's growing up now. But they could see up there and when they'd see the dogs running the goats, they'd call Fred and he'd take off up there. And he killed 47 dogs, he and other people, too. The old trash dump used to be on the west end of the mountain and people just dumped it on top of the ground, they didn't bury it. People would bring their dogs and cats up there and dump them out and they'd live off of that garbage.

He didn't have a dairy farm during my time. Years ago, Fred used to milk, I think it was, 50 cows by hand. I think he had one fellow that helped him. But that was before my time.

Fred raised beef cattle. We'd winter about 300 steers and then sometimes we'd buy them in the spring. He built that big barn down there and he was wintering them. The water was heated so they'd drink a lot. He'd keep about 300 steers and then some years before he built the barn, he would buy the cattle in the spring and sell them in the fall, just graze them. Sometimes if he'd get a good buy, he'd buy 50 or 60 cows and a bull and raise a crop of calves. He was a good farmer. He didn't miss many opportunities in that line. His cousin [Dean Colvard] turned out to be the dean of agriculture at N.C. State.

Fred only had one brother living, Lynch. He was the one that ran the mill across the creek there, the old water-powered mill. Two sisters, Mary and Helen, also lived nearby on family farms.

When Lynch had the old overshot wheel in there, he could really grind. It was a good wheel. He got rid of it and put a little turbine in and it wasn't much good. One of the boys was watching him grind and he said (his old mill was one of those old slow ones), "I could eat that as fast as it's coming through there." And the old miller said, "Yeah, but how long could you do it?" And he says, "Till I starve to death." That's the way Lynch's second mill was with the old turbine. He put in a little old turbine. Fred called it a coffeepot. It was about the size of a coffeepot. It's still in, I guess. I don't know whether it is in operation now or not. No, it couldn't be. The building is still down there, but the mill race is gone. [Note: The mill building no longer stands in 2000.]

You can still see the rocks at the site of the old Absalom Bower mill down the river from the Walter Sheets Bridge. The old logs were still in there back when I worked down there. I think Fred told me it was an undershot dam. It was just something to pile the water up. But I don't know, I didn't pay a whole lot of attention to it. It was there a long time ago, way back in the early 1800's, I guess. There was another one there on Fred's place where the creek goes through a gap in the hill down there. There was an old mill in there, too. Fred got one of the logs out of the creek and it was a big log that had a fork in it. He wanted to have it sawed and make some bookends out of it. So this L & E Lumber Company was cutting some timber for him and he got them to saw the log. Charles Edwards, he was the "E" in L & E, told me about it, but I don't think he ever told Fred. He said they started in that log and they hit a big flint rock right where that thing forked. He said those saw bits flew all over the house. I said, "I'd have made Fred pay for them." He said that he'd been too good to them, selling them timber and stuff. They didn't say anything to him. There was purple swirls in it from where it'd been in the water so long, prettiest piece of wood you ever saw.

Those old logs over in the river, I guess they're probably still in there because they last forever, you know. That was the site of the Absalom Bower mill. That was the one over on the river. They lived over there on the river. They would set fish traps. To make fish traps, they'd take a white oak log and they'd split that thing, like the splits that they bottom chairs with, and make a fish trap out of them. Then they would pile rocks in the river, angle them down the river, so that the fish, when they would come up, would dodge those rocks and come in where they'd have the fish trap set. They'd guide them right into it. The rock angle was still over there in the river. That

Fred Colvard (1896–1984) by the New River on Bledsoe Road at Roan's Creek, looking toward Mount Jefferson about 1980 (courtesy of Annabel Harrill).

whole family, he used to tell me about his grandmama sitting out there on a big rock fishing. The rock's way up from the river now and was when he was telling me about it. It was in the river, or right in the edge of the river, in the 1800's.

His folks have been here for two or three generations or more. They're buried down there in the Colvard cemetery, the Bowerses are.

I used to get a big kick out of Fred. That's the reason I worked for him so long. I liked him, he was a friend. There were five or six fertilizer companies and they all had a salesman and they all had a story to tell when they came. They don't do that any more, I don't think. They advertise on TV. Insecticide salesmen would come in. I remember a lot of the stories, but some of them I couldn't tell in mixed company.

Fred used modern methods, the latest thing in his equipment and fertilizer and everything to get a maximum yield. He was the first one in the country around here with irrigation. He used the river and the creeks. He had three complete irrigation engines and thousands of feet of pipe for each

Fred N. Colvard exhibiting crop of green beans growing on the hilltop beside the New River, about 1950 (courtesy of Annabel Harrill).

particular engine. We'd build a dam on the creeks. We'd lay sandbags across it. It didn't have to be very deep for the suction pipe. Walt Sheets, Wade Vannoy, and Fred used to pump Naked Creek dry. The one down the creek would have to quit till the others got through pumping. We irrigated everything — potatoes, beans, cabbage. He had two 500-gallon-a-minute pumps and one 1,000-gallon-a-minute pump. One of them was gasoline operated and two of them were diesel. We had overhead sprinklers. Each one of the three spigots of the 1,000-gallon-a-minute pump would cover a little over an acre.

As to how I spend my time now, I'm a hermit. I read quite a bit and do things outside. I've got a little orchard, but my neck got sore and I got so I couldn't prune the trees, so I have about let it go. I keep a few cattle in the summer time. Fred died in '84 and that was when I quit. The farm is no longer going.

It's a golf course now. I've talked to several fellows and they'd say, "I bet old Fred'd turn over in his grave if he could see this." I'd say, "No." Ed Weaver was a fertilizer salesman for International Fertilizer Company, and they sold a lot of fertilizer to golf courses. I didn't think of it at the time, but some of their biggest consumers were golf courses. Anyway, Ed said that someone wanted to know if Fred would be interested in selling this place for a golf course. This was years before this thing came up. Fred said, "Yeah, I'll sell it. I'll sell anything I've got." They said, "Well, what will you take for it?" Fred said, "I'll take a million dollars." That was just 700 acres there where the packing house and his house was and a 100-acre plot outside of that. After Ed left, I said, "Fred, you know if he comes back here and says they'll take you up on it, they'll buy it for a million dollars, you'd back out." He said, "No, I don't believe I would. I could take a million dollars and buy me a farm that didn't have any rocks on it."

You take this little old rockpile I live on here, I bought it in '45 and paid $30 a acre for it and everybody said I got cheated. And I did at the time, because it had sold at auction sale the year before or maybe earlier in that year for $1,000. These people that I bought it from, the guy that bought it at the auction sale sold it to them for $100 profit at the sale, before he ever got out. So he paid $1,100 for it. He sold the timber off of it for $1,400. Then he sold me the rest of it for $30 an acre. Everybody said, "Boy, you really got took." But I saw it before the timber was sold and this was the prettiest place you've ever seen, great big old trees up there and a spring, all walled up where the old house place was. I owned some land out here at Beaver Creek, good property. I paid $800 for 14 acres. When I decided to buy this, I sold it for $1,200 and man, I thought I'd really hit the jackpot then. I've got 105 acres here. It's steep and rocky, but these tax people, they really burnt me this last time. It's valuable, I think, because of the golf course down here and this development and I'm sandwiched in between. I can't complain, I guess. It's a beautiful place. Our kids, Robert, Sarah, and Barbara, will get it, as I have no intention of selling.

JOHN C. MILLER, 77

July 19, 2000

At his home in Fleetwood. His wife, Virginia, is present.

My name is John C. Miller. I am a native of Ashe County. I was born and raised in Ashe County and have spent basically all of my life here. My father's name was Fred C. Miller. He was at one stage in his life a school teacher back when the requirements were not so strict. My mother was Pearl Reeves from Alleghany County. There were five of us children, three boys and two girls. I'm the second oldest. I was born in 1922 when Ashe County did not register all births. Probably my birth was brought about by a midwife and, therefore, there was no record of my birth. When I got old enough to require a birth certificate, I had to go to the family Bible and get whatever information was there, and from my father, and send it to Raleigh. Then they mailed me back a delayed birth certificate. The odd part of the delayed birth certificate was that it said one of my parents was white and other one was black. Therefore, I had to send it back, because both of my parents were black. When I finally did get it back, I had it registered. I guess, to tell the truth, most of my brothers and sisters got their birth certificates that way. They were birthed by midwives and there were no hospitals at that time, or at least most black people could not afford a hospital birth.

I grew up in Ashe County like most farm boys. There was a little school near us, an elementary school that went from grades one through eight. My father had the unique idea in his mind that he would like for the boys to get at least a high school education. He had this philosophy — he believed that if the girls were good girls, they would marry good husbands and they would look out for them. He realized that the boys needed to be prepared, if they were going to marry and to take care of their families.

When I finished the little school here, my father arranged for my brother and me to attend high school in Wilkes County, Lincoln Heights High School.

Both of us stayed with white families. My brother stayed with the one-time sheriff of Wilkes County, Claude Doughton. I stayed one year up on Kinston Drive with the Rousseaus, Mr. Rogan and Mrs. Nell Rousseau. She was a teacher and I stayed with them the first year and attended Lincoln Heights School. Then the next three years, I attended Peabody High School in Troy, N.C., Montgomery County. The reason for the change was a man from Montgomery County was teaching at our black school. He had recently married and he asked me if I would like to finish my high school education down in Montgomery County. I was young and I did. I went down to Montgomery County and finished Peabody High School. It was at one time an academy.

When I finished high school, I was young and foolish like most young people. The lady that I stayed with, Mrs. Anderson, had obtained a scholarship for me to Talladega College in Alabama. She was a graduate of Talladega. Schooling or learning was no problem to me. I generally made good grades for it wasn't hard. It was easy to make good grades. But being young and immature, I didn't take advantage of being able to learn easily. When I finished high school I came back to Wilkes County and began working at Smithey Hotel in Wilkesboro. I worked there for possibly two years. Then the draft came along and I was drafted into the Army. I was drafted with inductees from Wilkes County because I was living over there then. I spent about three years in the military service. That experience probably taught me more than any school could possibly have taught me. I had some experiences in the military that let me know very quickly that if I didn't put something up in my head, somebody would be knocking on my head the rest of my natural life. I decided when I got out of the army, I was going back to school, going to college. And I did.

When I got out of the Army in March I went to school that fall at A. & T. in Greensboro. Of course, everything was in my favor then. I didn't have to have the money because the GI Bill basically paid for my education. I went on to college with no basic idea of what I wanted to do other than just get general knowledge in my mind, and be able to utilize common sense. But there in school I got interested in teaching and, therefore, I majored in English and Social Studies. I had a double major. I was an honor student in college. I had no problem there in college.

When I came out of college, I had one or two job offers. I was offered a job by the man that I worked for in Wilkesboro at Smithey Hotel. I told him I had an offer for teaching. He wanted to know how much I would be making. If I remember correctly, that was in 1950 and teachers with their A certificate and a B.S. degree with no experience were making $225 a month. When I told him what I would be making, he said, "Oh, I can't pay that kind of money."

So I started teaching here in Ashe County at a little all-black school.

The county had consolidated the black elementary schools into one school and they called it Bristol Central. It had grades one through 12 and only three teachers. You can imagine a school with three teachers, each one with four grades, trying to teach children all the things that they would need. It would be almost impossible. It was not an accredited school by any means, but I stayed there until integration came along.

When integration came along, I was offered a job at a new high school just opened in Ashe County, Northwest Ashe. I didn't learn until later that at the two existing high schools, Beaver Creek and Ashe Central, both the principals indicated to the superintendent that they'd be glad to have me. I went to the new school and I stayed there until I retired in 1988. I had approximately 38½ years in the classroom, plus military time, about 41 or 42 years and it was time for me to retire.

Teaching was fascinating. When I went into the integrated school, I didn't know what to expect, but I had an open mind and fortunately the school had a principal who was a young man and most of the faculty were young. The young principal laid down some rules that I think was the pattern that that school followed. He put it in simple terms like this. He said, "We're not going to have any cliques, we're not going to have any little groups getting off and drinking coffee. If one drinks coffee, we'll all drink coffee. And if we can't do it together, we won't drink any coffee." The rules that he established were followed throughout the years that I was at Northwest. I don't believe anyone in the world could have found a better school to have worked in than Northwest Ashe. Then when the time came to retire, I retired. Since then, I've been just working for John.

At Northwest Ashe High School, I taught English. My choice was ninth grade English. I've taught tenth and eleventh, but my choice would be ninth. All the years that I was at Northwest, I don't really think I ever had a problem student. If I had a student that I had a little problem with, my simple solution was the next day and the days that followed I'd meet him at the door and I'd call him by name. Every chance I'd get, I'd call his name. That kind of broke down any animosity that, I think, might have been there. Students sometimes come to school with a chip on their shoulder. It wasn't directed at you. It might have been something that happened at home, something that happened anywhere, but if they had a chip on their shoulder, you were in the way and it might sort of come your way. So you had to offset those kinds of things. I had good rapport with most students. I enjoyed the years that I did teach.

I think growing up in Ashe County wasn't the easiest thing in the world. About the only jobs that you could find would have been service jobs like working at a sawmill or farming. I have worked on a farm, I have worked at a sawmill. I think my first job was working at a sawmill raking dust during the summer. Back in those days when they sawed, most sawmills didn't have chains that pulled the dust out. You had someone there with an old wooden paddle and he pulled that dust out from under the saw. It paid five cents an hour. Most of the work then, if it was farming, was 10 hours a day. Then pay went up to seven and a half cents an hour. Finally, wages went up to 10 cents an hour. By that time I think I had finished all my schooling and went into teaching, so I didn't keep up with the wages any more. Ashe County did not have a lot of factories for people to get jobs in.

At the time I was growing up, the problem of discrimination was there. Most of the jobs you'd get would have been menial. Now on a farm, there was no difference in the work. I never worked a day in a factory in my life, but I have worked on a farm. Most of the things to do around a sawmill I have done. I have turned logs, I have tailed an edger, I've run a cut-off saw. I never did any sawing. It was hard work, but I learned in life that hard work is really no problem. I'm a firm believer that nothing that we ever get in this life comes to us free. We've worked for it.

During the years when I was growing up on the farm, Dad had a little place in our community of about 20 acres. He would rent land from different people that he knew to plant fields of corn, and he would raise corn. Now on his own place he would raise basically a garden. In the garden he would raise enough potatoes to last through the year. He'd raise beans and sweet corn and squash and tomatoes and pumpkins and different types of greens, like mustard and turnip greens. Then on my dad's farm, we were fortunate to have several apple trees. The apple trees would furnish you with fruit for the winter. If my mother didn't can it, she would peel it and then quarter it and soak it in salt water for just a little while to make it a little tough, and then just string it up on a string, hang it on a rack and dry it. I've seen them build a rack out over the old cook stove with a wire bottom and spread the fruit over there and then they'd have dried apples. With pumpkins, my dad would pile him up a bunch in a field and when we cut corn, we'd shock the corn around the pumpkins. They would stay there all winter long, as long as that corn was around them, or, you could bury them in the barn in hay. Most farms at that time raised pigs or hogs. An annual hog killing was the normal thing. You'd kill those hogs in the fall of the year when you thought they were fat enough and neighbors pitched in and cooperated. When they'd kill hogs, every family would kill their hogs. They'd all join in together. They'd work over here today and over in the next holler on another farm the next day. That way they'd help each other to clean the hogs and to hang them and to dress them out. It was sort of a cooperative venture.

My dad used to raise molasses cane. In the fall of the year we had to strip that cane and hope that no wind storm would come and blow it over. That cane would grow up to six or seven feet and maybe taller than that. If a wind storm occurred, it'd just blow it and twist it every way. Before we harvested that cane, we'd strip it as far as we could, as high as we could get and pull all the fodder off and then we'd cut the cane. Down near the ground where it grew up, it had a lot of brown leaves or blades, and my father said you should get all those off. After we cut the cane, we'd haul it to a mill. The first cane mill I can remember was just up the road, not a quarter of a mile. The mill had steel rollers and a long tongue attached to the roller, and you'd fasten a horse or mule to the tongue and he'd go around in a circle turning those presses. You'd feed the cane in and the juice would come out of a little spout and drain into a barrel and then you would strain it. You had a boiler, sort of like a furnace, built up with rock, laid up by some person who knew how to lay it. Then they'd put this boiler on there and they would strain the juice into it and start cooking the juice. The women and the children would have to stand by with what they called strainers. They'd take an old top off of a bucket and drive it full of holes, then fasten it to a three-foot handle. As that juice boiled, it formed sort of a green scum on the top and you'd have to skim that off and throw it in an old bucket. Every now and then they would hold that strainer up and count how slow or how fast it would drip. They could almost tell you when the molasses was done. You could almost tell by the smell anyway. You didn't want to get them too hot or too cold, you wanted to keep them boiling. You could make them too hot and you could scorch them. They'd begin to cut down on the fire. When that green material stopped boiling up, then you'd have a yellow sort of a foam begin to form on the top of the molasses and you knew it wasn't long then until they were done. Then you'd get men to set the boiler off of the furnace. It had handles with poles on each end and they'd set it off on two logs and then they would have their jars or their cans. They would have a clean cotton sack, I have an idea that most of them came from old chop sacks. They would pour those hot molasses in the sack and strain them until all the molasses were in cans and seal them up. When I was a little boy, I used to love to play on the crushed cane stalks while the molasses were boiling. I used to play on those until they'd find something for me to do.

The community used a horse or a mule to turn the rollers that crushed the juice from the cane stalks. If a man had a horse, they'd use a horse. What was interesting to me, we had one man that had a mule and he took an ear of corn and fastened it just out of reach in front of the mule. I guess the mule would always try to get to the corn. A mule is slower walking than a horse. They tell me a steer is the slowest of all. I don't think I ever remember seeing a steer being used to turn the cane mill because I think one would have to drive him to keep him going. We had one man that had mules, and I used to think that mules were the most stubborn animal in the world.

I had an experience with a mule one time that proved to me that they're pretty intelligent. My father plowed some ground not far from where we lived and he was going to plant buckwheat. He'd plowed the ground and he had me harrowing the ground, using one mule and one horse. The horse belonged to my dad or my grandmother and the mule belonged to another man. My dad said, "You just keep harrowing all over the field until I get back." The first round or two was good. Then the old mule looked around and he saw a little old fellow. When I finished high school I was four feet, 10 inches tall, and weighed 72 pounds. You can see I wasn't any size. The mule looked around and I think he decided, "He doesn't have any control over me." When we got to the end of the row and I tried to turn him, the old mule just wouldn't go either way at all. He just stopped. The only way to get the mule to follow the horse was to let the horse drag the harrow up on the mule and the mule would have to move. Then the horse would just literally pull the mule around. The mule did that until he saw my father walk in the field and then he'd do as he was supposed to do.

My father would always try to rent river bottoms, because normally the river bottoms were much more fertile than this old upland that he had here. Back when I was growing up, I can't remember that there was a lot of fertilize. If there was fertilize, most people would get manure out of their barns or a barnyard and scatter it over the fields before they plowed it.

We'd plant that corn and hoe it. After you planted your corn, you had to hoe it three or four times, all summer long. We have been in there chopping weeds out of corn and the corn was 10 to 12 feet high, couldn't see a person all day long, just chopping weeds. You'd sow your grass down the last time you went through it and plow it in and you'd chop all the weeds out. Back then there was no corn picker; you'd just shock it up, or you could shock it up and go back and shuck it from the shocks or you could top it — cut the tops out just above the ear and strip all the bottom off and tie it up in bundles. Then in the fall of the year when it'd come a freeze or a good heavy frost or two, you'd take the wagon through the field and pull off the corn, you'd slip shuck it. You would pull off the whole thing. You'd take out the inner part. You'd take the corn with several shucks on it and throw it in the wagon.

Most people planted white corn, very few planted yellow corn. Now yellow corn is probably much stronger for fattening animals and hogs, much better than white corn. The idea of it is nobody wanted yellow corn in his meal, so everybody would plant white corn. Later in years, my dad would plant yellow corn because the strength in yellow corn was much stronger. I can't ever remember seeing any yellow corn being ground. I've carried many a bag of corn, half bushels, over to the mill and watched it ground. The miller would always take his cut or toll.

I believe Mr. Frank Blackburn ran the last mill that I can remember there in Fleetwood. Now there was a water mill on up above Fleetwood., but Mr. Blackburn ran a gasoline engine. The water mill was about a quarter of a mile from the Blackburn mill on Old Field's Creek, I believe, and he had a big mill pond and ran that one by a water wheel.

A lot of people raised buckwheat and rye. I can't ever remember my father having any rye ground. Buckwheat would be made into flour; I don't know where he got that ground. Most people would use buckwheat to feed chickens; however, buckwheat flour would make delicious pancakes. So, some farmers would raise buckwheat, and there was another grain they called duckwheat. There were numerous quail when I grew up. When people quit raising buckwheat and duckwheat, the quail population began to go down. When they raised rye and the other, you had more birds like quail than you do now.

My mother died when I was about seven years old and my grandmother lived right near where I now live. My mother's sisters in Alleghany County said, "There's five of the children, and we'll take two." My grandmother was a pretty hard taskmaster, but she had a heart of gold. She said, "No, I want them all to stay together." She had raised my father and his brother and his sister. She'd raised one family. She took all five of us children to raise and the youngest one wasn't but about three or four months old. She kept us and raised us. She had a heart of gold. We were her grandchildren, and she accepted the responsibility. I think by and large she evidently did a good job.

I was pretty high tempered when I grew up; I didn't have control over my emotions as I should have. My grandmother would always be telling me, "You'll be in the chain gang before you're 21." I'd always say to myself, "I won't either" but I wouldn't say it to her because one didn't say anything back to people in those days. I'm about 78 years old and I've never been in a jail other than to go there and cut somebody's hair. I've never been involved in any kind of criminal activities in my life. So she evidently did a pretty good job. Then the Army also taught me that if you don't control your emotions, somebody else might control them. So I had to conquer that thing called a high temper.

When I met Ginny, my wife, I was in the service. We began to correspond, and then when I came out of the service, I went to see her. I began going to see her now and then, then I went to school, and from school I kept up the pattern of going to see her. She lived in Salem [Virginia]. After I graduated from school and landed a job, I proposed to Ginny and she accepted me. We did not have a big wedding. I had arranged with a minister in Greensboro whose church I had attended during the years that I was at A. & T. Even working on my master's degree, I would always go to his church. He was a Presbyterian minister and I asked him if he would marry us and he told me "Yes." So I got the marriage license and we both got our blood tests and just the two of us were there and Rev. Douglas married us. The marriage has survived 50 years.

Ginny has always been a stay-at-home wife. We kept thinking we would have children, but we never did have. At the time when we married, we lived at first with my father, and then I began looking around trying to get the money to build a house. I went through the Federal Land Bank first, thinking maybe that I had a good chance. I got the idea that I was getting the runaround and I'm pretty sure I was. I was teaching then and making money. My grandmother, after she died, her land went to the county because she had been drawing old age assistance. Then they sold the land at public auction and I bid it off. After I bid the land off, I had that much money in the bank but I didn't want to use it. I went to two banks and they told me to get one black landowner and two white landowners to sign for me and they would loan me the money. Again, I guess my temper got the better of me and I said to myself, "That will never happen." I didn't do a thing but go to North Wilkesboro to the wife of the man I used to work for, Mrs. Smithey, and I told her I needed to borrow some money to buy my grandmother's land. She reached and got her checkbook and said, "How much do you want?" I told her I bid it off at $875 for eight acres. She wrote me a check for it and I brought it back and laid it down in the Northwestern Bank over here and it sort of scared them. They saw whose name was on it. Mr. Smithey was one of the founders of the Northwestern Bank. They said, "You know him?" I said, "Yes, I know him, I know a whole lot of people."

After I got the land and wanted to build a home, I decided that I was getting the runaround. I had developed friends with some people here in Ashe County. One of them was Mr. Robert Burgess. He was the owner of Burgess Furniture Company. He told me, "John, I hear you're looking for money to build you a home." I told him, "I am." He said, "Go up to Ashe Federal Savings and Loan and put in your application." He had a son, I didn't know it at the time, that was working there. Within a week's time they called me and said, "Whenever you're ready to build, your money is ready." I think I borrowed $12,500 to build this house. I was working at Northwest High School then teaching school. When I went to get the money, one of the ladies that worked there, Mrs. Knox, said to me, "John, come in here, I want to talk to you. I want you to be my student." She had me to sit down there in Ashe Federal Savings and Loan and she told me things about building that I would have never learned in a lifetime. She told me, "Don't pay your contractor any money until you see a bill for every foot of lumber, whatever goes into your house, make sure that you have a bill for it and that bill is paid before you ever pay your contractor." The good part of that story is years later — Mrs. Knox is dead now — but I met Mrs. Knox in the grocery store one day and I told her, "I want to take this opportunity to thank you." She just stood there with tears in her eyes and she said, "You're one of the few people that have ever come back and said anything." Mrs. Knox I considered to be a true friend because she gave me some knowledge that I don't think I'll ever forget. I had a friend that built at the same time I did, and when he paid his contractor the contractor had never paid for any material or other expenses associated with the building, and he had to go into a lawsuit to get it straightened out. She had given me all this information, what to do and what not to do. Her husband, years ago, used to run Knox Knitting. She was a real friend.

The years that I taught at Northwest, I developed a lot of friends. I had some friends that I didn't even know I had. The years I was there, I was just like I am now. I tried to be just a down-to-earth person. The children that I taught were like children of my own. I tried to do what I thought was best for the children. I can even now be somewhere and a child will come up to me and say, "Mister Miller, you don't know me, do you? You taught me in eighth, ninth, tenth grade years ago." I run into former students in stores in Winston, sometimes as far as Roanoke. That's the great reward in teaching, you run across people that say, "You helped me somewhere along the line." It didn't take me long to realize that children look at people as people, they don't look at you as color. I'm inclined to believe that they look at you as color only if they're taught that. They look at you as a person and if you treat them fair and square, they don't care what color you are, green, yellow, blue, or brown. I tried to be just as fair to the students as I possibly could. Most of them didn't ever forget it. They have a lot of influence on their parents. We used to have parent-teacher conferences, and I looked forward to seeing their parents as much so as I would relatives of mine. That's the one thing I miss about teaching is the parents and the association with children. As long you're around young people, you stay young. You've got to stay young, and you've got to think the way they think. If you don't, they'll run you out of the classroom. If you stay young, you stay one step ahead of them. When I retired from teaching, I got in the old rut and aged considerably. At least, that is my belief.

I was going to tell you the fishing story. I fished in the river. I had an old man in my community that I called Uncle Roby, and I guess he was by birth related to my uncle, and he loved to fish. He didn't have any children, just he and his wife, Aunt Belle. I was living with my grandmother then and when he would get ready to go fishing, he had a peculiar whistle. He'd always whistle and tell me he was going fishing. I'd run and ask my grandmother, "Can I go fishing?" She'd look at me and she'd say, "When you get your kindling in, when you carry your water, all the chores, feed the hogs. If you do that, you can go." I would follow him off over to the river and I developed the habit of fishing. In fact, that's the only pastime a person in a rural area

John C. Miller, in 2000, shows typical size of fish caught in the river.

has, either fishing or hunting. I used to love to do both, but the fishing has stuck with me, I still love to fish. It's not so much the fish, because the fish are immaterial. I'd rather buy one slice of salmon to eat than to catch a dozen fish out of the stream. There are some fish that I do like to eat, like a wall-eye and a catfish or a trout if they're a decent size. If one really enjoys fishing, it can be the most relaxing thing one could ever do, I think. I can sit on the banks of a stream and the problems that I might have just disappear, they're gone.

I still love to fish. At that time the New River had smallmouth bass, red-eye, white suckers, hog suckers, horneyheads, chubs, and a few catfish. There were a very few trout in the river. Back when I first started fishing, stocking was not one of the things that they did. The only trout that I really found in the river then was when someone had a pond and it washed over. The trout would get in the river. I think the first big trout I ever caught was somewhere up the river. It might have been up around where Mr. Bart Brown lives. He had a pond and the stream came and washed some big trout into the creek. The first rainbow I ever caught was about 18 to 22 inches long. I caught him in the river where it had washed down. At that time, it was no problem finding any place to fish. Today, it's a little different story. I knew practically everyone, I believe, from Todd up and down the riverbank. Today the land has changed hands and when that land changes hands, then the use of the land changes, too.

Hunting is the same way. I used to keep beagles, rabbit dogs, and loved to rabbit hunt. I loved squirrel hunting and I loved to hunt grouse. I have a gun down there in the case that has not been out of the case in five years, other than to just check it out. I can get out in the yard here and see five or six rabbits. If I wanted to kill one, I'd hate to kill one I'd walked around all summer long. Rabbit is a good game; I love to eat rabbit. Squirrel is good eating. Grouse are slowly fading from the scene. You don't find grouse like you used to. Turkey, I have no desire to kill a turkey. I see them all the time. For the preparation I would have to go through to kill a turkey, I could buy enough turkey breasts to last me the rest of my life.

To get from here to Fleetwood, you go back to US 221 and turn left. After you pass Fleetwood School, the first road to the left would take you back down to Fleetwood. There was a little post office there called Fleetwood and it is still there. When I was growing up there was a mill over there. There was a post office and two general stores, if I can remember correctly. When I was growing up, the N & W Railroad ran to Todd. You could catch a train into West Jefferson. Even when I was younger, there was a railroad that ran, following the river, and ran up Gap Creek here. There were a lot of big logs up Gap Creek and those little spur railroads would go and get those logs. When timber cutters cut a big tree in a marshy place and they couldn't get to it, they'd leave it in the woods. When I was young, my dad used to go down there, and a lot of that land belonged to the Cole family then. My dad would get permission and we would go to the logs left and saw those old pine logs into shingle length and split out shingles for houses. Most of the big logs were left in marshy places where it was almost impossible to get them out. The spur line, I think, went almost up to Deep Gap, along Big Gap Creek. Then when the spur lines left and the N & W left, the little stores that were at Fleetwood began to deteriorate. People would go to West Jefferson. There weren't many hard top roads. In fact, I can remember when to get to a hard top road, you'd have to go to Baldwin or up to Deep Gap to 421. Those were the only two hard top roads I knew of. From Deep Gap to Baldwin was a gravel road and most rural roads were gravel then. At one time a person could, if he wanted to, follow Big Gap Creek from Deep Gap to the river and never see a soul, for it basically was a wooded area. You crossed this creek prior to turning onto the road I live on. It had deep water. There'd be holes four and five feet deep.

Let me name some of the things that I do. I'm one of the Ashe County Trustees for Wilkes Community College. I'm a member of the Council on Aging, I am one of the directors of the Chamber of Commerce, and I was one of the directors of the one local bank, but my term expired on that. I teach a Bible study course every Wednesday night. I'm a Sunday School teacher; I'm also treasurer for my church, and I'm a trustee for my church,

Pleasant Grove Baptist. In addition to that, I take care of the church yard all of the time. The church wasn't always there; our church used to be across the river. I'd like to show you that old church. It's just the shell of a church over there now. We used to walk over there, about two miles, all the time. There were a lot of black people that lived over in that area towards Baldwin and even on up towards Todd: the Grimeses and Boydens and Harrises and Hamiltons, but they're all gone now. When they disappeared, the people in this community decided to build us a church here. Our church now only has about 12 members. We're sort of stubborn. We only have preaching services once a month, every third Sunday. We have Sunday School every Sunday. During this time of year, there's a little black church in Jefferson called St. John's and another one at Crumpler called Cox's Grove. We go to Cox's Grove every first and fourth Sunday for worship service and to St. John's every second Sunday for worship service, and this one every third Sunday, so we've got a church to go to every Sunday. These three small churches are members of The New Covenant Baptist Association, which is composed of 13 churches in North Carolina and Virginia. Most of the 13 churches are small ones. During the summer months the 13 churches have their annual homecoming. They call it the August meeting or homecoming and we generally go to them and get to meet and fellowship with other people that we know and have known for years.

I'm an avid reader. I do every crossword I can possibly find. I don't use a crossword puzzle dictionary, either. I have had people give me crossword dictionaries, but I like to figure it out myself.

There's been a lot of changes in Ashe County, all of them for the better. I can remember when I was young there was no mail route. We'd have to walk across the hill to Fleetwood and it's about two miles. The land we once traveled across now belongs to a businessman in Boone. At first when we started walking over there, they had this old railroad trestle, the spur line came up here, and you could walk across that trestle. When they took the railroad out, the people in the community put a boat in there, stretched a cable across the river, and fastened the boat to the cable. If you were on the other side, you'd just pull the cable to get the boat to your side and go over and if anybody else came, they'd pull it back and go across that way. The cable was on a pulley. At one time there was just an old boat there that you had to pole across. Most people don't know what poling a boat is. You can only pole a boat in fairly deep or calm water. If it's swift water, you can't do much poling. It's easy for someone who doesn't know how to pole a boat to let the boat get away from them.

When I was young, one of my responsibilities was to go to the post office and carry the grain to have the meal ground and carry a gallon jug to get kerosene for lamps. If I remember correctly, electric lights did not come to this area until 1938, when REA put in electric lights. If you had a radio prior to then, it was a battery radio. No one in my community had refrigerators because we didn't have electricity and no one delivered ice. There was an ice plant at Fleetwood where that rolling mill was that Goodman operated for a number of years.

When I was young, I would dread going to the store because if you happened to meet a school bus, you would always hear some derogatory remark one way or the other. Even if I was fishing along the river bank and the school bus passed, I'd hear a derogatory remark. You just had to ride with the tide and forget about it. You can't hold that against people. Times have changed and the attitudes of people have changed.

I think it's for the better. I don't say that all animosity between races has gone; it has not gone. But the younger people in the world today come in contact with people of race, on the job, wherever they go, more so than ever before. Before then there were no integrated schools and if there was a factory, there were no blacks in the factories, so there was no contact with people of a different race. One had little or no opportunity to learn what a black person was like. I believe you only learn people when you know and associate with them closely. So a lot of that animosity had no way of getting out. Young people with their thoughts and ideas, and then a lot of old people, began to realize that times change. I don't know what their thoughts were about the Bible, by holding animosity. We're pretty bad to interpret things the way we want to interpret them, not necessarily the way they are. There's a little animosity in the world today and there will be when I'm dead and gone. There will be 40 or 50 years from now, but I don't think that hard core animosity is there. I can't see a modern-day parent teaching their child to hate someone of a different nationality. When I was growing up, 70-some years ago, I could see it then. But times have changed and they will change even more, I hope.

Speaking of Appalachian State University, when I was in school in Greensboro I met Dr. Dougherty. I was coming home one weekend from Greensboro and the bus stopped in Wilkesboro and Dr. Dougherty was on there. He was a couple of seats in front of me and, naturally, I was on the back seat. When he got off, I didn't think he was going to get back on and he'd left a book there. When he came back on I was reading it. He got back on and he came back and sat down beside me. He said, "Can you read?" I told him, "I think so." He said, "Do you understand what you read?" I told him, "I think so." From there to Deep Gap, he asked me some of the strangest questions. He finally found out that I was in college. At that time, I couldn't go to Appalachian. He owned a farm down on the river, too. It was a big dairy farm. There's a building there now just before you get to the river. From where you turn off 221 onto the road I live on to the river was all part of that farm, or the Dougherty property.

Teaching was rewarding but it wasn't easy. The attitude of children changed. I know when I first started teaching, about every student that you had had a great deal of respect for teachers. As years went by, they had less and less respect for teachers.

Bruce Eller, 74

February 18, 1999

*At his home where Buffalo Creek comes into
the New River in Warrensville.*

I was born and raised in Ashe County in the Clifton section as it was referred to at that time. It's no longer the Clifton section, but it's called Warrensville. I lived there basically all of my life. I've been out of the state for short periods of time but no extended, long period of time. I don't have a vivid memory of my childhood like some people I've talked to. I can remember growing up and I was small. I was born July 16, 1924. Of course, my younger years were spent through what we call now The Great Depression and times were very hard. My mother was Ethel Graybeal. My father's name was Guy Eller and his father's name was Josh. Josh's father's name was David and David's father's name was Jacob. They settled about a mile up Mill Creek from where the power dam now stands on 88 and the North Fork of the New River. They had several children. The story has been passed down to me that they had 19 children and about 13 of them died when they were infants or very young. Most of the family is, of course, passed on and gone. But some of them I can remember very well.

Getting back to when I was born, times were pretty hard. We raised about everything then that we ate. We didn't go to the store and take a grocery list like you do today. We kept a few chickens and sold a few eggs, something like that, to get some flour and sugar and coffee. We raised our own corn and had it ground at a local, I guess you would call it a small rolling mill. That's where we got our cornbread.

The person who ran the mill, the oldest one I can remember, was Oliver Eller. He lived about half a mile below where I was born and raised. We were no close relations. I guess probably all the Ellers' generations are related some way, but no close relation. I don't know if you've heard of Wade E. Eller or not. He was in the Ashe County history. They was a pretty good article in there on him. His father and my grandfather were brothers, is how I'd be related to him. He was principal at Riverview High School for several years. He was quite a character. There's a lot of history in the Ashe County Public Library that he compiled. After he died, his family — his wife was from Texas — and she moved back there before he died. I guess they were what you'd call separated; they never divorced. They had three children and they went back to Texas. His wife is still living as far as I know. She would be up in 90 now. They were raised just about a mile down the river from where I live.

Getting back to my childhood, we thought we were living pretty good. We had plenty to eat, enough to wear. We didn't go hungry, we didn't go naked. But times were not then like they are now. I can remember one Christmas, I don't know what age I was, but I was pretty small. I don't know what I was expecting, I can't remember that. But I remember I got a sweater and a little bag of candy and an orange. I was pleased with that just the same as a kid would be now, I guess, with a new automobile.

For the first six years of my life in school, I walked across the hill and went to Staggs Creek Public School. It was then an eight-room schoolhouse, but they were only using about four rooms at that time, as I recall. No convenience of any kind. We took our own lunch. Sometimes I can remember taking milk and bread. We'd put it in a trough that had water pumped from the other side of the hill to have water at the school. When I was in seventh grade I started school at Riverview — it was the high school. I went there as long as I went to school.

I can remember as a kid trying to make a few dollars. The first work that I can recall ever doing, I helped Arthur Roland. He had a little truck farm. He raised vegetables and took them to Charlotte and different places and peddled them out. I worked for him for 10 cents an hour, which is quite alarming, I guess, to people of this day and time. Ten cents back then would buy more, I guess than maybe 10 dollars would today, I don't know. Anyhow, there's a big difference.

I met my wife, Willa Dean Richardson, in school. We were married at a pretty early age. After we were married, I went to Blackstone, Virginia, the first public work that I ever went to. I guess that was in 1942, to the best of my remembrance. I hired on as a carpenter's helper. We were building army barracks for 67 and one-half cents an hour. After I came back from there, I went to Kingsport, Tennessee, during WW II. I hired on over there as a carpenter's helper and I stayed there till my father had a serious stroke the latter part of 1942 or early 1943. He was a semi-invalid for 13 years. My wife and I came back to live with him and my mother. We lived there up till the time that they died and up till the time that we moved down here in 1968. We moved here on October 15, 1968. This pretty well covers my life as far as I'm concerned.

Getting back to the things you said you were interested in about the river, of course, you weren't here in the flood of 1940. Well, I'm sure other people have told you about it. We didn't live right on the river, it was less than a half a mile, but we were pretty close. I can remember going down and seeing the river when it was at its highest. It was something to behold. We've had other high waters later in my lifetime, but none quite to equal that. There was a little house that Ernest Bumgarner lived in up there at the little power dam and it washed that little house away. It was the only one in that immediate section that it washed away that I'm aware of. No one that I recall lost their life in this period due to that flood. In about 1977, I guess it was, I'm not positive about the date, was the highest water that's been here since I've lived here at this present location. It was very close then to what I remember about and what people's told me, where the high water mark was. It lacked a couple of feet or something like that of being as high as it was in 1940. It did not get to our house, not this one here. It would have had to get three to four foot deeper before it got to the house. Distance wise, 10 or 12 foot from the house. I'll show you later where it got to at that time.

This river we were talking about, it got up, since I've lived here, till it got up to our water supply down here. We had to clean it out, disinfect everything. We've got a three-family water supply, a spring. I've got a well and so have the other houses, but there's too much iron in the water. We can't use it with any satisfaction at all. The spring water is good.

After I came back from Kingsport, Tennessee, living with my mother and father, I tried a little farming, raised beans and one thing and another and cattle, kept a few milk cows, sold a little milk, anything I could do to make a dollar and put food on the table.

I have two sons. The oldest one is named Joshua Bruce and we call him JB. The youngest one is named Charles. I have two grandsons, two great-grandsons, and one great-granddaughter. They all live in the county. One of them lives at the old homeplace where I grew up. The grandson is building a new house on the same property, not at the same location where we lived but on the same property.

After I came back, I did what I could and then later on, somehow, I got started in construction work, road construction. I worked at that for approximately 10 years. I never moved away. My family stayed here and I'd be away at least a week at a time. I never stayed much more than that unless we had to work through the weekend. I was home practically every weekend. I worked in different parts of the state, around Asheville, Jonesville, Waynesville, Canton, Sylva. I spent several months in a little town they called Andrews.

We were between jobs and I wanted to draw a little unemployment — never had in my life. I went down here to what is United Chemi-con now, which was Sprague Electric at that time, and applied for a job. They called

Bruce Eller at his desk at Sprague Electric in January 1977 (courtesy of Bruce Eller).

me to work. That was a hard decision for me to make. My boys were in their early teens or a little younger and I felt like I needed to spend more time with them, so I started to work there for about half what I was making. I lacked just about three months of being there 30 years. I retired in 1987 from Sprague Electric.

I lost my wife to cancer in 1995. She had had cancer since January of 1990. It was, we thought, in remission, but she had a reoccurrence. Not of breast cancer, but they thought of her liver and lungs. She was diagnosed with that at Ashe Memorial Hospital, took her to Baptist Hospital in Winston-Salem on a Saturday and they gave her a preliminary examination and more or less agreed with the diagnosis that had been made at Ashe Memorial Hospital. She died Sunday morning about five o'clock with a massive heart attack. We lived together for almost 54 years before she passed away.

I married Lorene Powers from Lansing two years ago this past January 30. It would have been 1997. We get along good and have a good life. I didn't know her from school days; she worked at the same place I did. I knew her through our work relationship. A little funny note about that. You know these sections that are in the paper seeking partners. Her husband had died several years earlier and just to be mischievous, I'd always take that part out of the paper and lay it on her desk. When someone in our surrounding community would get married, I'd tell her she'd missed the boat, too late again.

Buffalo Creek, left, joins the New River behind Bruce Eller's home.

It never entered either one of our minds that we would ever, in our wildest imagination, wind up together. We worked together 11 or 12 years, I guess.

You ask about some of the changes in the county that I remember. Well, getting back to the roads, I can remember when 88 was rebuilt and paved from Warrensville on up 88. One winter it was real bad, and they were taking a bulldozer to pull the school bus through a lot of places. That would have been in the late 30's, '38-'39, I guess. Before that, it was just a gravel road, no asphalt, no pavement on it. There wasn't too many automobiles back in my time. Lloyd Mitchell had the first automobile that I can remember and he lived pretty close to us. I can't remember the model of it, the year model, but it was a Whitley automobile. You've probably heard of them. That was quite a show to us back then.

They's been a great big change in the river where I presently live from the time we moved down here till the county decided that they had to do something about the garbage and the trash that was being dumped in the river. They put these dumpsters around in the communities back then. When the river would get up, the milk jugs and anything that would float was terrible. I guess up there at the little dam on the river, what they used to call Sharpe's Falls, they was a place where the current didn't hit it too swift and those jugs and everything would wash over in there and bed down and the grass would

The Rev. Jimmy Eldreth baptizes Amy Turnmire, as Bernard Calhoun assists, in the New River behind Bruce Eller's home (courtesy of Bruce Eller).

grow up and the next winter they would be two foot deep in there. There's still too much garbage being dumped in the water. I'm thankful for the progress that's been made. That was one mistake I think the county made when they went to these recycling centers. I think they would have been better off—they're going to have to do it eventually—to have door-to-door pickup. My opinion wasn't rated very high. I did go to some of the meetings, but it didn't do any good.

I moved down here in 1968. About 1970 I joined the fire department up here and I've been a member ever since, still I guess what you'd call an inactive member. I'm past president of the fire department and I've had the treasurer's job for the last several years. I answer some calls, but I don't try to fight any fires. I wouldn't even begin to think about that unless somebody's life was in danger before I would even attempt it any more.

I just keep a fire department vehicle here because we don't have any room to put it in the fire house. We've got it full. This was about the handiest place. Since I've got the age I am, I don't respond to any emergency calls. I've had some heart problems and a serious prostate operation. I'm pretty healthy, I guess. I haven't gotten too fat. I can brag about that. In 1956 when I started working at Sprague Electric I weighed 178 pounds. Last month when

I went for a regular checkup, I weighed 179.3. That's about the only thing I can really brag about; I've maintained my weight pretty good. I don't have to watch my diet a great deal. I watch the amount I eat, but I eat about anything I want.

I've been a self-styled Baptist minister for a lot of years. I've belonged to Sugar Tree Baptist Church for years. After moving down here, I moved my membership to Phoenix Baptist Church, the church on the bank just down the road here. I do very little preaching any more since my health is not too good. I guess my mind's a lot older than my legs are. My memory's got real bad. You were talking about the Pond Mountain section. I pastored a church back there for a few years, the Big Springs Baptist Church. I have a lot of fond memories about those people back in there.

I have always been a church-going person. My mother and father were raised as Methodists. They raised me as a Methodist. There wasn't a Baptist church in our community till about the time I was in my late teens. They established a Baptist church in my community and I joined the church and have been a Baptist ever since. I have good ties and good connections with different denominations. I feel like that's essential to feel like that you're in fellowship with people, I shouldn't say different faiths, but for want of a better word, that's what I'll use. We're all of the same faith.

When I was growing up we went to what they called Mill Creek Methodist Church. Just go on up Mill Creek and there is an old church house still up there. They don't have service there and haven't for years, but that's where we went to church. My grandfather, I've been told, was one that had a big hand in building that church. He was David Graybeal. He had two sons that made doctors. Dr. A. B. Graybeal moved to Marion, Virgina, when he started practicing. He stayed over there as long as he lived. The other one went to Montana and lived out there for years and years. He finally came back in his later years to Marion, Virginia. They would have been my uncles.

BOB CORNETT, 73

December 15, 1999

At the Riverview Community Center.
His wife Darlene is present.

DARLENE: Bob grew up here near Creston. We live at his home place. We don't live in the house. We have a trailer. It is on Highway 88.

BOB: My dad and mother's names are John Monroe Cornett and Rosa Belle James. I'm the thirteenth one in my family. They's 11 girls and four boys. Six of them is already dead. I'm the third youngest; two more are younger than I am. I grew up right here in Creston on the North Fork [of the New River]. My grandpaw was John Calloway Cornett. I can just barely remember him. He's my dad's dad. I can't think of my grandmother's name on his side. My mother's mother was Sally James from over at Laurel Creek.

My dad and my grandpaw worked in a sawmill and they did a little farming. My mother was a midwife. She never did tell me any stories about midwifing. One time she got a calf for delivering a baby. That was over at Mountain City. I had to take her over there and bring her back. I took her in an A Model Ford. We put the calf in the back seat. There wasn't too many doctors around, just Doc Robinson up here, but he was out.

My dad worked away from home at a sawmill at Mountain City. He'd come in on the weekend. It was a long way then because he had to walk. While he was gone my brothers and I always had to get wood. We'd go to school and at recess we'd come home and get enough for dinner. Then we'd go back to school and at recess come home again and get enough for the night. I went to school at Sutherland. The building is tore down and gone now. I went to the eighth grade. Some of the teachers there were Ray Knight, Josh Spencer, Earl Sutherland, Arlene Cane, and a Knight woman. They kept us right on the grindstone. They didn't put up with any foolishness. I never got punished.

188

The John Cornett family around 1930, showing 14 of 15 children. Back row: Edith, Mary, Birdie, Alice, Milton; second row: Sarah, Rena, Clyde, Celie, Bob; front: Hazel, John, Rosa, Belle (on lap), Eula, Charlie. Beatrice had married and moved away (courtesy of Bob Cornett).

We used to play ball right above the house. My dad had a big swing. They'd be about 100 there every weekend swinging in that swing. My dad would pull it with a rope to get it started. It had a big crank on top of it and then when one got in each end of it, he got it started and you just kept going. There would be four on it at a time, two to a seat. He also made a ferris wheel.

Out there when the river froze over, my brothers would get out there and ice skate. There'd be about 30 or 40 out there. It doesn't get that cold any more. Then the river would be so iced up it would hold several of us. They could drive horses across it, drag wood across it. My brother made him a pair of skates out of a piece of steel. He put them on a pair of roller skate frames, tied them around his feet with twine string. It was a single blade. I never did try to ski. I used to take an old car hood and get up on top of the hill and ride it off.

One of my brothers got killed in a car wreck up highway 88. I seen him get killed. He was driving an A Model Ford and when he come around the curve, it just stood up on its end and fell over on top of him and drug him down the highway. I raked the gravel out of his head, got him down off the windshield. They was running too fast when they come around the curve and it just turned up like that, just turned plumb over.

My wife and I got married about 30 years ago. We've got a daughter 20 years old. She works up at Wal Mart at Boone. Her name is Janice Lee.

When the flood come it was up to my shirt pocket. I went to get my hog out of the field. I was already wading up to here. I led my hog to the road, turned her loose out there in the road. She stayed all night. The next day after the water went down, I went out there and she went back to the pen with me, went right back in the pen. The flood come up all of a sudden. It just took about 12 hours and then it run down.

I forget what date the cemetery slid off but it was back in the '40's. I would say it was right after the flood of 1940. There was so much water in the ground, it pushed out 28 graves. Well, it didn't push them all out. It just pushed three of them out in the edge of the road. The rest of them we dug them out and took them to another place. Took part of them up on Round-about, some to Mountain City, two of them to West Jefferson, two of them up there on my place. They're just scattered around. We buried part of them back at the upper side of the cemetery. It's called the Cornett Cemetery. It's just below my house and it's still there. My dad and mother is buried there and my two brothers and a sister. We had to dig some of the graves up and put them back someplace else. We moved about 20 of them. The rest of them we put back in there. We finally got a little help. Nobody didn't want to help, but we had plenty of lookers. They's about 100 standing around there. They wouldn't turn their hand, though. When we'd open a grave up they'd run. See, it had an odor to it. When you uncovered it it'd puff up in your face. They's paying us $2 an hour. They didn't embalm people and put them in heavy steel caskets back then. All of them was in wood boxes. Probably all that would be there was just the handle. That soldier boy was in a casket with a glass top on it. His beard was about an inch long. It growed in the box. He slid plumb out in the road. He was a distant cousin. He died in the second World War.

I've just done farming most of my life. I worked 12 years building fork lifts down in Lenoir. Six years of it I drove back and forth every day. Then I worked three years in Hickory wood carving, turning out chair posts. The rest of the time I've been on the farm. I done a little dozing, digging base-ments, and building roads. Then I drove a school bus for nine years. I drove it here [Riverview] a little over three years and then I drove at Watauga High School in Boone. I lived up here at Sutherland. I drove to Pottertown and then back out and through Trade into Boone. When I drove here, I just went above the house, turned around and come back.

Bob Cornett points to family stone in the Cornett Cemetery.

I'm 73 years old. I was born May 26, 1926. I'm retired now.

I never did fish any. The only way I fished, I just took a seine and went in there and dipped them out. My family ate them. I don't care nothing for them. I used to go seining all night long. I'd go plumb into Pottertown and come down to here dragging the river. We got down in there and waded. There would be three of us.

I used to bird hunt. My boss man, Glen Snyder, he's on the other side of the railroad track and I's over here. I come up over the top and he shot. Shot just covered me up. I went to the house. I quit right there. That was a good time to quit. It didn't hurt me too much. It just burnt my face a little where the shot hit. I don't like to shoot anything. I don't even like to kill a snake. Black snakes do some good; they catch mice.

Back when I was growing up we lived on a farm and all the children had to work. My daddy had a gristmill and I still have that gristmill. It's been in the family for about 90 years now. I ain't used it in about a year. It could be used. All I have to do is throw a switch. It's got an electric motor on it now. It did have a little gas motor, a hit and miss motor. It'd hit a lick and then quit. He used to have a water wheel back yonder, back in the '20's, my dad did. It was beside the river. He had a #10 sawmill boiler a-pulling it, heating water, to get the steam out with. Then he sold that and bought that little five horsepower hit and miss. Then we got a six horsepower, a bigger one, and pulled the mill with it. I used to pull it with my car. I had a '38 Ford Coupe. I pulled it with that for about two or three years. I bolted a steel pulley on the wheel and put the belt on it. I used to grind anywhere from seven o'clock to midnight. Used to grind for Stevens up there, store merchant. He'd bring a wagon load. I'd shell it and grind it. I had a hand sheller and the motor driven mill. This was when I was young. If I didn't have to go to school, I'd go in at seven in the morning and go to bed about midnight. On Saturday I'd stay all day. My dad was working at the sawmill. I'd bag up the meal for the store, put it in 25-pound paper bags. It had a label on it, Stevens Store. I don't have any of those old sacks left. The mice got in them and cut them up. That meal made the best cornbread. You can't buy it now.

I had to stack a lot of hay back then. I cut it with a scythe. I cut seven stacks every year. I cut a stack a day and my sister would stir it out, stirred it with a fork and turned it and just spread it out. When I mowed it I piled it up and they'd come and scatter it back out to dry, then we'd roll it up. Up there on that steep hill, start a roll at the top and go to the bottom. We rolled this with a fork. Then we'd put a pole in the ground and stack it.

I still trim all the fencerows and everything up the highway and around with a scythe. Ain't too many people knows how to use a scythe. Most of them cradles it. That's the way my brother does, he cradles it. I leave my scythe on the ground. I can cut it just as close as you can with a lawnmower, by letting that blade run on the ground. It's hard on your back, though.

Back then I had seven or eight milk cows. That's what we lived on, that milk. We had one horse. She was about 30 years old. She plowed in the spring for us. My daddy had 16 acres in all. Now it's all growed up, except about three acres of it. I had chickens and hogs and dogs.

DARLENE: Now we're down to one cat and one dog.

BOB: They'd be about eight or 10 cats around there and about 25 or 30 chickens. We made pretty much everything right there on the farm, except a little sugar and baking powder or something like that. I run that gristmill and made about all my feed there. We had corn planted. I made enough to make bread out of the mill charging tolls, half a gallon of corn to a bushel. I never ground any flour, but I done a little buckwheat. We didn't sell milk to the dairy, just had enough for our family. It took a whole lot of milk for that many. We milked three cows.

DARLENE: Bob said back then when they's all little, when they'd go to the table, they wasn't even allowed to speak. Their daddy was real strict and they wasn't allowed to speak to one another when they's eating.

BOB: We just spoke when he asked us to. You could hear a pin drop around that table. We didn't hear the dishes rattle.

DARLENE: I can't imagine 15 children and them being that quiet.

BOB: My dad and mother lived to be old. My dad was 94 when he died in 1976 and my mother died at 81 in 1971.

I can just barely remember when they started up the Knox Mill down here [at Creston]. It was open a few days when the flood came along and washed a lot of it away. It didn't wash all of it. They rebuilt what tore out. The building is still there. They did run it and make socks there. Seems like somebody else took it over. I'd say it's been quit several years. But they's somebody has got something in there. I don't know what he's a-doing.

DARLENE: They was making Christmas wreaths in there this year. Somebody was.

BOB: Basil Barr had a gristmill, just above his house. The old building fell down last winter. It was up Three Top way there. Instead of going across Three Top, you go across like you was going to Muddy Branch, up around the Peak. Last winter when that big snow come, winter before last, it fell in. I went down there and bought the belts out of it to put on my mill. No, he didn't make any furniture here, he made it down in Jefferson. Well, he had a little old shop up there. They was furniture parts in it, but I think he done everything down there [in Jefferson], except he brung some up here. I don't know of any other businesses or factories around here or around Sutherland. It's just been farming country. They just ain't much a-going on up there no more. Everything is growed up now.

Back in the 1940's, the church folks at Sutherland Methodist were having trouble climbing up about 40 steps to get in the church. The church is about 40 feet long and 30 feet wide and it was built on a pretty high hill. So the decision was made to lower the building several feet by digging out from under it. We would dig out a little at a time and put logs and slabs to make pillars and then with hydraulic jacks—big railroad jacks—would let the building down a little at a time so as not to ruin the floors. The minister, Rev. Short, myself, and several others had it almost dug out about nine feet when the minister let his jack down too fast and it pinned him down. We had to jack it back up to get him out. They still have church at Sutherland twice a month.

It'd be hard to say what it's going to look like around here in a few years. It's all going to be growed up. You can't see nothing. Nobody's clearing it up. All the young people's quit. They don't do nothing, very little farming. They's a few cattle up there. Now it's gone to Christmas trees. I did think about putting mine in trees several years ago. Glad I didn't now. They's enough around. I'd have to let mine grow on up. It's just tree farming now. I wouldn't be aggravated with it.

DARLENE: That's dangerous spray that they have to use on them. I believe that could get in your water.

BOB: We've not had too many water shortages in the wells and springs around here. They's a few of them. All the weather springs went dry and they

A scene on highway 88 with the Sutherland United Methodist Church resting atop a hill in the center of the picture.

had to dig wells. They's a lot of wells been dug. Wells are holding up all right. My spring went dry in July and it come back the next year, but I had a well dug. My spring is still a-running, but it's just a-dripping. See, when they built the highway back in the '40's they sunk my spring. You could go up yonder at the spring and you could hear it a-running. I worked several days trying to punch a hole back through there to see if I couldn't hear it. Down here at the highway, it's coming out in the ditch line, but I can't head it up there. The road commissioner was going to come back and fix it, but he died before he got back. I complained to somebody else, but they wasn't nothing they could do abut about it. My millhouse is four feet on the right of way. When they built the road, the commissioner said just to leave it right there. If it has to be moved, I'll come and move it, he said. So it's still yet sitting in the same place, but it's a-falling down. I'm going to have to tear it down and rebuild it.

All they grow now is silage corn. Don't nobody grow no white corn. Farming has gone. The younger generation ain't going to come back here and bring it back. They's so much stuff in the ground now, nothing won't grow, so much of these chemicals and stuff they spray on these pines. I've seen a lot of difference in it. It'll just grow up so high and stop. I used to grow tomatoes and now I can't. One side of them turns black and that's on account of that spray.

JOHN LITTLE, 70

November 14, 1998

At his home on Highway 88 near the New River.
His wife Edna is present.

I was born here in Clifton, the son of Jake and Katie Sutherland Little. I had three brothers, Herman, Paul, and Jack; one sister passed away at birth. I grew up along the river here and went to Riverview School to about the ninth grade. I didn't like school, so I dropped out. I helped my dad farm and when I got old enough, I went to farming a little on my own. Me and my wife, Edna, started growing beans, back then that was the money thing, and tobacco. I can remember when we first married, we had a patch of beans across the river over here, about an acre, a bunch of beans, and we done it by hand. She'd bake gingerbread for our lunch and take the gingerbread and some milk, probably, for lunch, and our hoes. We'd hoe them beans and take care of them till we'd get them to market. Back then you didn't know if you's going to get a quarter a bushel for them or 10 cents or a dollar, you just took whatever they offered you, just about had to take it.

Just a few years of that got me into growing apples. I first started and had a few milk cows and sold milk for a while. I had to build a silo back in the hill and we'd fill it full of corn silage for the cows. I thought ahead enough to think about that, that was right back in the hill and cemented up, and I thinks now, I'll go to growing apples; I can store apples in here. I seen the milk business was going out. I got a carpenter, well, it was two guys helped me, Paul and Don McCoy. They redone the building for me after I quit fooling with cows and I turned it into an apple house. It's still there and we still use it for potatoes and what few apples we have anymore and anything else we want to store. It's dirt floor right back in the hill. I put me a little shop up overhead where I can saw boards if I need something to repair things with.

195

John Little stands in his tobacco patch with apple trees in background in 1980's (courtesy of John Little).

My orchard gradually grew from the old apples, like Smokehouse, Pound apples, Virginia Beauties, Sweet Rusty Coats, June apples—red Junes—and Transparents. They might have been a few other old varieties that we started out with and then it started growing. They come with new varieties like Mutsu. It's a Golden Delicious and Japanese apple crossed, and the big yellow Pickens, they was a fall apple. Everybody loved them for apple butter, applesauce. I think we had horse apples, they called them, long shaped. The later ones, Red Roans—they're real red—and the Mutsus, and they's a Jonagold that's coming on now that's real popular. It's a cross between a Golden Delicious and Jonathan. There was Sun Gold; it's a small Golden Delicious with a red sun blush on it. I just got one tree of them left. They won't be here after this, I don't guess. It's firmer and juicier and a little more tastier than a regular Golden Delicious.

I set out the trees myself. I grafted the trees, most of them. I ordered a few of them. Then I collected sprouts from some of the other growers in different places, and I grew some of the trees myself. I got into the dwarf and semi-dwarf, got away from the big trees and got them down where we could work them a little easier. Semi-dwarf is best anymore for commercial apples. The dwarf trees don't bear enough bushels to pay. They've got so expensive to grow them, you've got to have a lot of bushels to make them pay. It's

John Little and Lindbergh Eastridge unload apples. Mr. Little's granddaughter Catherine Sexton plays on trailer, in 1990's (courtesy of John Little).

getting so a little grower just can't be there, that's all. It's going to the big orchards. I don't know how long they'll stay in business, just don't know. I had probably around 300 trees at the peak.

It's a year-round job. In the fall after the crop is harvested, about the first thing you've got to start thinking about is ground mice and field mice. They'll work underground and girdle your roots and either kill a tree, or it will stunt your apples, stunt the growth of the tree, and then your apples are stunted and don't get the size. They've got chemicals for that. Probably the next thing from then on to spring is pruning. You've got to get that done. Of course, you've got a lot of time in there to do it, but that's according to the weather. If you have a lot of pretty weather, you can get a lot of pruning done. If you don't, you can't. Then in the spring after the pruning is done and the brush is all hauled out and burned or whatever, the spraying schedule starts. That's usually when the buds swell and the tips breaks open. They used to tell us, state college people, when the leaves is the size of squirrel ears, that's pretty small, you put on a dormant spray. Used to, it was just a simple oil spray, mix it with water. Now the new bugs and diseases that's come on, it takes about three different chemicals in that first spray. The next thing you've got to worry about after a week or ten days, is scab, that's a spotted disease that gets on the apple. You may have seen them. It's just a black, scabby-looking splotch on the apple. You've got to start spraying for that pretty heavy, about once a week for about four weeks. Then you can go about two weeks for cover sprays to keep the leaves and little apples covered with chemicals for bugs and diseases, the rots, and the different kinds of things. I imagine red mites and coddling moth are probably the worst two bugs. The coddling moth, he comes in during the night and gets around your lights, you've seen them, I'm sure, an old gray moth. They'll sting that apple and when they begin to get ripe, then they're wormy. So you've got to keep that on there.

Most of my trees are down in the valley, down low and that's bad, because elevation has got a lot to do with whether the apples gets killed in the spring or not. There where you live, a lot of times you'd have a crop of apples and mine would get killed or badly damaged. The frost settles in the lowlands like I am. I've never lost but two crops, but I've been damaged several times with frost. It can really hurt you after all them months of work and all at once you get up some morning and they're all gone. If you know a bad freeze is coming, you can put out smoke pots and the smoke would hold the heat in. I've done that a few years. I'd take a few bushels of sawdust and make a cone out of it and bore a hole down in the middle and pour motor oil in it. You get that sawdust to start to burn, if you ever got it started, you know how a sawdust pile will burn. It'll just burn and burn, mostly smoke. I've done that for two or three years. I finally decided it wasn't worth it to set up all night. We didn't have too many trees at that time. It wouldn't have mattered if the whole thing would have been in trees. That smoke stirs the air, makes the air move, and that slows the frost down. It's not the heat, I don't think, as much as it is the smoke stirring the air. It moves the air, in other words, maybe makes the wind blow. You get out sometimes, build you a fire when you're cleaning things up in the spring, it'd be nice and quiet. You get the fire to going and the air will start moving, the wind will blow. It'll do it almost every time. That's one way, but it got to where it wasn't worth it.

They used to tell us in apple school to get big or get out. I never will forget that. I didn't have nothing else to do, four or five milk cows and a few apple trees and a tenth of tobacco, maybe. I've set there and listened to them doctors from state college talk and they'd say, "Get big or get out." I thought to myself, "Now, I don't have too many trees and as long as I can do that work by myself I don't have to pay nobody, just the chemicals and a little work. I could do it myself, no expense much, I could make a little." So I've done that for years. Kept planting more trees and more trees and the first thing I knowed I had too many trees for one man. Then back in the '60's I started working at Sprague Electric. I seen I had to do something besides farm and grow apples. I worked down there 26 years and about 20 of that I took care of the apples and worked full time at the plant, too. That helped, got our insurance, you know. But I'm paying for it now with bad knees from climbing trees.

The sprays didn't hurt my breathing system and I never did use organic sprays. All the teachers and experts that I ever heard said you might try it and grow you a crop of apples or whatever and you'll come up with a wormy crop. I don't think anybody would know, yet, hardly how to do that. That's reversing nature sort of, don't you think, I mean reversing the thing. I remember when they first started growing beans, you didn't have to worry about nothing for a few years. Then the old Mexican beetle come into existence. Then it began to get a little worse and a little worse, nailhead rust, and I can't remember what all could get wrong with beans.

Getting back to the chemicals, I never felt they hurt me at all till this past winter. I got sick and couldn't breathe, my breathing almost stopped, and I went to the hospital. That was last Christmas. The doctor said I had double pneumonia. They kept me in there for three or four days and Christmas day I talked them into letting me come home. Naturally, I wanted to come home for Christmas. So I come home and was so weak I just laid down here on the couch. It wasn't but a day or two and my breathing didn't get any better; in fact, it got worse. I called the doctor and he sent me oxygen. I stayed on oxygen there for, I don't know, off and on all winter. They wound up sending me to Winston-Salem to a lung specialist and I've not got either doctor to this date to tell me what was wrong. My family doctor said, "Pneumonia." The specialist at Winston-Salem said, "We just don't know." He said, "These things can come back on you." I told him about how I worked in chemicals at the plant, too, bad chemicals, and I told him I thought the combination of the sprays at home and the chemicals at the plant might be the problem. He said, "There's no way to tell if that's the bigger problem or not." I still sprayed my trees, a few trees, not many.

How did I market my apples? Years ago when I first started we tried to haul them to Johnson City, Tennessee, and Bristol, Virginia, and try to sell them that way. I seen you'd starve to death at that. Sell somebody a peck of apples for a buck. After three or four years, I hauled them to West Jefferson, just wherever I could get rid of a few apples. I told my wife, I never will forget it, I said, "We're going to sell them here at home and we're going to quit. I'm not going to haul them all over the country and beg people to buy them." After that it wasn't no trouble to sell them here at home and let people come and get them. I could sell acres of apples if I had them right here. I always got rid of them. I could fill my apple house full and sell them all winter if I needed to. That was what pleased me about getting away from that bean buyer. The beans had to go and I had to take his price, but I could store my apples back in the hill up here and sell them all winter if I needed to. I done pretty well at it. They sold good.

I've got a friend that's got a big orchard. My orchard's gotten so small the last two years I started hauling them. I can go right into his orchard and load my truck and I've been selling his apples and mine, too. I have so many customers that have come for years and years. I can back right into his orchard and I help him grade them, run them over the graders, and load them right on my pickup and they're fresh, picked that day probably. It's out of the county, but I can go and pick up a load and help him grade them and get them loaded and be back home in a day, so they're fresh.

That's the way it's going to be if I keep my health. If I can do it next year, I'll bring some in, have them for people. People comes from Florida. I've sold them to people from

John Little shows "Siamese twin and triplet" apples in front of his sales warehouse behind his home.

New York and Pennsylvania, I don't know all the states. Reno, Nevada, I believe, was the furtherest off I ever sold apples to. They stopped, and then called me wanting me to ship them some. I wasn't big enough to get into shipping apples, so that was the end of that.

I've got a son and a daughter and two granddaughters. The granddaughters are almost more interesting than the first ones. My son lives over here. We see them every day, the little one especially; I have to go pick her up at school. My daughter works for FHA, Farm Home Administration, In Jefferson. My son, Tommy Little, has an automotive paint place in Boone, High Country Paints.

Getting back to my dad, I found something that might interest you. Him and his brother, Ben, after Dad got out of the Army in the first World War, they went in the sawmill business. The first truck that they ever owned, I've still got two of the old wheels off of it up there in the garage. They're big old wooden wheels with wooden spokes and solid rubber tires. One of them is still in good shape. This was a letter that my dad wrote to that company. Something happened to the truck and he wrote and asked them how to repair it. This was back in the '20's. This was the answer he got back in September 1925:

> Gentlemen: The material ordered by your letter of September 11, confirming telegraphic order was shipped the same day we received the wire and is, no doubt, in your hands by this time. This will also acknowledge receipt of your letter and order dated September 11 ordering more parts for truck C671. We have in stock and are making immediate shipment by parcel post. In reference to the summary in view: washers in the hub positions are as follows: the thin washer takes first place inside the hub, then the felt washer and then the thick washer. These parts may be placed in the recess in the hub.
>
> Very truly yours,
> D. Elder Motors Corp., New Jersey
> Sept. 14, 1925

Evidently D. Elder was the name of the truck. It had a Wisconsin engine in it. This was right after World War I, 1925. He may have had the sawmill earlier than this, though, but I couldn't say. See, that was back before I was born. I was born in 1928.

My dad went to France in World War I, but he didn't have any injuries or anything. I think the day he landed the armistice was signed. This is his discharge from the Army. Looks like they awarded him a button there for something, what they call a Bronze Victory Button. I just kept them things. I think I've got one of his love letters that he wrote to my mom. She was from here. She was raised up at Riverview. You know Nell Sutherland. Paul, Nell's husband, was my mom's brother. Thomas Sutherland is another one of them, he used to run the store there at the school. He had a pretty big grocery store and post office. The old house, they've remodeled it there where you turn up Rich Hill. You know where Nell lives now, there used to be a post office in there in the house. They just had a special room set aside, and Walter Joines would come down there on horseback with the mail and sometimes it'd be a-pouring the snow and him riding horseback with the mail. That post office was called Fig. Nell's my aunt. Her and Paul went with us to get married. They was our witnesses. That was a big wedding, me and my wife and Paul and Nell. Me and my wife just growed up together. We got married in Warrensville at the Methodist parsonage. Best I remember, I had $25 when I got married. I give the old preacher $20 of it. Back years ago you got by on a pretty small amount, had to.

We go to the Baptist church, but I grew up in the Methodist church. Then, of course, when I got to courting a little bit, I wound up at the Baptist church.

I remember a ghost story. It's unbelievable, but it's true as I'm setting here. Us kids was 'possum hunting one night with dogs. They was an old colored graveyard up the mountain there, over on the ridge, and these boys told me about seeing a light in this colored graveyard. We stopped under an apple tree, I never will forget it, picking us up some apples to eat on, you know. One of the boys said, "There's that light." I looked over there on the ridge and, sure enough, it was white and, oh, it looked like a light that big around, about a yard across. The thing was bobbing up and down like that. In a minute it just disappeared, never seen it no more. My brother-in-law, he was hunting with us and he's scared so bad, and he come home. We was walking, and I had to walk out of the way and take him right to the door and let him in the house, he's scared so bad. I had to go on home by myself. We never saw it no more, but I heard of other people seeing it.

The next biggest story that I can think of would be the '40 flood. The water was up on the floor of the bridge out there. My dad had a sawmill and had a lumber truck and the neighbor up the river here, the water was getting up in his house and he didn't have no way to get his furniture out. So I reckon he walked over across this bridge to my dad's, and my dad let my brother take his lumber truck and go move them out. My brother, he's sort of a wild driver anyway, he come up to the bridge over here and the water was up on the floor of the bridge and he said he looked at it and he didn't know whether to try to cross it or not. But he decided he would. He backed up to the curve over there and put the truck in gear and give it all it had, I think it was a '38 Chevrolet, and he give the old truck all it had and crossed that bridge and it throwing floodwater all over the place. He's going after the man and his wife and their furniture. That was pretty risky.

The water got up in my wife's family's house. She's got pictures of the old house there. They had to move out of there in the flood. That house was right down the river here just a little ways. Water got way up in it and they had to leave out. They's a swinging bridge there they had to cross on foot, and the water was right up almost on it. I think it washed the bridge away.

There is another story right here I could tell you. They's a deep hole here in the river and years ago us boys, we'd go in there swimming. Some of the older boys built a swing, put in two long poles and a cross, it must have been 30 foot high, and made a rope swing. They could back away up on the bank over here and they could swing across the river. They's some colored boys, they's two colored families lived up here, and those boys, back then they didn't mingle with the white folks much. So these three colored boys come down there and was wanting to play in the swimming hole. They got in there and didn't know how to swim and two of them got in there and didn't get out. They drowned. I'll never forget, it was on a Sunday. I walked down there and saw them after they got them out. They had sheets over them.

There used to be, back in the '30's and early '40's, three or four families here in the community, colored people and they's nice people. You could deal with them. You could be a neighbor to them and feel good about it.

GRACE RAY

August 6, 1999

At her residence in Jefferson, N.C.

I lived at Todd up on a mountain when the snow was so deep on my birthday, on Old Christmas. That was on Old Christmas, and they made New Christmas. Old Christmas was way back when the cattle got down in the barn and mourned when the Lord was born on the hay.

I don't know the year I was born. My age got burnt up in the Bible. I had my age down, and all, but my Bible got burnt up.

My mama and daddy is dead. My mama had heart dropsy. Daddy had phlebitis and his leg was swelling and they had to take him to the doctor. I had a feeling, I was out on the back porch, and something come to me and talked to me and I believed it was the Lord. I said, "Mama, Daddy won't be back." And sure enough Daddy died.

I've got three brothers and two sisters. Two of them are here with me, Charles and Letcher. Mattie and Gert lives in a nursing home, my two sisters.

We farmed for a living. We had potatoes, we had corn, we had beans, we had onions, we had cucumbers, we had tomatoes, lettuce. We raised every bite we eat.

I had two kitty cats, and two doggies. One of them come up on my lap and sung to me, a white Persian, the prettiest thing you ever saw. He'd get up there and just sing to me. When our home got afire, they got out and took off to the woods, both of them. The fire was about two or three year ago.

I've cooked all my life, from a girl up. We had beans, October beans, and I had cornbread and I had milk and I had potatoes, fried potatoes, buttermilk, sometimes we'd have buttermilk and butter. We had a cow, so we's raised on the farm. I done the cooking after Mama died. I did before she died and I took training when I's just a little bitty girl. I'd watch my oldest sister cook. I took all my training from her, every bit of it. I done all the cooking.

I went to school until I was in the second grade and I was picked at, run over. I used to wear my hair long and they'd get a-hold of it and they'd jerk it before I got to the schoolhouse. It was at Todd School.

I never had to walk to school. I rode on the bus. Daddy made us go, me and Charles and Letch. We all went. Gert and Mattie went to school at Mill Creek, too. I got sick and I had to quit — epilepsy. I have medicine now to take care of it. I take

Grace Ray and her painting (year 2000).

medicine to keep from having those spasms. They don't want me to run out of it at all. I went to Preacher Ed Blackburn's church when I was young. It's a Methodist church. I went and joined that church, got saved and baptized and all. I was young then. Oh, I just cried if I didn't get to go to Sunday School. I wanted to go. I went up there to camp and stayed up there at Elk Shoals. They had camp houses that we stayed in. I'd go up there and stay, and we'd read the Bible and we'd sing. I'd go there every summer for about eight years. I enjoyed that, buddy. They've got their picture up there at the church, Ed and Ollie Blackburn. Ollie is his wife. They have a road named for him, Preacher Blackburn Road.

I've done a lot of work at home. I've washed dishes, I mopped floors, I'd sweep, I've scoured the walls and painted the house myself. I painted our room before our home got afire and burnt down. Cleaned it up and painted the walls. My daddy built the house. I's just a little girl when he built it. I remember crying when he tore down the old house. It was my grandparents' house. The new one was a wood house. It was pretty. He made the porch and all. We could sit on the front porch, in the summer time, we'd sit there and I'd sing "Jesus Loves Me." We'd string beans and break them up for supper. We enjoyed it. Boy, I missed my mama when she's gone, though.

Grace Ray and her crafted flowers (year 2000).

The river was down there at our neighbor's meadow on down as you go across towards the highway. It's about a mile from the highway to our home. We didn't get flooded when the flood came. You see, that creek down there got up and when it got up, it got up booming and you couldn't cross it. It didn't have no bridge across it, didn't have nothing. It done that way all the time. Me and brother Letch had to wade it to get across to get to the highway. It got up high. I wouldn't try to cross it when it got up too high. We didn't take any chances on the river. My dad would have whupped me if he caught me into anything. He wouldn't let us.

We've had a wood stove all my life. We didn't have electricity. We had old-time lamp light. We's raised the old-time way. We had an old antique round table and an old washing machine, hand washing machine. We's raised the hard way. We carried the wood up, me and brother Letch, and piled it in behind the stove. We had to carry water, too. We carried water from a spring that come out of the mountain to out here. We had good running water there, cold water, cold as ice. I like spring water and I like my own cooking.

My daddy's name was Jess, Jesse Ray, and my mama was Ruth Ray. She was a Greer. The Greers lived out from us, out in the hollar from us. Ellen was my grandmother's name. Heart dropsy killed her, too. I don't have it.

All of our people lived across the hill. We had to cross that mountain before we'd get to see them. A lot of time, though, they'd come over there, when we got sick or anything. She was a doctor, she doctored, Maw Minnie did, many times. She used the old herbs to doctor people when they was sick. She doctored Mama when her children was born. She doctored her many a time. She delivered the babies. She was a midwife. We had another one that lived out from us and she helped, too. Mama didn't have to go to no doctor. They's all born at home. They took training, though, for that.

Our house was at Todd, off the highway, straight up a hill, up on the mountaintop. They's a meadow down below it and you go straight down through the meadow and you cross a creek down there and you go straight up that mountain. It was off the Old West Jefferson Road. You can't see it for the trees. It's growed up. I ain't been back in I don't know how long. When my daddy was growing up, they had houses all the way down through that meadow when Daddy got married to Mama. Doc Blackburn and everybody lived there. It's a pretty place, good laying ground and everything. They had horses back then and wagons. The ground was rich close to the river. They call that the bottom land.

Walter Davis had cattle on that land. But he'd let anybody they was go through there. They had a road in there then. We still own the land. I guess it's about 12 or eight acres, somewhere along there. Letcher, he's got bees up there now, honey bees. He can't get up there to gather the honey. The bees will die. They'll freeze to death when winter comes if you don't rob them, take that honey out of there.

Yes, I'll sing a song for you, but let me pray a prayer first.

She sings "Precious Memories" and "Jesus Loves Me."

Grace Ray was featured in an article entitled "New River's Deep Soul" in the June 1999 issue of National Geographic, *pp. 120–137.*

BRUCE MILLER, 67

August 19, 1999

At his home in the Staggs Creek community.

Four generations of Millers have farmed the place here at the house where I live. This is the house that my father built in 1905 and he did it all himself. That's when he first started out in carpentry and architect work. He built other houses, too. The house that was sitting here before belonged to my great-grandpa, the old log house. It was taken down and moved two-tenths of a mile down the road. My grandpa built a house and he added it onto it. Then this house was built where the old great-grandpa's house sit. The material, my father told me when he was living, that he hauled some of the chestnut logs or timber on a sled with a yoke of steers about two and one-half miles down what they call Stikedale or the Mouth of Long Branch and had it sawed, then he'd bring it back. He'd work on it a week or so, do with the material he had, then that's the way he built the house and our home.

I'm out of a family of five kids. I was born here and I'm 67 years old. I'm working on trying to get the house on the National Register in the Parks Service in D.C. I've got somebody that's supposed to come and help us shortly about writing it up into nomination. It is eligible. We've done had that checked out. I plan on using it for viewing purposes and into history where we can make a little money by visitors, by displaying a lot of farm items that we've had here all down through the years, farm equipment, mostly hand equipment. We didn't have tractors and 'dozers and things like that to do any work. There were very few tractors when I was a kid. Nobody didn't have any farming equipment, much of their cultivating was just by hand. They done it the hard way with horses and steers. But they made money. They got as much money as you would now if you was into farming with a tractor, 'cause you've got a lot of expenses.

We had cattle and we milked cows and used the milk and sold the calves,

Charles Miller and family. Left to right: Ella Mae, Charles, Lillie, Hattie, Howard, Clifford (sitting), in the early 1920's (courtesy of Bruce Miller).

and sold the cows at the end of the year. Then we raised corn and beans and potatoes and made a little money that way.

My father got into playing music. This is why we're restoring the house, where he practiced his music here. He had a band called the Carolina Night Hawks. My father was the manager of the band and he played the guitar and my brother played the violin, or the fiddle we call it, the old-time music. They recorded in Atlanta, Georgia, in 1928. They recorded one of their first recordings on Columbia Records, the old 78 wax records. After that, they played music for all the schools in the area and they'd walk a lot of places. I remember we walked down to Lansing, down where you turn off of Little Horse Creek, just above Lansing. The train would stop there. We'd stick our hand out and the train would stop. They knew my father because he'd ride the train into Abingdon, play music there, and then he'd come back on the weekend.

He had friends that owned the Trailway Bus Company, the Woodies out of West Jefferson, back in the '20's and '30's. It would take them into Atlanta to record. After that, he got into building again, went back into carpentry. He also built musical instruments. He built guitars and mandolins. I've got

Carolina Night Hawks, about 1928. Left to right, top: Ted Bare, mandolin; Charles Miller (father of Bruce), fiddle; left to right, bottom: Howard Miller (brother of Bruce), guitar; Lester Miller (distant cousin of Bruce), guitar, who also played with the North Carolina Ridge Runners (courtesy of Bruce Miller).

a brother that built banjos. He died about two weeks ago. He's got some of the beautifulest banjos you've ever saw. I've got another brother, he's been dead probably 15 years, and he built violins and guitars. He was a window and cabinet and door maker in the county.

I carried on and worked on the farm and made a little money. While I was growing up on the farm, we had the old milk cans, and I had an aunt that lived down near the main road, and we used her spring. As I went to school I'd take a wheelbarrow and roll a five-gallon can full of milk down and put it in her spring. Then the milkman would come up that day sometime and pick it up and take it into Lansing. They had a Coble milk plant in Lansing, one of the first ones in the county. Kraft Foods could have been the first, I'm not sure. I think it was 40 cents a gallon they got paid for the milk. They'd get paid every two weeks and that helped buy our clothes.

I walked to school two and a half miles down to what they called the Staggs Creek School, and I walked back. Then we'd get back early; they'd knock off the classes early. I would walk in the mountains. I got as far as I could go in the school where I went. It only went through the sixth grade. All the old people like my father and everyone — I admired the old people because they'd teach all the children how to work and how to not run around. You know how young folks are now, they want everything and it's hard to pay for it. Then we had plenty, never worked too hard, eat good. My mother, she done all the canning and done all the housework and helped milk the cows.

We walked to school, walked a path or the road up by the river there. The road didn't quite go to the river, but it went near it. Sometimes we'd follow the road, but that was the long way around. You could go quicker through the mountains where the cows go. I started when I was six years old. We used to wear what they called the overalls; most of us would be barefooted.

I remember one time I was in the school and along about 12 o'clock it started snowing. About 1:30 the teacher said we needed to turn the school out. He looked outside and he said we'd already got about eight inches of snow. He said, "You little kids may never make it." So we started cutting through the edge of the woods and we saw my father and the other boys' fathers coming down the road. They was pushing the snow and they was carrying some boots for us. So we met them and went across the valley and over into the road and we got up to what used to be the Comet Post Office, down the road about a mile and a half. I think the first post office and country store they had was named Edison and then converted to Comet. We got up to the store and the little post office, and the guy built us a big fire in the wood stove and we warmed our feet and got on home. That day it was pretty rough, pretty hard walking.

The old school was two large rooms downstairs and two large rooms upstairs. On the back was a little gym of a place and it had two entrances to it, one on either end. Upstairs was an open place where some of the littler kids played sometimes when it was bad. On out to the side of it, they had a spring there, a little water pipe that come over in a spring box. We'd carry cornbread and milk. We'd take our cornbread and milk and set it in the spring box and when it come dinner time we'd eat that and go back in and finish up our school, along about two o'clock.

Mr. Floyd Jones was one of my teachers and Edna Walters McNeil was one of the ladies. I thank God for the good teachers we had back then. They were really good. You didn't run around and play ball and forget everything. You learned what you's there for. There were two teachers in the school. I think they's three grades to each one. So I got a good education. I've got a high school education, which I got later. After I got out of construction work and electrical contracting and helped there for 20-some years, then I went into electronics and went to school for two different trades. I took a GED course through a community college. I've done all types of work. I'm capable of plumbing and carpentry work and things like that. I've helped a lot of people.

Then I went into construction. I hired in as a masonry helper, making up mortar for two brick masons and block masons. Back then it was hard to find jobs in Ashe County if you didn't have a trade. I was lucky to have an employer like Witherspoon Construction. It was in the early '50's, and is now Vannoy's. The first building we built in the county, I guess, was the Northwest Food Market and the Sutherland Store there at Riverview, which may be gone now. I got 60 cents an hour and the foreman, Mr. Vannoy, got $1.00 an hour. That was good back then in the early '50's. Then I went into Ohio and worked and come back to Salisbury, made a trip up in Canada and back.

They used kerosene lamps and woodstoves and fireplaces in the Teens and Twenties. We got our house wired in 1948 or '49 and the electricians that wired it, I helped them a little bit. Then later, they said, "Well, you're good at this so why not come up and help us work a little." So I went in 1950 and started helping the electrical contractor, Yates Electric. I worked with them off and on several years. Then Sears come along and I went in and helped them. I retired back on the farm here and that's where I've been since '78.

Still we do a little farming and work on our rentals and outbuildings. We've got a few rentals we maintain and that's how I make a little money.

As far as farming, my dad when he was younger, with his father, they would sometimes bring a thousand bushel of corn out of the mountain back here. They had all these mountains covered in corn, which you couldn't do it with a tractor, but they used horses and cattle. They'd have what they called corn shuckings. Somebody had a cane mill and they set it back here and ground cane. They raised a lot of cane in the open spots. All this farm was in grass, some for hay and some woods back on the mountains. Now it's growed up since the past 60 years in large trees. They had turkeys, too, back then, several turkeys. Back when the chestnuts started dying, they had big trees and we would pick up chestnuts and sell them. They'd gather roots and herbs, ginseng, mayapple, all different kinds of herbs. We had several different kinds of herbs here on the farm to make a little money.

My mom, she was a Barr, and she was related to the Elliotts, and her great-grandma was a Hubbard. I think most of them was out of Saltville, Virginia, or from New York into Saltville, Virginia, and then on into this area. She was into quilt-making and she made old knit-type rugs.

In the '30's, they had their big fiddler's convention on the Whitetop Mountain. It's all gone now. My brother, Howard Miller, went and played the fiddle, and I think he always got first prize about everywhere he went, a blue ribbon. They went there one weekend and the First Lady, Mrs. [Eleanor] Roosevelt was there, and they talked to her and played some music for her. She said that she'd like for them to come up and maybe visit in the White House sometime, but they never did get a chance to do that because they didn't drive and there were not any buses up that way. I think my brother or my father was telling Mrs. Roosevelt about my mom making those little rugs. She said she'd like to have one for her and Franklin in her bedroom. My mom knitted one and put different colored flowers on it and she rolled it up and mailed it. I don't remember whatever happened to the letter, but they wrote her a nice letter about how they admired the rug. They used it in their bedroom. At least she got one rug in the White House. She made them around for everybody and helped make quilts and she was good at canning and cooking, the old-time cooking.

They had these big dinners at the church back when the prisoners would go around and work the roads, and they'd take dinners out. When they ate there everyone would sing some old songs, working the roads. We don't have much better roads now than we did then.

Talking about walking along the New River, on the weekends it was close to the river and we'd talk about fishing. My father would go with us and we'd just walk on around the curve a little ways and hit the river and walk right up the

Bruce Miller, about 12 years old, in rocking chair that his father made and in front of rug that his mother made. A similar rug was given to Mrs. Roosevelt following the Whitetop, Virginia Festival in early 1930's. Bruce's father and brother played in that festival (courtesy of Bruce Miller).

edge of the river. It's very close to what they call the Sharpe Dam up there. I don't know why it's called the Sharpe Dam. We just call it the New River Dam. We'd go fishing and right below it was a foot bridge or a swinging bridge. We'd get scared, we'd cross it every time, because you'd get a swinging feeling. It was pretty high across the water. We'd cross it and go up this side of the river part of the way and then we'd go back and cross it and go up the other side and fish the river. Down below the dam was some big holes. When the water would get low, it would stop the dam off and them fish would be trapped in them holes and you could go in there and catch them with your hands, which we've done a few times.

They was mostly bass and a few trout, the old-time trout, and some of the older catfish. They wasn't too good. A lot of the old people eat fish along that river. All the way down to Lansing, we'd fish. A lot of times we'd walk down to Lansing. That's Little Horse Creek and Big Horse Creek combined that goes into the river down at Bernard Miller's. Just out of Lansing right near the Deep Ford Road, you go right on down and it goes into the North Fork of the New River right there. We'd walk through there and fish just everywhere. When we needed to go to town we'd walk down to, they used to call it, Stikedale. It was back about a half a mile or three quarters of a mile from where the depot was in Lansing. We'd just catch the train there. It cost us 20 cents to go to town and back. That was per person. Most of the time, though, they didn't charge us anything. That was from Lansing to West Jefferson. We crossed the river two or three times that way on the train.

You can see a little of the railroad bed in different places. You can follow it into Damascus, through the Whitetop and Green Cove and back in there. They've got some road, some of the beautifulest places you've ever seen, little waterfalls, and you can see part of the track yet at places back in there. It come down through Big Horse Creek and through Lansing.

We had a lot of friends around that had horses and wagons. We didn't have tractors back then. We had tractors and old cars later, when I got older. Charles Davis come and plowed our fields. He had some fine horses. He got them in the west. He stayed in the west a lot, and herded sheep and cattle in Pentlan, Oregon. He was our cowboy, we called him.

I've got family everywhere, really. I've got a sister in Fairfax and a sister local. Two of my brothers is dead. My great-grandfather was Ely Miller and his wife was Mary Ham Miller. Then my grandpa Monroe Miller had the farm here, he got it later, 250 acres. He married Ely's daughter, Amanda. They only had one daughter. Ely and Monroe was way distant relatives. But Ely Miller was the first land owner here. His house set here where this one does, an old log house, one room with a half story over the first floor. This one's got a few logs under here that was left. Then Monroe married Amanda and she got the 250 acres. When he married her, he built his house down two-tenths of a mile where there is a big trailer in the pines. Right there is where the old house sat. Somebody tore it away in the '50's, which there wasn't nothing I could do about it. I was younger and had to work and travel around. What I want to do sometimes is make me a sketch of the log house

Charles and Hattie Barr Miller, parents of Bruce Miller, at home where Bruce still lives. Built around 1905 (courtesy of Bruce Miller).

and maybe get some good artist to do it in charcoal, bring it back to what I remember.

I've got some of their equipment they had there. I've got an old coffee mill they used to grind their coffee and an old clock or two, a few items that come out of the old house. We've got a lot of furniture my father, Charles Miller, built years back.

My mother, she was a Barr. Her dad and mother was Harrison and Elizabeth Barr. They're buried on Little Horse Creek where the road goes into the top of the mountain, what they call Roaring Branch. I've got some pictures of them. My mom was related to the Elliotts, the Barrs, and the Hubbards. I'm related to a lot of the Elliotts back in this section. I'm related to the Barrs in West Jefferson a little bit. Robert Barr, he was a little bit related to me.

Basil Barr was in charge of building the dam up here for the power plant. Some people say that dam was built under the WPA and some say it wasn't. The Sharpe Dam, the only thing I can figure out, Mr. Will Sharpe, he owned land back up in the holler on the right of it. Will Sharpe raised a family in there, and his land may have come down to the dam there. The farm was right above it. That may be why they call it the Sharpe Dam. They made a lot of electricity with it, and it closed there for a while. Then they reopened it. I think it makes enough electric for three or four hundred homes, maybe more, when they need it.

My father helped build the Conawingo Dam in Maryland. Then after that, he come and went to Fort Bragg and helped build the old Army barracks. He was one of several carpenters, finish carpenters, and he done all the fancy cutting for them, kind of a supervisor, too. After that he come back and went back into building crafts and sort of retired, didn't do a whole lot, lived simple. He built several houses here in the county.

My father built about three houses on down this Staggs Creek section. You go down Staggs Creek by the big house where the white fence is, the old David Miller place, the next house on your right down below the road, my father built it. You go on down and turn left at the stop sign like you're going back to highway 88, where there's a tree farm and there's another white house there, he built that one. There are several places he done.

I married Dorothy Hardin from Beaver Creek and we have one daughter, Marie, and she's married to a Jordan. She lives in Elkin and she's got two daughters, Kayla and Bridgette. We took over the farm back in the '60's and '70's and started using it. We live here now and Dorothy works at a restaurant. Her father was Carl Hardin from Beaver Creek and her mother was Ada Cooper Hardin. She was related to a lot of Coopers. There was a Wentford Cooper, he was in the chicken business in Wilkes and Ashe Counties.

We never see a lot of history about Ashe County, because people who never talked about their history are just now turning up. People are realizing now that old houses and historic places are getting gone and we're going to need to talk about it. We never thought much about it back years ago.

Our land here does not go all the way down to the river. Ours is a mountain farm, North Carolina Century Farm. The Agriculture Department in Raleigh gave it the name. They've got a book about it, a big book. There's only about two or three in the county and one or two of them ain't even in operation. As far as I can tell, this is the only farm that's in the fourth or fifth generation that's still in use. I can go back right near 200 years on the same place here, still in the family. I've checked everybody and I don't know of any other place that has that long a history in the same family. It seems like that everything's got sold away. The younger folks, it seems like they're anxious to sell it away to a realtor and move. They don't care about keeping it or farming.

Another thing I plan on doing is put this farm into a conservation easement for the New River. I got Jeff Scott [from the National Committee for the New River] that's supposed to come some time and he's going to help me with it. Then I'm putting in some hiking trails and primitive camp sites and let people that wants to use it. Maybe I'll have a little donation box to help keep the tax paid. Then it's passed on and took care of after we are gone, however they want to do it.

I've got plenty of good people that's been a-visiting. I've had several out of Raleigh and Mikki Sager, she's good at it. I was talking to the National Audubon. I'm a member of it. There's a chapter in Chapel Hill and I called this fellow and he said he was interested in a place like this, high up, and he'd be glad to talk to his attorneys and help me get it on an easement through them. We've got a lot of wildlife here, a lot of rare birds. We're getting a lot of deer that we didn't have, wild turkey, a few black bear, and a few wolves and coyotes has been seen — maybe not on my property but within 10 or 12 miles. Nature Conservancy is on the Bluff Mountain. I'd be interested in getting something about the Audubon here if I could, get enough members, maybe use this place as a meeting place, or for field trips to look at birds and have a museum farm with garden trails, too.

There's some more open property back here. It's our friend's. We all just use it and walk it. You can see back to Whitetop and Mount Rogers and back in near Tennessee and Three Top and all the Blue Ridge range back this way. The trails go up about 3,700 feet.

The way I see life as being different now from the old days is making more money and having more. But I don't know if it has changed much or not, because the more money you make now, the more you've got to spend and you've got to "keep up with the Joneses," as they say. If you make more, you spend more and you pay more taxes. It seems like your food and everything is not like it used to be. We raised our own food and things on the farm. Nobody got sick back then like they do now. I'm not sure that's what it was, but back then people didn't use chemicals on the crops. I'd say it's a little better now than it was then because you can get around better, meet more people. Back then you didn't meet a lot of people. About the only way you could meet a lot of people was at church or school or have a reunion or something. My grandfather, back when he needed help, he'd have neighbors come in and help him on the farm. He'd pay them in farm products. If he had hogs to kill for their meat, he'd give them part of that. They'd work for things that he had on the farm. He had big grain houses down here and kept his grain, ground it, thrashed it, had thrashing machines.

I've got a corn mill back here and a mill house, but I don't remember ever eating any of the ground meal off of it. It was just stored there. But it is in workable condition. They used to operate it with a gasoline engine. I think before that it could have been steam, I'm not sure. I've got an engine down here that pulled the cross cut saw. It's been on the farm here for years. It's still in operation. I intended to take it to a county fair some time, but we don't have a fair. We need to get one started.

My father built a lot of his old tools, sort of blacksmith type work, too. He had an uncle that was good at it. They built waterwheels. I know on down just around the curve there, there's a little lane that goes up. There used to be a trailer there, and off in there was an old mill waterwheel. I think the little mill he pulled with it was just a real small one. It wouldn't pull a very big one. He had a little old grinder, he'd grind axes and things on it.

My father and his brother worked together. They invented a few little things. My father invented a little miter square for a saw table, a T-square to where you could turn it to cut a 45-degree angle like a picture frame. Somebody saw it one day. He had it on his old wood-cutting saw; he built it, too. He was cutting a 45 with it like the old boards they used to put on a house; they'd cut them at an angle before they weather-boarded it to make it steady. They said, "Where did that come from?" They'd never seen one. He said, "I made it." They said, "Why don't you get a patent on that thing?" So he decided he'd send it in to the patent office. They sent it back in about a month and said they'd already got one invented about six months earlier. That's all he ever heard about it. Then my uncle was the one that built the waterwheels.

My uncle invented a thing that counted chickens. He had a lot of chickens. He invented a counter to count from one to 99 or whatever, maybe two or three little wooden wheels in it, like a wooden clock. He had a little canvas thing at the bottom of a door, an eight- or ten-inch square hole and the chicken would put its head through that cloth and when it crowded on through it would push a little lever and roll that wheel up one and two and when it got to nine it would roll it to zero, like the odometer in your car. Each day when his chickens come out, he'd look to see if they'd all come out or knowed he hadn't lost one that night. He tried to get the patent on that but he waited too long.

When my father and his group played music, they played at a lot of the old schools for dances. They went to the fiddlers' conventions back on the Whitetop. Then later they had them in other places. The Woodies out of West Jefferson, two brothers, one of them was the millionaire Evert Woodie. He used to come here. We've had several come here, pretty good musicians. My father taught one of my nephews, Earl Sexton in Maryland, and he plays like Chet Atkins, the guitar, and can play anything. I've got pictures of the band group. I've got pictures of the family with their music. My mom didn't play, though, and I didn't play and one of my sisters didn't play. But one sister and two brothers and my daddy played. They played everywhere. They played at Fleetwood and played in all the old schools. The Woodies first started out with an old station wagon bus, had several seats in them, looked like a Model T Ford. They had two or three of them and they got to hauling my father's band around and some of them, I think, was in music. They took them to

Atlanta and got to recording in the late '20's. Then the Woodies finally bought out Trailways and they used buses a lot until they got to riding the train.

I remember when I was real little they practiced music here and several people come that played real good. I remember one time Frank James, the superintendent of the schools in Ashe, he played the mandolin a little bit before he was married. I've been told that Carl Storie's been by here one time to visit, the one that recorded on the Bluebird label, I believe. He was out of Tennessee, somewhere in Mountain City. But he didn't have his band with him. Then we had the guy that recorded religious music, E. C. Ball, out of Grassy Creek; he's been here with his singers. Albert Hash, the fiddle maker, is all friends. Seems like they told me The Carolina Night Hawks recorded five different records, but a lot of them wasn't released, I don't know why. Local people couldn't afford to buy them anyway back then. They give out a lot of free records back then. I've got one copy, that's all I could ever find. Several people said they'd seen them and had them. Then I've got a little story about it written up by somebody in Raleigh. I believe that some of the information is in the Archives and History, too. They won several blue ribbons. They made pretty good money at it.

I do some crafts. I do a lot of old-time clock work, repair old spring-wound clocks. There's not many of them left. I can do that, "tinker" they call it. I've got several wood-working tools and I operate them some. My father, I guess he's the only one that built spinning wheels in the latter days before he died. He built a lot of them and he sold them in several states. A lot of people have still got them. He built little corner shelves and little cabinets. He turned everything on a hand-turned lathe. Back there in the shop I've got two of the lathes that he used. He got into the Bell Saw Magazine. He got his picture in that for being one of the experts for turning.

My father helped the state some when they were cutting old wooden bridges. He helped them cut some of the miters where they put them beams. I remember they'd call him to come and help them half a day or come after him to help them get started on a bridge. He's really good at architect work and figuring house patterns. My father made money several ways. He had a shop one time in Lansing. He built windows and doors and cabinets, like kitchen cabinets. It was right across from the old Coble Milk plant, his little shop was. He rented the building from Mr. Wade Weaver. There's an old house right below it. Mr. Wade Weaver, his son was a ball player, Monte Weaver, a ball pitcher, the only one in the county. He played with a major league.

I had a Barr on my mother's side that was a shoe cobbler, made shoes back then. He used wooden tacks, locust pegs. He'd use thick leather for the bottoms. He had a metal form to fit your shoe over. He sewed his shoes by hand. Once he got everything sewed he'd put the welt in there to tack it to,

Bruce Miller shows location of old springhouse near his home, in 1999. He plans to rebuild the spring house.

then he'd put a leather sole on it. He'd drive them pegs in there, they'd spread out inside and outside, too. They never would come off. I know a lot of people that said they used some of his shoes. He was good at it.

Back when we was growing up, like when I was five or six year old, we didn't have a lot of money to buy toys. It seemed like everybody had to have a little something, and my father built us a little wagon, used blackgum and made wooden wheels and put a little band around it and a tongue to pull it. You could get on it and ride it down hill, pull it up hill and ride it down hill. Things like that helped the kids be happy. He made some wagon wheel light fixtures and large wagon wheels for horse-drawn wagons. We never knowed about these fancy things which they got now, electronic, remote controls.

We had an old battery radio and we could hear the Grand Ole Opry on Saturday nights. They started making the old radios in the '20's. I believe the one we had was built in '25. In the late '30's, I remember listening to it. I've got an old wind charger, but I think one of my cousins had it. He had it on his house and it would charge a battery for his radio. An old windmill had a generator on it. I've got it. They'd charge the battery and play the radio a week or two and then they'd charge it again. When I got older, we had some of them old engines around and I got me an old generator off of a car and charged our battery to have a light. We had a light in here in the early '40's. It used a six-volt battery, maybe two of them, and I connected them together and took that old kerosene engine and charged the battery and it would last about a week. We had a light bulb that would hang down in the center of the room, used it and the old kerosene lamp, and it was pretty good light back then.

We couldn't get the electric until 1948 or '49. The guy that put it in here pulled the poles in with a horse. There's one pole out there and one laying out here beside the branch, them two are still there. I remember a lot of people wouldn't sign the right of way for the electric line like they do now about the roads. We had a time with some of them, kindly afraid of it, never heard of it. Some of the old people called it juice; they didn't know what else to call it.

It was a lot of fun growing up. I figure I got a lot better education that way than I would have if I'd went away to college. At Sears I worked in West Jefferson, N.C. as an electronics technician in televisions and some in refrigeration, and combustion furnaces; I done that some. I went to school on that later. I didn't work for Sears too long. I got back doing what I wanted to do, staying around my farm. My hobbies are collecting antiques, native American artifacts, rocks, and gemstones.

EDMUND ADAMS, 65

February 17, 1999

At his law office in Sparta.

I came to Sparta January 1, 1970. I guess it is fair to say I was recruited by the county commissioners; they needed a county attorney. Mr. Floyd Crouse, who had been the county attorney since sometime about 1930, had passed away. I bought his office building from Mrs. Crouse and started practicing. As you would understand, in a small county, the county attorney's job is not a full-time job. Unlike Virginia, we don't do any criminal work; we just do civil work for the county. So the county was just another civil client to me and I was expected to practice law and make a living and not be supported by a county salary altogether.

At that time, the county commissioners needed to know what the issues were and in effect they really wanted to know whether or not they should oppose the Blue Ridge Project, so they sent me to gather such information as I could to assist them in making that decision. We found a lot out from state government. The state government had a very good staff of people at that time. Governor Holshouser had borrowed some very good, bright people from the universities in the Raleigh area and the man that I relied on most, Dr. Arthur Cooper, is still teaching at North Carolina State. He is one of the brightest men I've ever met in my life. He was very wise and he helped me out a lot. He pointed to the studies on economics and environmental matters that had been done at the University of Tennessee.

I like to say that the University of Tennessee has studied TVA [Tennessee Valley Authority] to death and so there were a number of publications and books that I was able to get from that university. Indeed, I interviewed some of those authors about the economic impact of a dam project such as the Blue Ridge Project. I relied on them a lot.

Eventually we did decide to oppose the Blue Ridge Project. That was

Sparta attorney Edmund Adams (left) and attorney Lorne Campbell, Independence, Virginia, worked together on the fight to save the New River from the Appalachian Power Company's proposed dam. They are standing on the old steel bridge over the New River at Mouth of Wilson, Virginia, February, 1976. If the dam had been built, this place would be under water (photograph from *Philadelphia Inquirer*, courtesy of Edmund Adams).

not only for economic reasons, which is really all the reasons we needed, but because of the severe social impact that it would have had on our communities. It was interesting that it was such a great controversy that the notoriety that the New River gained from that has caused it to become a very popular recreation area and, indeed, there has been an awful lot of development of vacation, second homes along the river banks today. That's interesting from the point of view that we had our cake and ate it, too, because we kept the river and yet we got probably just as much, if not more, development than we would have gotten if we had had a flat water lake shoreline to develop. It is sort of an interesting, ironic twist to the whole affair.

Today, people still live in the area and the farms that existed then are still in production. I thought it was interesting that I had to try to determine and found out from the Department of Agriculture about what the actual productivity of the valley that Appalachian Power wanted to inundate was.

I analyzed the farms that would have been put under water, for one year —
and you know the Department of Agriculture has extensive records. The
farmers report quite a bit of information about the milk and meat and
tobacco and other products that they sell from the land. According to their
records, in the three-county area that would have been under water, the
actual sales of farm products exceeded 13 and one half million dollars. That
was one of the things we pointed to; it was going to be quite an economic
loss to the area. It would be interesting to go back now and take a look at
this same land and see if it is still in production. I know some of it has been
developed as actual subdivisions. I know there's one active farm right there
at what we call the low water bridge at Piney Creek that is a campground
and has numerous houses on this land today.

The products have changed somewhat since then. We didn't have any
Christmas tree farming then. If I understand it right, the local Christmas
tree farmers are producing Fraser firs and these have become more popular
than a tree — and I've forgot the species, I think it's some kind of pine that
is produced in the Great Lakes states and Midwest. I know of one farmer
who actually moved down here from up there. The Christmas tree industry
has really burgeoned in recent years and is probably the leading agricultural
activity here today, because of the depression in the price of milk. You hear
about another dairy farm going out of business almost every day. I don't like
to see that. I don't know what we can do about it. The price of milk is reg-
ulated, but I'm very concerned about that.

There's an awful lot of beef cattle here and some sheep, too. Again,
prices are way down and beef is even worse than pork because we don't produce much pork in the mountains. I don't know about lambs, but I do have
a friend or two who have quite large flocks, and they seem to be doing well.
James Coman is still raising sheep over here. He's the biggest one I know of.
I know it's a big event when they shear the sheep. His whole life stops for
days while that's going on.

Environmentalists say a monoculture is not good and it's almost come
to that in the mountains with the Christmas trees. I don't know what anybody can do about it. There's one beef cattle farmer over in Laurel Springs
who has a big old place. They took the cattle off and planted Christmas trees
on all that pasture. It's just good, rolling pastureland. I know of one guy that,
I think it was four years ago, his gross sales went over a million dollars. He's
got a lot of land that he's either bought or leased out, planted in Christmas
trees. That's fairly labor intensive, so we have a lot of seasonal farm laborers
and there are some that stay here year around.

Then there are the pesticides. That's one thing that we did for the farmers through the National Committee for the New River. About four years
ago, we got most of the Christmas tree farmers in the area together and, through

the efforts of James Coman — and this also included the folks in Virginia as well — through the Department of Agriculture and the local extension services and everybody, to teach them the best management practices to keep the rivers clean. The basic idea is that there are numerous techniques that you can use that cut down on the use of chemicals for application on one particular insect, a mite, that attacks the firs. Then we have herbicides that some use to retard the growth of the weeds and grass in the fields. There's concern about that. In this program, we've just had all-day classes for the farmers on the best use of these things to make it less expensive for them. There are a number of techniques that they can use that may be less expensive than just going out and buying a lot of chemicals and using those. I think that's been fairly successful, but I'm sure some of them are still using some environmentally hazardous things.

The National Committee for the New River [NCNR] in recent years has taken a greater interest in the land trust approach. It's always been my dream that the NCNR would be an effective land trust. What we do is try to keep the land along the river in agricultural production or in forests and not developed. If it is developed, then it's developed in an environmentally attractive and sensible way. For instance, you might see a piece of land, and I think the Sue Smith farm at the Mouth of Wilson, which is partly in Virginia and partly in North Carolina, is a good example. We bought the development rights. Mrs. Smith and her family are going to continue to live there indefinitely and they can sell the farm. But nobody can develop the farm as a cookie cutter subdivision, as we call it. They've got to keep it in forest or pasture, as it is today, agriculture, so that the scenery will be preserved. It's strange, because when the settlers settled along the New River, they cut the forest and farmed it and had pasture and corn and other crops. Today, I don't think people would want to see all of the land returned to forest. I think people love to see a nice, open pasture or cornfield. And the lovely old farmhouses, I've had so many friends and people who have never been here before to say that they thought the pastoral scenery was some of the loveliest to be found anywhere in the country. So we try to keep that image.

One of the things you can do to develop second homes and vacation homes is to subdivide into larger parcels. I would say nothing smaller than five acres, more like 12, 15, maybe 20. You get a landscape architect to design the parcel and then that way you tell the buyer where they can put the house and the outbuildings. You keep some control over the design and structure of the house. If you get in a boat or canoe and go down the river, you don't notice a lot of these houses because they're brown and they blend in with the countryside. We've been able to persuade a lot of those who have built along the river not to paint them sky blue or that kind of thing.

I don't think any of the mountain counties are zoned, as we call it, or even have subdivision regulations. The county government, in Alleghany or Ashe, does not have any control that's imposed by county government. We have state laws that do apply to some extent on subdividing and house building. But there's very little of that, so it's a matter of persuasion. Most of the developers want to keep their subdivisions as attractive as possible and do impose restrictions that prevent people from doing outrageous things. They keep pretty tight control over the kinds of houses that are built and keep them attractive. Log houses are very popular and most of them like to get the old-timey looking ones. You see so many of those new houses out there that if you look at them from a distance, you can't tell them from one that's 150 years old. So, many people like those and that's been a big help, I think.

The economy now is in good shape in this county. In the last decade, the Chamber of Commerce here in Alleghany has really taken hold and we've tried to diversify. We did recruit the Bristol Compressors plant which has been here five or six years now. That provided industrial jobs and just last year the Magnolia plant was built on the outskirts of Sparta. That's provided about 100 very good jobs for our people. What's happened is, with these new industries, in addition to those that are already here, the housing market has been under the gun and all the contractors are very busy building homes for people, especially in the Sparta area. That helps the economy quite a bit. Of course, the industrial jobs do, too. I think they are very good, clean industries like we like to have. That's spurred a lot of interest in better roads. The real concerns I have right now are about the prices of some of our products, primarily beef and milk. That's caused a depression in those areas of farming, but the Christmas tree business is really good.

As for the economic future, I think that we can continue the trend that we have, especially if we can get milk and beef back on their feet, we'd be doing very well here.

Another interesting trend is that there are more and more intellectual people moving in. For instance, a friend of mine sells insurance and he has a highly selected clientele all over the country. He can live anywhere he wants to. You take authors and writers. They used to like to go to New Hampshire. We're seeing some of those come into the area. Sales people who have to travel over a wide area don't want to live in the urban areas so much any more, so we see more and more of those coming here. Computer people, any number of those who can live anywhere they want to, are here now. We had an artist, one of his pictures is here on the wall, who settled here and had a great career. There are others. There are two great potters in our area, David and Sherry Hoffman over in Independence. You need to meet them, very bright people, great musicians, Hoffman Pottery in Independence. Then there are Robin and Bet Mangum at Turkey Knob, right outside of Sparta about six or eight miles. The Mangum pottery is very well known. Another very interesting little industry is something called New River Artisans at Piney Creek. The old Piney Creek High School building was worn out, very old, but it was still useful. New River Artisans set up shop in there and they have about 25 or 30 employees. They made these rugs that you see in the hallway and I'll show you one upstairs. They have artists on the staff and they make all kinds of nice rugs. They use all wool yarn. You can design your own. As a matter of fact, the most interesting thing I ever saw there was a great big eight-foot round one that was a picture of Lee Iacocca. So if you really want to give a great Christmas present, you can go there. They go to shows in Atlanta and New York. It's very exciting.

I think that we have succeeded in our way without the use of government to keep the area pretty clean. If you look around Sparta, you won't see many neon signs and this is mostly on a voluntary basis by the merchants and the business community that realize that a neon strip is not desirable and they keep control of themselves pretty much. As you know, we've got the President's river initiative, of which we were the first. Through our Chamber of Commerce director and his staff, they hired somebody to work on the New River Initiative, which has already been incorporated and organized and is a working plan that's been approved to improve the economy and the environment of our area. In addition to that, we [in Sparta] were the first really small town to get a redevelopment downtown grant. We're going to be rebuilding our downtown to make it more attractive to look at and to help our downtown merchants share in the economy and growth that we see. I think that's very exciting. One of the things I'm looking forward to is to—I don't know how we're going to do it—make the downtown area more friendly to pedestrians.

DONALD SHEETS, 62

April 22, 1999

At the home of Donald and Shirley Sheets on Bare Creek Road, east of Jefferson. They see turkey, deer, and small land and water animals from their home.

When I was growing up we lived in a two-story house on the South Fork of the New River. I had eight brothers and sisters. My father's name was Walter Sheets and my mother's name was Nettie Perkins Sheets. My grandfather was George W. Sheets and my grandmaw was Sessie Little Sheets. My grandpa lived with us in the old house that he built in the 1800's. The house was later remodeled by my uncle and it still stands. I was living in it, but I've moved out now.

We were farmers. My dad, he hauled produce to raise the family. He hauled produce from here to Charlotte. He trucked to Charlotte twice a week. We raised lots of vegetables, potatoes, cabbage, and beans.

I can well remember when we had the big flood in 1940. The water lacked about a foot of being to the ceiling on the first floor of our house and everything was destroyed. There was six children then and then later there was five more born. There was a covered bridge that caught everything coming down the river and backed the water all up in the house. Mother carried us all out of the house down into a barn that stood out from the house. The water was in the barn, but not much. It was a little higher up than the house. The water was all down the highway in front of the house. My father was in Charlotte then with the produce.

They had a water gauge setting on the river, the U. S. Geological Survey, and my grandpa looked after it, then my father, then I. What it was there for, they got gauges in the tank and a float sets on the water inside the tank and as the water rises and falls, it's got a graph that records that to tell how much water went down the river. In the flood, it washed out. They also

228

Spectators survey the damage to Sheets bridge on highway 16 South following the 1940 flood (courtesy of Annabel Harrill).

had a cable across the river that they took water samples with temperature, water speed. They sent bottles to my grandfather, well, all of us, and they could tell how pure the water was. Back then the water was really pure in the early part.

The flood happened in 1940 when I was just past four years old. I can remember the logs in above the house and all the water getting up. My grandpa was there and he had my mother to get the kids and get out. There was one girl younger than me and then one born the same year. This covered bridge was probably 100 yards above the place that the new Sheets Bridge is now. They just put this one in five or six years ago.

My father had about 360 acres or something like that in the farm. We raised probably 75 to 100 acres of crops—about 50 acres of potatoes, around 35 acres of cabbage, and around 15 acres of beans on the average. My mother cooked for the work hands. She was a wonderful cook. She had to do a lot of cooking to take care of everything. All the family worked on the farm and helped raise crops. There was about eight or nine other than family that worked for my father in the fields to raise the crops. They had a crawler tractor; they called it the Oliver Crawler where they done the plowing. We used three horses to pull the plow before they got the tractor.

When I was a little fellow we played hide and go seek. We had a big cardboard box and I got it in the middle of the road and got in it. This lady come by with her husband in a car. She told her husband, "Don't you run over

Donald Sheets stands by the U.S. Geological Survey gauge near the Walt Sheets Bridge, which spans the South Fork of the New River east of Jefferson.

that box. One of Nettie's kids may be in there." She lifted the lid on the cardboard box and there I sit in the box. That was the first and the last time I sat in the middle of the road.

One time I had been to the neighbor's house and was coming back in and my brother, he got him a sheet and hid behind the truck and he jumped out with the sheet. I had a stick in my hand and I went in and told my mother I'd killed a ghost down the road. It was my brother. I didn't kill him, but I hit him pretty good. He never scared me no more. That was Doug, the one next to me; they was only 17 months between me and him. About two years between all the rest.

Sometimes it was cold enough to freeze the river. I can remember when they worked horses on the river, logging wood out. There was a bud they called bam bud. They'd cut them down on the ice and it'd shatter a lot of buds off and they'd sweep them up and pack them. They hauled the big wood to Wilkesboro for pulp wood. They'd log that out on the ice with horses. The river would freeze up. There'd just be an air hole here and there where horses or cattle would drink water.

That bam bud tree, it was my understanding they made some kind of medicine out of the buds. We would sell those to herb companies. Jobs were scarce and you had to do anything you could. We gathered a lot of herbs. They had a leaf called a beadwood leaf and a wild cherry tree. We skinned the bark. Sassafras, we dug it and peeled the root. We'd sell burdock or yellow dock. Where they plowed a big field, we'd get that poke and chop it up. I've eat poke salad, dandelion, plantain, dock leaves, and that little bright-colored weed, lamb's quarters, it's good to mix in mustard greens. It mellows the mustard greens out. I love it. It comes up about the same time as mustard. Poke, you get it when it first comes up when it's real small.

We grew most of what we eat. We raised big gardens. My mother done lots of canning and they raised hogs and beef. We had chickens, ducks, turkeys. Got all our eggs and then we milked eight or ten cows. They sold that milk to Kraft Cheese over in Jefferson.

There were four girls and five boys and my mother's last two was dead — they was a boy and a girl. In order was Willard, Richard, Willeen, Douglas, Donald, Raychella, Marguerite, Frank, and Beverly. Then the two infants, a boy and a girl that lived around a month. I can't even remember their names. Seven of these are still living. Richard, he died in 1989, and my brother died this year, Willard, the oldest one. My father died in 1975, my grandfather in 1956, and my mother in 1994. My grandfather was 97 year old when he died, my dad was 69, and my mother was 84. She was born in 1910. My dad was born in 1906.

Used to they'd all come from town and everywhere to go swimming in the river. In my life I pulled three from the river that was drowning. One time my scout master, John W. Lute, brought a bunch of boy scouts and we were all swimming and they had a big raft on the river. One got in under the raft and didn't come up and I dived in and pulled him out and Mr. Lute give him mouth-to-mouth resuscitation and got the water pumped out of him. Then another time I drove up and this man and his wife and little girl was at the river and she's in the water. I saw her go down two or three times. I hollered and they wouldn't pay no attention and I run in and got her out. I thought how my scout master had got the water out of the little boy, so I tried that and the water just run out of her mouth and she started breathing. I put her across my knee and pushed on her back and that water just run out. I had a first cousin and he was in water and he got scared. I finally got him out to the bank. His name was Paul Sheets. I didn't have to do him the same way. He just strangled bad. He had a-hold of me and I finally kicked him off of me and got a stick and got a-hold of him and got him out. He just got scared. That's the cause of drowning, 90 per cent of the cause is that they get scared and just start fighting. If they're bigger than you, the best thing to do is get something and not grab a-hold of them 'cause they'll hold you under.

We had an old wooden boat. Everybody had one on the river. We done a lot of fishing out of it. We had cattle we milked on the other side and we used the boat to cross the river and bring the milk back. My brother had a canoe and we'd ride it and fish and just ride to ride. I've still got an aluminum boat to fish out of. We catch small mouth bass and a fish called a redeye. There lots of species of fish in the river — trout, bass, carp, horneyheads, catfish. I've caught some large cats out of the river.

I fish a lot of the river, a lot of remote areas, too. Before the Appalachian Power Company talked about building a dam on the river (which was never built), you'd hardly ever see a canoe, maybe two or three during the summer. Then it got to be a big, big thing. Before they put these dumpsters in, when the river would get way up, you'd see lots of trash, a lot of jugs and stuff going in the river. After they got them dumpsters, it cleaned the river up lots. My mother started the slogan, "The New River, as it is." They was a bunch come there of newspaper reporters and they asked her about the river and she said, "Leave the river like it is." She sure did. That bridge down there has always been called the Walt Sheets Bridge. They just recently put the official name on the bridge. It was named after my father, Walter Sheets.

My grandpa, he was a horse trader. He didn't smoke, nor drink no alcoholic beverages, didn't use tobacco in any form, my grandpa didn't. He'd trade horses with everybody, I reckon, that would trade with him. He had several horses there. There wasn't too much transportation, mules.

I can remember when they put the road back in after it washed out. It was in the same place it is now. The water got up that high. It washed a lot of the pavement out between there and where the road leaves the river. That covered bridge caught everything and when it went out, the water went down. My grandpa had a meat house there below the old store and he carried all the meat out of that and put it up in the store. My uncle, he come over and he thought my grandpa was in the store and kicked the windows out and the stuff floated down the river, the groceries and stuff. What it didn't float out, though, the water destroyed. But the meat, he saved all of it. My uncle said about the time he got over there, they was a lamp burning in the meat house and that house just floated right off, just raised up out of the water and floated away. He said he just knowed his dad was in there. When the flood come, Ed Jenkins over there, he come down there and told my mother and them to get out, that the river was from hill to hill up towards Boone. And I reckon they just stayed in there.

Nobody died as a result of the flood that I know of. On up above us there, on the far side of the river, that house, just barely the top of the roof was showing. Glenn Mash and some of them marked a mark on the old house where the water got up to. My mother and dad both could play a piano but none of the young'uns could. They had a piano and the water got up in it and ruined it. That's the highest I ever saw the river, but I've seen the water up to the porch two or three times since then.

The river gets a little bit lower in the late fall, but this is the lowest I've ever seen the river in the spring of the year. I had a key for that tank down there and I lost it. I could tell with them water gauges there. They've got a computer in there now and that guy told me that in 30 seconds they could tell what the water was there on the river. It was run by a battery. It had a clock, a water clock, a clock that run with water and it had a graph in it. Every 30 minutes it would punch a hole through this graph and they could take that graph out and read the graph and see if it corresponds with the water clock that moved a line up and down on the graph. That way they could tell how much water went down the river. That still operates in there, but it's solar now. They've got a computer in it now that transmits the information and that solar keeps that computer operating. It was read at a geological station in Statesville, then they moved it to Marion, Virginia, and back to Statesville, is my understanding of it.

Tank holding devices for measuring the New River, which runs a few feet beyond the base of the tower.

My mother and father raised nine kids and they finished school at Jefferson High School. My oldest brother went in the Navy and then come back out and finished his schooling, but the other kids all finished school at Jefferson High School. Marguerite and Beverly and Frank finished at Ashe Central. Raychella is the last one that finished at Jefferson. We always had school buses to ride. We had to walk a long ways to get to where the school bus stopped. Part of the little schools, we had to walk to them, when we first started. When school was out at Jefferson, they'd have school over there at Orion and I'd go over there and play with all them other kids. When I was growing up you didn't lay out of school. If you did, you had to work. School was a lot better than staying at home.

I can remember when we used the lamps, but we had electricity about as far as I can remember. Television, we didn't have one of them until way up in the '50's.

When we were growing up mostly we went to school. We played on the ball team and my sisters was all cheerleaders. I played basketball and softball and baseball and we'd pitch horseshoes and play marbles. We played kick the can, and all those little games, hide and go seek. They had a game where you put your face down and somebody would try to creep up and get a thing behind you. If you heard them, you'd bark. If they got the eraser, they got to be the one that sat there. They always used an eraser at school. You'd hide your eyes and you'd hear them a-slipping up after you. But if they wasn't slipping up after it and you barked, you still lost your turn. Everybody wanted to be up there to hear them a-coming.

Cable across the New River still stands behind the old Walt Sheets home.

Our teachers were pretty good to us. One teacher at Jefferson taught all of them. Mamie Smithey, she was the fourth grade teacher. She was a good teacher. Well, they's all good then. I can remember all mine except my second grade teacher.

We used to stand on the side of the road and put chinquapins in a glass and sell them for 10 cents a glass. You have to hull them before you eat them. They look like a small chestnut.

I never played any instrument, but I remember my mother and dad playing the piano when I was real small. They played religious songs, hymns. My mother would get us all ready and Sunday morning we'd walk to the Orion Methodist Church. C. C. Murray was the pastor.

My mother was born in Ashe County, but they moved to Virginia when she was small. They used to go to West Jefferson to go swimming. They had to come into the house to change their clothes and bathing suits. That was a big, big thing in the summer time. Down where one of these guys was drowning at was where they used to swim all the time. It was on Carlton's farm down there.

All I heard was our ancestors was German. Grandpa's daddy and his brothers settled, one of them in this country and one in Wilkes and one in West Virginia. Those three brothers came from Germany. The name Sheets may have been spelled a little different back then. I've heard them talk about some of them from West Virginia, but I never did know them. My grandfather had four brothers, I guess.

The biggest change I've seen since I was growing up is transportation, I guess. They wasn't no vehicles back then. Mighty few people had a car or any transportation. Back when I was growing up, my dad had a big two-ton truck that he trucked with, and people from all up in this country would walk in there on Wednesday. That was family night at the theater and he'd take them all to the movie. They'd ride his truck there and back to our house and then they'd walk home. They had a serial that they had on at the show, and everybody had to go so they wouldn't miss it. I can remember that good. That was in the '40's.

Electricity, that's another big change. I can remember when my mother done all the washing in tubs. We had water piped into our house. They built a spring box.

Sam Shumate, 62

August 4, 1999

At his home on Buffalo Creek in Warrensville.

I was born April 19, 1937, in a little house about a hundred yards from here. My parents broke up before I was able to even know them and I was brought to live with my grandmother in this house. This house was built in 1912 by my grandfather. They were Johnsons and they came up here from Yadkin County, bought a lot of property on the North Fork of the New River, from the mouth of Buffalo Creek all the way up past what they call the "old house," which is the log cabin. There's a date on the chimney — about 1872. At one time they owned all that property. Today I don't think any of it is in Johnson hands.

I grew up here; went to school at Warrensville Elementary, two class-rooms, grades one, two, and three with one teacher, and four, five, and six with another teacher. It was actually a four-room school. A third room was a place to play when it was too bad to go outside. The fourth room was a lunch room where you took your bag lunch to eat when it was too bad to eat outside. This school was located over on Buffalo Creek. It's the old B.R.O.C. [Blue Ridge Opportunity Commission] building today. We walked to school, even kids two or three miles away walked to school and thought nothing of it.

Growing up in the 40's, we were pretty well isolated, because we didn't go to town. All of our activities were limited to walking distance. There were times as I got older that I've walked to West Jefferson and back, but I can't say that I enjoyed it. We used to walk across the bridge and cut down on the creek bank, what we called "the jungle" because it was grown up in those big tall weeds and we were small people. It just seemed like a jungle to us. We always had a path through the jungle. After we got big enough to roll a wheel, that was taking about a 12-inch steel wheel off a wagon, an old wagon

236

wheel. There were a lot of junk farm wagons back then. You'd get you a good strong piece of wire and cut it in a U and if you'd got skill you could roll that wheel with one hand and just make turns and put it anywhere that it could go. We had to roll that wheel to school with one hand and carry our books in the other. Even when we went to the grocery store we would sometimes have to make two trips because you had to have one hand free to roll that wheel. We used to roll it over on Campbell Road to the Campbell boys, Buford and Gwyn and Wayne. They always had a shop and they were always improving on things. In fact, they improved on our wheel. We were always wearing out the wire down there with the friction. They found if you put a wooden

Sam Shumate, age 14, in front of the house where he now lives (courtesy of Sam Shumate).

spool on there before you made your final bend, you had a bearing. To roll with the Campbell boys, you had to roll it across a swinging bridge. That took a great deal of skill, because if it went in the river, you had to go in after it or you lost it. It was a lot of fun growing up here.

We were all poor, but nobody told us, so we didn't know. We wore patched jeans; blue jeans were cheap, $3 a pair, and any kind of a shirt we could get. If a kid came to school wearing jeans with holes in them or ragged, that was a slam on their parents because the parents didn't think enough of them to at least patch them. That's just kind of a turnabout for today. I've often wondered if today our kids are kind of rebelling against the better economy they have today, trying to look poor by wearing ragged and patched jeans when they don't have to. Jeans back then was the cheapest attire; today they're some of your most expensive.

Back then most every farm only had one vehicle and it was usually a pickup truck. It was embarrassing, but if you took your girlfriend out, you had to take her out in a pickup truck. Today the young people, even the girls, want a pickup truck. Of course, Lord have mercy on anybody that throws anything in the back of them, because they don't want that paint scratched. Seems like it isn't very practical to have a pickup if you're not planning on hauling anything. I think that, too, may be a reflection on the rebelliousness of kids toward our economy. Until they've heard their parents, and especially their grandparents, talk about how things used to be, it was tough.

We were lucky. We had an uncle, my grandmother's brother, who ran a store. He was an old bachelor and when great-grandmother Jones died, he moved in with us and he agreed to furnish the groceries. That was the best deal we ever had. We didn't have to worry about where our food was coming from any more.

We loved the creek. We dammed it up and we played in it. We even had a diving board where you could dive off. I know there was two or three years we couldn't go near the water because of the polio epidemic. They felt like we might get polio out of the creek. We had friends who had infantile paralysis and if the creek caused it, we were not going to get close to it. Those were kind of sad days when you couldn't get close to the creek. But when that was over with, we dammed it back up and went in again. Every flood that came by washed our dam out and it was to do all over again. It was a lot of fun, it kept us busy, and it kept us out of trouble. There used to be a bridge across the mouth of Buffalo right where it enters the river; the old Joe Badger Road used to go down under the big bridge and across the mouth of Buffalo and on down the river.

When we would play ball at school, the only ball we had besides what we took, was a volleyball. We didn't know it was a volleyball because we didn't know what volleyball was. We played kickball with it. About time for the bell to ring to take up books, we'd manage to kick it in the creek so we could chase it down the creek and skip school a little bit. If it got over to where we could get it, we'd usually throw rocks at it and knock it back out in the middle of the creek because we could always get it on the low water bridge. We'd just walk on the bridge and get it before it got in the river. About 20 or 30 minutes later, here we'd come tromping triumphantly back into the classroom. We'd retrieved the expensive kickball. I don't know if my uncle, Lee Jones, the teacher, ever got wise to that or not, but I'd say he probably did. He wasn't a dummy. It was an automatic whipping if you fell in the creek, no questions asked, zero tolerance.

In the winter time when it'd freeze over, we loved to get out and skate on the creek. Of course, we'd never heard of ice skates. We'd just get out there and get a good long run and see who could skate the farthest with their shoes. One day I had on my Sunday-go-to-meeting leather bottoms. I thought I'd try them out. The other boys had skated and they'd marked their spot. I got me a big run and those leather bottoms went down through there so far that I even went into the swift water and I got wet. "Well," Uncle Lee said, "Sammy, go home and change clothes and as you come back through the jungle, break me off a keen willow and I'm going to check to make sure it's not notched." We's pretty bad to take a knife and notch it about halfway through in three or four places so it'd break right quick. He was wise to that. I came home and I was really dripping. I got upstairs to change clothes and my grandmaw had just done the washing and I had about 12 pair of clean underwear. Uncle Lee was not a leg switcher, he'us a tail switcher. So I put on every pair of underwear I had and put on my old jeans and I marched back over to school. I went through the jungle and I got me a nice keen willow and I took it in and he checked it and he laid me over his desk and he just let me have it. I didn't feel a lick, I was well padded. When he was through, he stood me up and said, "Now students, let that be a lesson to you, and may I say that that is the way to take your punishment, not all this hollering and screaming. You did fine, Sammy, sit down." I didn't tell him that I didn't feel a lick.

We used to take our fishing poles to school over there as we went as young boys. The boys' toilet was down by the creek, the girls' toilet was around behind the school. In the morning before we took up books, we'd set out fishing poles. Then we'd take turns being excused throughout the morning to see who'd caught what. They'd go down and come back from the toilet and tell you what you'd caught and who'd caught what. At that time, usually it was silversides, a little old fish about six inches long that I've never seen since. I don't know whether it's extinct or what. At the end of the day we'd divide up our fish and head home. If Uncle Lee knew that we were fishing down there when we were being excused so much, I don't know. We took advantage of the creek; we enjoyed it.

We liked to go to the river. It was a good place to swim. Right down below the mouth of Buffalo was what we called the Carter Hole. One of the Carter children was drowned in there years ago and our parents always told us to beware of the Carter Hole, that it had a suck hole in it. So we never went close to the Carter Hole except to fish off the bank. There was an old man lived down there that fished there constantly. He'd take his fish up and keep them in his spring box until he was ready to eat them so they'd be good and fresh. We were fishing the Carter Hole. He considered that his private fishing hole, but he couldn't say anything to us because it wasn't his property. But if we were fishing down there and he was fishing, if we caught something, he would come up and say, "How about you putting in somewhere else. I believe I'll fish here a while." And we would. We'd go down there and if we'd catch one down there, here he'd come, "How about you putting in somewhere else. I'll fish here a while."

I still enjoy fishing the New River, especially the North Fork. One of my favorite places is to wade from the old log cabin back up the river, because when you get up there just a few hundred yards, you're out of any type of civilization whatsoever. You've got a rock cliff on one side and a rock cliff on the other side and if there's not an airplane going over, you could have been there 500 years ago and it'd look probably the same. It's too rugged for people to have logged the timber. I was fishing there not too many years ago and it was awfully still and you could watch the wildlife. Fishing, to me, it's kind of getting back to nature. I rarely ever keep the fish unless it just happens to be a particularly good one. I usually just throw them back. I was fishing this one day and I heard the awfulest splashing coming down the river and there was a curve and I couldn't see what it was. I stood there and thought, what in the world is that? It got louder and louder and around the curve came the biggest buck deer I've ever seen running right down the middle of the river, just as hard as he could go. I thought, well, this rascal is going to run over me, and I moved. When I moved he realized I wasn't a tree or something and he did a right turn and went up that rock cliff. I've never seen a deer go up a cliff like that, pretty sure-footed.

Along with the creek and the river, we also took advantage of the railroad. I hate the railroad's gone, but we sure did enjoy it growing up. Little Doc Jones was the depot agent and he usually welcomed us boys in to visit because he said it was a pretty lonely occupation except when the train came in or went out. He had the warmest place in town in the wintertime because he didn't have to buy the coal; Norfolk & Western Railroad furnished it. We invented a game called Prisoner. We'd divide up into teams and one-half was the prisoners and the other half was the guards. That came natural because the bridge camp down here was once a prison camp. Then when it closed, they had another prison camp up Buffalo. So, we all knew someone who worked at the prison camp. We used a box car as the prison. We'd lock the prisoners in there and it was their job to escape. Then, it was our job to catch them and put them back in. We were playing Prisoner one day when the train came by. It unhooked and backed up there and pulled out of the station with two boys in it, Pig Turnmire and Gene Goss. Gene used to be our sheriff. It hooked up and started to West Jefferson and those boys was back there just screaming bloody murder. We went in to see Little Doc and said, "Doc, we'us playing Prisoner and Pig and Gene are in the box car." He said, "Yeah, I know. That's all right. They had to take it to town to get the one behind it. They'll put it back as they come back." So they got them a ride to West Jefferson and back, two pretty scared boys.

The most fun with the old steam engine was greasing the track. Ernest Seagraves had a service station over here where Ivalee lives now, the big brick building. We'd spend a month draining the oil out of his oil cans after he was through putting it in vehicles. We didn't mess with that used stuff, we used the real thing. By the time we had about a gallon of oil, we'd take a brush and go up there above the depot and oil the track from out there to the Devil's Stairs 'cause it was an upgrade. Then we'd sit on the rocks right above where the engine would stop. It was really something to hear a steam engine try to take off and start to spinning. They really make a racket. The engineer would shake his fist at us and he'd say things, but it made so much noise we couldn't hear what he said. I think it's probably better that we didn't. He finally would back down to about where Northwest School is now and get a running go so he could get across it. They called it the Virginia Creeper, but when it was going across that oil stretch, it wasn't no creeper. In fact, I often worried that it might hit somebody at the Devil's Stairs crossing. But back then traffic was pretty slack and everyone knew when the train ran approximately and they watched for it. It got to the point where if we wanted to have some fun, whether we oiled the track or not, we'd just go up and sit on the rock. If we sat on the rock, he wouldn't even try to take off. He'd just back down to the school and then come across it whether it was oiled or not. He just took it for granted that if we were sitting there, it was oiled.

I left here in 1955 for two reasons. One was to get off my grandmother's purse strings. Like I say, we weren't economically well off. We weren't as lucky as some. We didn't have a pickup truck, much less a car. But another reason was to see the world. I'd been stuck in these hills for 18 years and I's ready to see the real world and get out of this God-forsaken place, 'cause I'd seen pictures. I joined the Air Force and in four years I got to see a lot of the world. I got out of service in 1959. I was ready to go to college then at about age 22.

I went up to Lees-McRae and talked to them and told them I didn't have any money and told them I didn't have a GI Bill. They fixed it so I could work my way through and I got some nice experiences, too. I transferred over to Appalachian after finishing Lees-McRae and worked my way through there by robbing trains. I robbed Tweetsie [Tweetsie Railroad, a recreation park near Blowing Rock] for $10 a day and I made an extra $3.50 a day making the bullets for us to shoot.

When it came time to do my student teaching, finances were getting scarce because I couldn't work. I'd written an article for a teacher at Lees-McRae who suggested that I send it to Reader's Digest for "most unforgettable character." This old colored gentleman who had encouraged me to go in the Air Force and go to college had burned up in his house. He was a teacher. I wrote an article on him and was encouraged to sent it to *Reader's*

Sam Shumate in U.S. Air Force, San Antonio, Texas, 1955 (courtesy of Sam Shumate).

Digest, which I did. After awhile I forgot about it. I went to the post office one day and there was a check for $1,500 from *Reader's Digest*. In 1962 that was a fortune. I paid back a lot of people.

By then I knew that I wanted to come back to the mountains, because I'd seen the rest of that world that I thought was so great. I was gone from Ashe County for 12 years.

About the future of this community, it's going to develop. I hope we have a little say-so in the development. I'd hate for it to develop kind of like between Boone and Blowing Rock or Boone and Banner Elk, just become a tourist trap. I would like to see some kind of planning and development take place. There's developments here that we're not even aware of. Just before you get to Lloyd Mitchell's on Sugar Tree, just as you start to leave the river, the road goes straight. That road used to go on across on the other side of the dam and come out across the low water bridge there just below the dam. But it no longer goes through there. Now it goes down into this Spicewood development. I noticed on Campbell Road, they've sold the other side of the river around on the Teaberry side and they're putting little houses and camping trailers in there. There's one development on the Campbell Road on the right just as you cross the low water bridge. It's happening and a lot of it we don't even know. These people come in and rent post office boxes or have a mailbox set up out on the road with these strange names and we know that people are moving into this area.

About my own children, I have two boys. Jon is 30 and Chris is 28. Jon works at Southern Devices. Chris is 28 and he lives next door in a house built by my great-grandparents, although it's newer than the house built by my grandparents. He married a girl who was raised over in Virginia and moved to Jefferson, Sarah, and they have a 16-month old girl, Cassie, our only grandchild.

I'll never be an expert at anything because I enjoy doing too many things. My wife is real crafty and we thought we'd like to do the craft tour, so we did that for four years.

I've always liked cars. I think the reason why is because we never had one and they always fascinated me. Today I've got to be careful or I'll buy too many old cars.

I had an apple orchard for several years. I also raised peaches, pears, nectarines, and apricots. I had apricots one year.

Then the idea came for Christmas trees. After losing all the money on the apples, I saved 20 over here just for me and the neighbors. I cut the ones down behind the house and planted Christmas trees, something that might eventually show a little profit. So we bought a little farm up at Clifton on the New River, North Fork, and planted Christmas trees. My oldest son, Jon, experimented with herbs, grew echinacea, sold a crop of that. Grew an acre of Asian burdock, sold that and made about $3,000 on that acre. It's a pretty good crop. Chris has a big crop of watermelons and cantaloupe he hopes will come in about the time the South Carolina watermelons and cataloupes give up. They're experimenting and I encourage it.

Sam Shumate, when a teacher at Northwest Ashe High School in the 1980's (courtesy of Sam Shumate).

POLLY JONES

August 22, 1999

*At her home in the Chestnut Hill community
on the South Fork of the New River.
Mrs. Jones is a teacher now.
She was for ten years on the Board of Directors
of the National Committee for the New River.
Her husband Ralph Jones is present.*

I guess you want me to start at the beginning. I really wouldn't have gotten involved in the fight to save the New River if Appalachian Power representatives had not made me angry. They told me I had to sell my land and take their price or else they would just put the money in the courthouse and it would stay up there until I took it. That really upset me. I decided then that I would join in the fight. I hadn't been too interested before that. I started attending the meetings at Oak Hill. The people that I remember working with the most were Sidney Gambill, Ed Adams, Joe Matthews, Wallace Carroll, Mrs. Anderson — the same people who came to the meetings. The meetings were emotional. You're taught not to make emotional speeches; you're supposed to have your facts and your figures. Nobody wanted to hear facts and figures. It was really how you reached these people, through their emotions, their land.

So, I made a speech at Jefferson High School. I went to Raleigh and spoke to the state legislature and was down there when they actually introduced the bill to make it a designated scenic river. Our representative would not introduce the bill, so we had to get to him politically. He eventually did introduce the bill to save the river in Raleigh. He did not want to do that. I was there; I was standing behind him, but he didn't know who I was. He told his supporters who were anti-river, "I don't want to do this; they have forced me to do it." I interrupted him and said, "We let you do this because we're being polite. We don't need you; we have someone from down the state to do this. We're just letting you do it as a consideration and a kindness because you come from our part of the state." So he finally did introduce the bill, but he didn't want to.

We went to West Virginia to Hawk's Nest State Park, I think it was, and attended several meetings. We drew up a coalition and usually it was just people from West Virginia; they were really more interested than the people in Virginia, I guess because most of the scenic part of the river, the really wild part of it, runs through West Virginia. We attended more meetings in West Virginia than in Virginia and North Carolina. I think the people in Ashe County really didn't know how to get organized. There was a lot of bitter resentment that outsiders came in and helped us. What they (the coalition) needed from people like me was someone who would do the grassroots work. I found that your government only works for you if you make it work for you. The people who yell the loudest get the things done.

I was amazed to watch these people work. Here I was a plain old housewife from North Carolina and working with these people who had power and position, who were Senators and Congressmen and newspaper editors. They had it all figured out. When we got down to the nitty gritty, I'm probably jumping ahead a little bit here, we hit the thing on three different fronts. I don't know if a lot of people realized that or not, but it was like a blitz. We took it to every newspaper in the country, in the whole U. S. There was a major editorial to save the river in practically every newspaper in the country. We hit it through the media. We hit it through the courts. It was going through the Court of Appeals and Sidney [Gambill] was spearheading that. Then we took it through Congress because we had to get Congress to pass the resolution. If Congress hadn't passed the resolution, then we would have had to pursue it in the courts. We never let the court option die down. We kept it going on all three fronts at all times. It was really a gigantic effort on the part of a lot of people, but really an inner core of people that dedicated a lot of time to doing it. I know I dedicated a lot of time, about ten years of my life. My children were small. I can remember my sons Charlie and Phillip saying, "That's our river," and if my children would see anybody in that river, they'd say, "Get out of our river." They felt like they owned the river, we'd worked on it so much. We had meetings here. We had suppers here. We went everywhere. I wish I'd kept the speech I made at Raleigh because one of the gentlemen down the road said I made him cry.

Another thing I did was go to New York to lobby. I hadn't flown before and I didn't want to fly. I wasn't crazy about flying to New York for sure. But we packed up and went and lobbied in the Plaza Hotel at American Electric Power Company's stockholders' meeting. We had a room that we had rented. We had done up some copy for New Yorkers who were interested enough to come in and talk to us. We had booklets that we had made. It was interesting to see all the wealthy people who came in to the stockholders' meeting who didn't care about the little people that lived on the New River in Virginia and West Virginia and North Carolina and how the dam was going to affect their lives and their livelihoods. They were interested in how much money they were going to get from their stock. But once in a while we'd find a little lady in a mink coat, carrying her little poodle, that was interested in what we had to say. The funny thing was, really, the New River Committee had given us a booklet that had a picture of the river, not in North Carolina but in West Virginia. They knew, they said, that part is not going to be under water. They didn't realize that if you dammed up the river up here, it was going to make the water less over there.

While we were in New York, we stayed with the granddaughter of R. J. Reynolds. It was interesting because the man she was engaged to was a teacher in New York. I learned a lot of things about the aftermath of World War II. We were up there one time in May and it was cold. We were going down the streets of New York, and we didn't have overcoats on. We had on light clothes, and it was cold and the lady who was working for Joe [Matthews] was with me. We had trash bags full of pet rocks for the stockholders of American Electric Power Company. Billie Moore, Sidney Gambill's daughter, had painted pet rocks and we took them up there, and we later sent pet rocks to the Senators and Congressmen. You can imagine two little hillbilly women walking down the streets of New York with a black trash bag filled with pet rocks, taking them to a power company's meeting. It was kind of interesting. Billie Moore got out in the river and collected those pet rocks. I've still got one of those; she made me a big one. But the small ones that she gave me I kept. The museum in Raleigh wanted them. So they're at Raleigh in the museum down there. They've got a lot of stuff I had and it's down there. She painted pictures on them — little animals, raccoons, o'possums, deers, snakes.

Whatever the Committee asked me to do, I always found some way of doing it. They had it all figured out when we organized the National Committee for the New River. Basically, the people were from Virginia, West Virginia, and North Carolina. We also sent this information to a lot of college campuses, because college students in the early '70's were still into things like this. I probably started in the late '60's. My sons were born in '73-'74, and I was working then. We had a lot of National Committee for the New River chapters on college campuses, especially in Ohio, at Kent State, and places like that, all the way to California, as a matter of fact. But most of the members were from those three states. We had a National Committee in a lot of states, practically every state. They may not have had a lot of members, but we did have those Committees. We did a lot of meetings, a lot of traveling, from New York to Washington, D.C., to Raleigh, to Winston-Salem.

We met in Alleghany County at Wallace Carroll's house [he was the former publisher of the Winston-Salem Journal]. It's just amazing all the things that we did, and a lot of the strategies that we used are lost. I have my notes as secretary, but we never did make those public.

The meetings were the big thing. We really had to work on the grass-roots and get all the people in Ashe County and Alleghany County involved that we could. If the people in your county who lived on the river didn't support it, then the politicians outside weren't going to support it. So we had to have everybody that we could get and most of the people in this section of the county did support it. So we had the grassroots effort. That's why I came in and I let them use me. I enjoyed doing it and I did it. I don't regret it. I think it was the right decision in the long run. It's a beautiful river. It was here before we were and it'll be here when we're gone. The river was here before the Appalachian mountains according to geologists; that's why it's flowing north.

Elizabeth McCommon, who wrote that song [about the river for the festival], I have not seen her or heard from her in years. Then Ronnie Taylor wrote a song. He works with Ray Taylor, his daddy, drilling wells. Elizabeth should still be living unless she got some kind of sickness. We did everything and it really was a grassroots thing. It was going on three different levels, through the media, through the courts, and through the legislatures in Raleigh and Washington. We did everything we could to draw attention to it.

I asked Appalachian Power Company if they were going to build a nuclear power plant on the river and they never answered that question. So my humble opinion was that was what Appalachian wanted to do was to build a power plant over there. They would not say they were not going to build a nuclear power plant. All the electricity that was supposed to be generated was going to Chicago and the bigger cities up north . That helped us to fight them. Another big arguing point was that it would take four kilowatts to produce three kilowatts of power. We had a professor from Wake Forest that worked with us on things like that. We had fact sheets that would tell you how much agriculture would be lost and the money it would cost the county in tobacco, in cattle, or whatever, and what you would get in return, maybe tourism, maybe somebody would bring a boat and put it on the lake. What I didn't like about it was the drawdown, because when you look at Butler [Tennessee] and you think of drawdown and you think of all those mudflats that are left, it would have ruined the best part of Ashe County. I'm not saying that the northern part of the county is not pretty; it is. But the bottoms are on this part. The river bottoms out and comes to where they join over there. It would have covered up the bigger bottoms in Alleghany and Ashe. If you want to see what a dam does, all you have to do is go over to Virginia, because they've dammed the river over there and it's ugly.

I worked with a guy from the state department, Art Cooper. He had Sarah [our daughter] in class after that at State. She got a degree in conservation and one in parks and recreation. We worked with him a lot, got to know him. He couldn't believe it when he met Sarah.

There are a lot of wild flowers up around Elk Shoals. The wild flower people helped on the dam. We took them up there. The North Carolina Wild Flower Association and Audubon helped us.

Another thing we did, like in Utah and different parts of the country, they were trying to get their rivers saved and so we traded favors with them.

In '75 we had the idea of having a festival on the river to let everybody come in and see what the river was like and to see really what we were trying to accomplish. We got a big, long bottom over at Lon Reeves's farm on the river, very pretty, and started working there. We had musicians come in and play country music. We had a lady that wrote a song especially for the New River. We had artists from Ashe County and Alleghany County and Grayson County, Virginia, bring in all kinds of art work and put them up on one section of the field. I was president of Ashe Central High School band parents that year. My daughter was in the band. Ashe Central High School Band did the food, did the whole plate lunches. They provided the food for between 5,000 and 10,000 visitors. I was working on the festival and organizing it and at the same time I was president of the band parents and organizing that so they could make a lot of money to buy new band uniforms. In addition to the food, we did have enough food for everybody, we had enough drinks for everybody. We had drink companies there. We had a huge stage set up for the musicians. Mrs. Eleanor Reeves wrote a history of the county and read it; it was really good. We dressed in old-timey outfits. We had the local power company run in all kinds of power poles so that we could have electricity. Actually, on one pole we put up a high water mark, that if the dam should come, it would have been so many feet up on the electric pole. That said a lot more than words did, because people could see that this is how much ground, how much land that this dam was really going to take. We had a tremendous outpouring of people. We had lots of musicians there and people came for the music and for the picnicking, came for playing in the river, came for the art. I looked personally at the license plates to see from what states the cars had come. They came from 21 or 22 different states that I remember counting. We had people from Georgia, South Carolina, Ohio. I did work on that festival for a long time. We published a little newspaper. It was just a time-consuming, big thing that was really enjoyable.

I think we went so far as to say it [the festival] was probably the turning point in our fight. Up until this point, I think a smaller group of people had been fighting. Most people had the idea that there was no point in fighting. We're little people, we're farmers, we can't fight a big utility company like American Electric Power. When they saw what happened at the festival and all these people coming together and that they had so much outside support, we thought that this was probably the turning point. We picked up a lot more support. Most of the people in the county and practically all the people as far as I can remember that lived on the river were against the dam. People who wanted the dam were people who lived in town. What they wanted was not a wild and scenic river but a dam where they could take their boats and go speedboat riding. Speedboat riding, you can go somewhere else to do that.

The Jones family at the time of the dam controversy. Left to right: Daughter Sarah, Polly, Ralph, and sons Phillip and Charlie (courtesy of Polly Jones).

We have 70 acres here. We don't farm it much any more. We used to. Daddy farmed until he got too old. We used to have cows and when you don't have cows, it grows up. But you can't keep cows because cows don't bring any money in. Since the boys have got through college, we've started back trying to work on the land a little bit. They will be the fourth generation. Ralph's grandpa lived there in front of us and Ralph's daddy lived up here behind us. Ralph's people lived in Alleghany County. His grandfather came from Wales and his grandmother came from England. The Richardsons came down through Virginia. I'm from over east of Jefferson. My mother's still living. My father was a Baptist preacher. He lived to be 94 and had 19 children. He was first married to Mary Jane Welch. They had 10 children and she passed away with a heart attack. Then he married my mother. She was 24 and he was 53 and they had nine children. He lived to see the baby at Appalachian State. He was a sophomore in college when my father passed away.

Our genealogy kind of ties to the river in a way. When my father was alive he would tell us about his family coming from Scotland. His family came from Scotland to Wytheville [Virginia] to Grayson, then into Ashe County over to Lansing to Piney Creek. The North Fork of the river is over there and, of course, we knew the Committee couldn't get protection for both, so we chose to take the South Fork. The North Fork was not protected [at that time]. When I was younger I didn't worry that much about heritage and I didn't worry that much about my family. When they'd tell us stuff it'd kind of go in one ear and out the other. Then one day my sister was talking about it. It's been ten years ago since we got interested in the genealogy. I've always loved history. One of our rallying battle cries was that the names on the mailboxes when you go down the road are the same names that you will find on the monuments and the same names that you'll find fought in the American Revolution. That struck a chord with me. It made it worthwhile.

The Committee told me to be prepared to get hate calls; the opposition would do that [during the fight to stop the dam], but I didn't get too many of those. I know there were some people who really got upset, because they really wanted the dam. They could see money, I guess, for the property that was around the edge of the water, plus they could see having a lake out there. At times I really faltered and I thought, maybe they're right and I'm wrong. My brother had just gotten back from Vietnam and needed a job, and they said they were going to hire all local labor. Then we got to investigating how they hired local labor, and they really didn't, they brought in their own labor. At times I've questioned if fighting it so hard was the right thing to do. In the long run, I think I made the right decision. Lots of people are moving into this section of the county. I guess some of the land Appalachian [Power Company] bought may still be vacant, but a lot of it has been resold and is building back up in this section of the county. Most of the people down this way sold because this was where the water would be first. For some reason, the Appalachian Power Company started buying down there and coming this way.

I hope people don't discover us. We're trying to hold the land for our children to come back, and our grandchildren. They've already picked a spot out. We worry about what people will do to our river bottoms. We're not going to do anything to it. Sometimes I'm for zoning and sometimes I'm against zoning. I really have put my head in the sand and not thought about which way is the best. I know in Ashe County people feel like it's their land and they can do what they want to with it. But I get upset when I see land that's been clearcut for timber and it's literally destroyed. The road on this side, Chestnut Hill Road, back in the 1700's was not on this side, it was on the other side, and I didn't know that until I did research. It used to be called Mulky Forge. You'd come down on the other side because there's no bridge up here. The water would have been a hundred feet over the bridge there at Scottville. Scottville River Bridge is what they call that bridge and the water would have been 100 feet over that bridge. But back in 1776, the road went down the other side, because there was no ford up there and so they came across right there in front of our mailbox. The horses and wagons came across there and went on down the Chestnut Hill Road.

I didn't grow up here, but I'm sure there were corn and flour mills up and down the river. There had to be. Ralph could probably tell you about that. We had that when I grew up. I can remember taking corn to Riley Dishman's to have it ground into meal. I guess his mill's been torn down. I can remember my daddy growing wheat and corn. We'd make pancakes out of buckwheat. He would thresh it at the house and take it to Boone to have it ground, and they would put it in commercial flour and buckwheat bags. I can remember the threshers coming.

I'd hate to see those threshers coming; it was so hot. I had to cook for them and I had to work. I can still see that in my mind, that big old threshing machine. Dad would need us to help and I've actually stacked sheaves of grain in a stack. You could stack it up in a big stack, and I'd stand on it. He had this long wooden pole with a little fork on it, and he would push it up and I'd stack it for him until I got it so high, way up. I was the oldest in the family. All the other children older than me were gone. People don't know how to work today. They think they do. They think working at MacDonald's is hard work. I guess it is, but it's a different kind of work. When I tell my students they couldn't keep up with me or they wouldn't know how to work, they think I'm not serious, but I really am. By the time I was married, we had tractors and things like that. There's a whole lot to be said for the old ways.

My husband Ralph went to Nathan's Creek High School and I went to Jefferson. Actually, he graduated three years before I did. I didn't know him. He was in the Navy when I met him.

We have three beautiful children, knock on wood, that never gave us any trouble. Sarah lives in Raleigh; she married Neal Tugman. She has three daughters. She graduated from [N.C.] State and is a housewife. I guess she'll go to work next year after the baby goes to school. Charlie went to Annapolis. He's a lieutenant in the Navy. Phillip's in Boston working for Raytheon, a defense contractor. He went to State. He's a mechanical engineer. We've been lucky with our children. We've been fortunate, because you really don't know who you're marrying when you get married.

Ralph supported me in the fight for the river. When we would go to Oak Hill — I've got a big mouth, you can tell how I talk. I could talk and when people make me angry, I can really talk. He'd say, "I want you to go over there and you sit down and you keep your mouth shut and say nothing." And I would. I'd sit out in the car and read Harlequin romances and he'd go to the meetings. I think they got him upset about something; I don't remember what they got him upset about. He said, "I really want you to start doing this now. I want you to get in there and say something." But he didn't want me to go until he got upset and angry with them. That's the truth. He knew I would get all involved in it, which turned out to be right, I did. He didn't want me to, he really didn't. It was a full-time thing, with two little boys and Sarah was in high school. They were naughty little boys when I got on the phone long distance, working on that festival for the river. They would pitty pat down that road and go just as hard as they could, or they'd pitty patty up this way and get in that creek, or they'd climb up the kitchen cabinets because they knew I was on the phone long distance and couldn't get to them. We had an Ashe County day in Washington, D.C., in the rotunda at the Capitol Building. We sent pound cakes, ham, cheese, everything from Ashe County, up to Washington, D.C. Lizzie Shumake and her sister, Ellen, made pound cakes to send and we sent people with musicians. We had a whole big hoedown in the rotunda of the Capitol. Anything we could do to make people aware of what was going to be covered up in Ashe County we did. We had some wild ideas, I guess.

That would have been in the mid-'70's. That was when Ronald Reagan was running and Jimmy Carter was president. Everybody who was president or was running for president or even thinking about running for president finally came out on our side — Jimmy Carter, Ronald Reagan, Gerald Ford. It was just amazing that we'd just politically maneuver and get people to fall into line. Your government works for you, but sometimes you have to make it work for you, and that's what we did.

When the 1940 flood came up, there's a house across the river, Luther Church's. He had four sons in World War II, and in the '40 flood the water came up to the edge of their porch and they stood out on their porch and kept the logs off their porch. The last hurricane we had, it wasn't Hugo, Hugo brought tornadoes through here and brought some rain, but not as much rain. You could see where there were swirls of tornadoes. If you think we don't get tornadoes in Ashe County, we do, because it tore the pine trees down right up there and you could tell where they'd gone around and around. One time we still had tobacco down there in the bottom when a hurricane came through. The water was up over the top of the tobacco. It was six feet in that bottom. It was muddy, but it drained it off. Some people had their trees cut and it just washed it on down the river. Ralph's daddy was living then and he was down there and I went down there to see about him. All you could see was the tops of the tobacco. That's a pretty broad bottom down there. Tobacco that year was high, it was over the top of my head. The water had to be about six feet there and maybe deeper than that. We get upset when we have a flood. Everybody's trash comes down and we have to go pick it up. The river, when it rains real hard, it will come up, it will get in that road right there. To go to work, several times I have had to walk out that way and across the hill and had to park the car out there because it's low right here in front of the house.

To get water to our house, we have a spring up in the mountain there. It's about to go dry because it's so dry this year. It's not been this dry since the boys were little. It got dry like this one time and I was afraid to use the water from the spring. We had a little pond out there in the creek and the boys would carry water to put on all the flowers. Charlie called the other day from Pennsylvania and I was telling him how dry it was and asked him if he remembered making that pond. He said he remembered. He was about five or six years old carrying that water.

BILL SEVERT, 57

August 15, 1999

At his home in the Boggs community.
His wife Lula is present.
His hay field by the New River was the site of
President Bill Clinton's visit on July 30, 1998, when
the New River was declared an American Heritage River.

My grandfather's name on my daddy's side was George Severt and his wife was named Betty Severt. My father's name was Gaither Severt. My mother's name was Saddie Mash. Her daddy was Bob Mash. Her mother was Ida Mash.

As far back as I can remember my grandpa, I think my wife told me he died in 1961, so I don't know how long the property had been in the family before him. But that would make it well over 100 years old. I was raised down along the New River. I waded in the water and I fished and I swam in it. In the wintertime, my dad and me would walk on it when it would freeze over with ice. It did years ago. I've put up hay along it in the summertime.

We had a farm, which consisted of the river bottom and most of the hillside. My dad and mom kept two or three milk cows and they would milk them. That produced our milk. We had a springbox that we set the milk in and kept it cool so it would not spoil.

We raised mostly corn down in the river bottoms. Sometimes we had a sugar cane patch. We'd have to go in the patch and pull the fodder off and cut the heads off of it and boil it down. Sometimes it would make pretty molasses and sometimes it would make tar molasses and you had to feed them to your cattle. My dad did his own molasses making. He used to have a grinding machine and a couple of boilers down there. He used to have a mill house down there, too. He had a grinder in there that would grind corn and make corn meal for people around. Most time he'd only open it on

254

Saturday. Saturday was the time for people that wanted some corn ground into meal to bring it to him. In the wintertime, I can remember his engine he used to pull the corn-grinding machine with; back then there weren't any antifreeze. We walked up to the spring and got water and carried it down to fill his tractor up in order for him to crank it up so it'd stay warm until somebody would bring maybe a bushel of corn and he'd grind it for them. Well, he didn't know if anybody else was coming or not, so he had to go out there and drain the water out of it to keep it from freezing and busting the motor. Oh, I got so tired of carrying water you wouldn't believe it. I finally told my dad, "You need to set up a schedule and if they're not here, tell them to wait until next Saturday." This carrying water was getting to me. He didn't have a real good setup, but it never did freeze and bust. The tractor had a gasoline engine, and after you got it started and warmed up, you could convert it over to kerosene. It was an old steel-wheeled Fordson tractor. This tractor had a pulley and you had to run a belt back inside the mill house to the mill itself. That tractor is what pulled the mill. It was something else.

Mom and Dad always had a big garden — potatoes, beans, corn, cucumbers, and tomatoes. We were really self-sufficient. We didn't buy much at the store. Dad used to put out corn in the fields down there and he wanted it hoed three times whether it needed it or not. When he put you to hoeing that corn, getting the weeds out of it, you'd best not leave any weeds or you'd have to hoe the same row again. He checked on you and if you missed a weed, you went back over that row of corn and hoed it again.

Mom and Dad also had chickens and pigs. They'd buy little pigs in the spring of the year. They would put two or three in a pen and raise them up by fall of the year. They would butcher the hogs themselves when it got cold weather. We had a meat house with benches in it. We used salt to cure the meat. We would put a layer of salt on the benches, and then we would lay the meat down on it, and then put another layer of salt on the meat. During the winter we would go up there and cut a ham to eat. It would keep until spring. Then what we had to do if it got warm weather, we had to go up there and take something like a white sack and put the meat in the sack and lay the black pepper to it to keep the bugs out of it and hang it up. Most of the time we'd have meat halfway through the summer. It had to be a pretty cold winter to do this, but usually it was very cold. If it's not a cold winter, it won't do to cure meat out like we used to do it. It has to get really cold to be able to do it like that now.

The closest store to us was out in Glendale Springs. The store's name now is Glendale General. Walt Bare had a store just across the road from Glendale General. I talked about my dad grinding corn for people and this engine he had was a gasoline engine. I can remember when I was little, my dad and me walking to Glendale Springs and he would carry two five-gallon cans to get gas for the tractor. We walked back down to the mouth of the creek, and at that time all that was there was a boat and we had to cross the river in a boat. That was the only way to cross it unless you wanted to wade the river. I remember my dad would walk to the boat before he ever set the gas cans down. It's a good mile and a half from the store to the boat crossing!

The road the way it is now is pretty much the way we went back then, up by the rock quarry. Glendale School Road is the name of it now. Where the bridge is now is where the boat crossing was, too. From the boat crossing up to where the President came, a little white house there in the holler, that was his next stop. He never did complain about carrying those gas cans and walking that far to get the gas. Now, if I had to walk that far, I'd probably have to call 911. Times have really changed!

I can remember well when we got electricity in the house, 'cause I would run in one evening down there and flip on one of those switches and the lights came on. That was amazing to me 'cause I'd never saw anything like that. It was back in the '50's, or maybe in the '40's. I hate to tell you how old I am. Anyway, I can remember stuff like that when I was growing up. Telephones came a pretty good while later. That was in the '60's.

I've got five sisters and two older brothers, which left me being the baby boy. The two youngest sisters went off to the school at Glade Valley, out on the other side of Sparta. It was like a boarding school. This left me at home by myself. But I got to tell you, it was hard on me being left alone. My brother Claude Severt was killed in World War II. His name is on the honor roll at the courthouse. My other brother lived in Maryland for years and years. He finally came back to North Carolina and was living in North Wilkesboro when he passed away.

You know where the President came; there is an old house below the road there in the bottom. That's the house I was born in. It's still down there, but it is run down. It used to be covered with old wooden shingles. As long as it rained kind of straight down, it didn't leak. I slept upstairs and in the wintertime when it was blowing snow, fine snow, I have waked up many a morning and throwed the covers back and snow would be on it. Back then I didn't have a cold; I didn't have to wear as many clothes.

Whenever I started going to school I had to walk to school. From where I was raised to where the school was located was approximately a mile. But we had a path through the woods that we walked up most of the time. If I had to come to school by myself, I walked up the road. I was afraid to go through the woods by myself. It was a one-room schoolhouse. It had an old pot-bellied coal stove that heated it. One class sat at one table, and another class sat up at another table; they had more than one class in one room. One of my teachers, Ona Darnell Caldwell, used to stay with my mama and daddy.

I can just barely remember it. Some of my other teachers were Myrtle Fletcher, Quentin Bare, and Mamie Wallace. That's the only four I can remember.

I went to Beaver Creek High School. I went one year, which would have been the ninth grade. I went one day in the tenth grade. My football coach made me mad and I would not go back any more. Mama and Dad begged me to. I said, "No, I'm not going back and that's it." They told me then that I'd end up digging ditches. And they were so right, but they didn't know I was going to get a backhoe.

Besides farming, I've got a backhoe and I dig ditches just like they said I'd be doing. But I do it the easy way. I've got a small 'dozer. When I dig those ditches, I've got a small 'dozer that I can level them up with when I get through digging. I've got a couple of old dump trucks. If you want a load of gravel, a load of dirt, mulch, something like that, I could probably haul it to you.

What did I do for fun as a kid? Sometimes my dad would get out and pass a baseball or football in the front yard. Every time we did that he tried to kill me with the ball. He was left-handed. I do remember somebody buying me a catcher's mitt, one of those big gloves. My dad, he would throw that ball and when it would hit, it would pop like a shotgun. You were afraid not to catch it; it would have killed you. That's the truth. Playing baseball is the only thing I can remember. Most of the time we had a hoe in our hand, hoeing corn and putting up hay. Putting up hay back then, you drove a pole in the ground and then you put the hay around it. Down in the river bottom, boy, I hated that because this old rich weed is what I call them, they grow eight foot tall. They'd get mixed up in that grass. They'd throw some hay up there for you to stomp down and them weeds would hit you down over the head and ears and it would hurt. I hated to have to get up on that haystack.

Lula's the only girl I ever met in my life, and we married. She lived up on the hill and I lived down along the river. In 1960 during the big snow, my dad had a horse, a work horse, and I would ride that horse from down along the river to the top of the hill and court Lula. I'd bring that horse an ear or two of corn, put it in a sack, tie it on the saddle, and come up here to court Lula. That horse waded in snow up to his belly. I took the back trails; I didn't try to come up the road. I remember the snow of 1960 well. The snow was in February. We weren't going to trust another bad winter, not being together. After the 1960 snow was over, Lula and I got married, July 9, 1960. It's been about 39 years, 40 a-pushing. I don't know if Lula would want me to tell you or not, but she's three years older than I am. She was almost 21 and I was 18.

I have two daughters. Tammy is the youngest; she works at Gambill Oil Company out at Beaver Creek. All these Citgo stations you see around here,

Lula and Bill Severt, July 1998 (courtesy of Lula and Bill Severt).

she helps tally up the gas and works in the office out there. Lecia, she's right now working up at the pawn shop for Joe Lyalls. I've got two grandchildren. Lecia has two children, a boy and a girl, Evan and Ashley.

You ask how it came about that they decided on our place for the President's visit. I cannot answer that because I don't know. They called me down there on a Saturday afternoon. Hollis Wild and Jay, he's the park ranger over the park. Hollis, his wife, called up here one Saturday afternoon and said, "Bill, could you come down here a minute?" I said, "Down where?" She said, "Down at your river bottom." I said, "Yeah, I can be there in five minutes." So I ran out there and jumped in my truck and got down there where I could see my bottom. The road was parked full of people, highway patrols, two or three of them were there. So I just pulled in there and got off the road the best I could and got out and two or three people introduced themselves to me, which I can't remember their names. Hollis came around there and said, "Bill, this person right here wants to talk to you." He introduced himself and I shook hands with him. He said, "If we decide on this place right here, your bottom down there, for the President to come to visit, what would you say?" I said, "I'd say 'Yes.'" We talked for a while and I came back to the house and told Lula what they asked me. Lula said, "Aw, Bill, you misunderstood them. The President ain't coming down there." They told me they'd let me know tomorrow, which was a Sunday. The next day, they called me to come back down there. This guy asked me, "When can you mow from this point down below the old house and get the grass out of our way?" I said, "Well, how long have I got to do it?" He said, "We want to start building in the morning," which would have been Monday morning. I came back to the house and told my wife, Lula, "They want me to mow that and get the grass up." She still really didn't believe me. But she helped me hook my mowing machine up and I went back down here on Sunday evening and mowed it. I came back and got my other tractor to hook to the rake. I went down there and started raking. Ernest, that married Lula's sister, he came down there and started raking for me. So I came back and hooked to my baler, which is a round baler. Before dark, we had that hay mowed, raked, and off of the ground so they could start building on Monday morning.

On Sunday they told me what they wanted done; they wanted to start getting prepared on Monday. And the President was here on Thursday. That's the first time since I've been farming that I mowed hay and raked hay and put up hay in the same day. I would have let it go a little longer. But it was no problem. I wanted to get it mowed so Bill Clinton wouldn't walk out there and step in a hole and break his foot or something. If they had showed me what route he wanted to walk going out there to the platform, I would have mowed it with a lawnmower.

The President did not come up here to my home. But, my wife, my two daughters, my grandchildren, and I got to meet him first down in the river bottom. I did not go out to Glendale and get to eat with him. I told the President that old house was the house I was raised in. He said, "You've let it run down a little bit, didn't you?" I said, "Yeah, we made a hay barn out of it." Orville Lyalls brought his big motor home down on the river bottom. Before the President got there, the Secret Service gathered my family and took us to the motor home to meet with the President. The Secret Service guys said, "Bill, when the President gets here, you introduce yourself and say anything you want to." I stood there. "What do you say, what do you say?"

Everybody thought he was coming up the highway and was going to walk down those steps. One of these Secret Service guys asked me to mow a trail all the way down through that bottom. I own the land down to the little white church. On down below the church near the bridge, there's a gate, and one of those Secret Service guys asked me, said, "Bill, could you mow with your mowing machine down there? Just mow the best trail that you know where they aren't any holes or anything. In case something happens, we may need that as an escape route." I said, "Sure, I'll do that." I'd have mowed the whole bottom if he'd asked me to. Anyway, he never told me anything, but that's the way they intended to bring the President in all the time. I kept standing there and this highway patrol came riding by real slow. I said, "It won't be long, he'll be here in a minute." I looked back around and

View of motor home where presidential party arrived. Speakers podium is near the river, with crowd beyond, July 30, 1998 (courtesy of Lula and Bill Severt).

there he was. They'd brought him up through the river bottom. The President amazed me for being there. But those Secret Service guys really amazed me for the work they did. I don't know how they do that everywhere he goes. I know it's a-costing us taxpayers, but there's somebody a-working their tail off if they're doing half of what they were doing down there. They're working their butts off a-doing it, they really are. It was amazing to me. I probably won't ever get to see it any more in my lifetime.

Talking about the New River down there, they asked me some questions about that, what my memories were about it. I said, "Well, the biggest memories I've got, I was raised up on the river banks here. I could go down there and swim in it, wade in it, and fish in it. In the winter time I could walk on top of it, really." It really was colder back then. I can see right now, me and my dad a-walking on the ice down there and you be able to hear that ice popping and cracking. I'd want to run and Dad would say, "No, son, as long as you hear that ice popping and cracking, you're safe. If you're out here on this ice and don't hear anything, you'd better get off of it, 'cause when you don't hear anything, it is getting rotten and you are subject to break through. " I remember that from my dad and he was right. You could see cracks coming up through that ice and it would scare you but it was just settling down. I wish this coming winter it would do that one more time. When the river freezes over any more, it just seems like, I call it, mush ice. It runs down, it just piles up and it looks jagged, and you don't want to get on that. You definitely don't want to get on that. Used to, the river would freeze over and it would be as slick as that glass there. You could ice skate on it. My grandpa on my mother's side, they say he had a pair of ice skates. There'd be channels in this ice six to eight foot wide. He'd come down through there and turn and jump and get over on the other side of that channel and just keep a-skating. I wasn't fortunate enough to see that. I was told he could do that.

We'd catch bass, what we call a red-eye — it's really a rock fish, slick heads, horneyheads, catfish, hog fish, suckers. Those are still in there. The river quality is pretty good now. The fish that I caught earlier is still in there. But I don't know if there are as many as there used to be or not.

I don't remember the flood of 1940. Mom and Dad were probably thinking about me then, but I wasn't born until 1942. I've heard tales about that flood. I'd have to take you down there and point my finger how far up it got. It didn't take our house away, but it took several houses and it left several houses that the water was real high on, but it didn't wash them away. The water got up in one house, almost to the ceiling.

Being close to the river, it is richer ground than up in the mountains. The only hay crop I had this year was down along the river. The hay fields we've got up here really didn't do anything this year because it was so dry. But down along the river, the river bottoms, we had a much better crop. If the river bottoms don't bring us through, we're going to have to buy some hay this year. Of a morning, the fog hangs along that river and keeps the ground moist, where up yonder in the hills, about time you get up you're gasping for breath. Sometimes I can walk out on my front porch and we've got a valley here and another valley over there, then the river. Sometimes I can walk out on that front porch and you can hear that river a-roaring just as plain as you can hear that fan a-running. When you hear that a couple or three days, you just as well get your umbrella, 'cause it's going to rain. You can hear it; it sounds like it's right here in this hollar. Sometimes you can hear it that clear.

At last, I am really thankful to know the place I was raised, down beside the New River, would one day be the scene of a visit from the United States President, Bill Clinton; Vice-President, Al Gore; North Carolina Governor, Jim Hunt; and many other top officials. it was an honor to have all these officials come together in Ashe County and to my "backyard" down along the New River, where they dedicated the New River to be an American Heritage River.

JOHN JACKSON, 52

March 13, 2000

*At his home on the Tom Jackson Road
in Watauga County near Boone.*

My name is John Robert Jackson. I'm one of several John Jacksons from my family. There are three or four John Jacksons in Watauga County and we're often confused. My roots are closely tied with the New River on both sides of my family. My mother, who was Marie Francis Jackson, came from Ashe County. She lived about a mile and a half from the New River in Ashe, which would have been the North Fork. My father, of course, is from this very farm right here. He was born right down here in this old house and we live about half a mile right over the mountain from the South Fork of the New River. So the river has always been a part of our lives.

I was born January 9, 1948, in Ashe County. I have lived all my life off and on in these two counties. My parents were school teachers. My mother was a fifth grade teacher and a librarian. My father was a high school principal. Before principals worked full time, we would live in Ashe in the winter where both of them taught, and then we would come back here in the summer where my dad farmed. The last year we did that was in '56. I can remember growing up off and on here on the farm and this has always been our homeplace. We lived in Jefferson and Ashe County and my mother was from Crumpler, Healing Springs.

My great-grandfather was Jesse W. Jackson. He was a member of the Guilford Rifles in the Civil War. He enlisted when he was just a teenager. The Guilford Rifles were a company in Robert E. Lee's Army of Northern Virginia. He was with Lee through most of the war. I have his pardon papers; I guess that's the best way you can describe them. When Lee surrendered at Appomattox, Jesse W. Jackson got a slip of paper and he could go home in peace. He was pardoned. He had an Army buddy whose name was Miller.

That's all I know; his last name was Miller and this family would have lived just three-fourths of a mile from here, from this homeplace. My great-grandfather went home with his Army buddy who was from Watauga, fell in love with his Army buddy's sister, and never went home, and we have been here ever since. That was 1865. Oddly enough, when they were married, their first home was on the banks of the New River. This particular place was purchased about 1870 and our family has been here ever since.

My grandfather, who was Jesse W.'s son, was Jesse Frank Jackson. He was born here in the orchard and he died in the little house below me. He lived to be 84. So this has been our stomping ground for all these years.

When I graduated from college it was the Vietnam era and I was going to have to go, and I just volunteered because I wanted to do something that

Jesse William Jackson, a Confederate veteran, and his son, Jesse Frank Jackson, age 5, about 1885, great-grandfather and grandfather of John Jackson (courtesy of John Jackson).

I would enjoy in the service, and I volunteered. I had orders for Vietnam and was ready to go. In fact, I flew to Fort Lewis, Washington, which was a staging area. The next stop would have been San Francisco and then on to Vietnam. Owing to the grace of God, I was turned around and diverted and sent back to Fort McGuire Air Force Base in New Jersey, I flew to Germany and spent one year and one month and one day. Now while I was there I made myself a promise that if I could ever get out and come back, this is where I wanted to live. And I did. I've been here since 1972 permanently.

I teach a rivers course in school and it's really sort of a mini-enrichment course. We have a free period or two at the end of the day. Students are sometimes assigned to my class or sometimes they want to come, and they sign up for it. We work about three weeks on rivers, the parts of the

Jesse Frank Jackson and his wife, Minnie Johnson Jackson. They were married in 1900. He died at age 84 (in 1964) and she, at age 81 (in 1965). They are the grandparents of John Jackson and the parents of Tom Jackson (courtesy of John Jackson).

river, the head of the river, the mouth of the river, tributaries and watersheds, and we talk about our river, the New River. I would like to get them in a boat and get a video camera and just take off down the river one Saturday. I think they'd really learn something. It really pleases me to see a child who's interested in where they have come from and their roots. I want them to be proud of themselves and proud of their river and their region.

The thing, I guess, that has provoked more interest in me about this river is the fact that I hunt. I have 'coon dogs and bear dogs. On one of my hunting excursions— and, by the way, I hunt along the river. It's been, I'd say, close to 20 years ago, I was in a particular region. I won't tell the name of it because I'm afraid someone will go there. Anyway, I was hunting there at night and I've gone back a time or two in the day. It was a long shelving rock. It must have been 50 feet long or more. It was high enough off the ground that you could walk under it. The further you got back, the ceiling dropped and eventually it would just coincide with the ground. I got to thinking, I bet some Indians camped under this rock. I have a friend or two who are good archaeologists; they're amateurs but they're really dedicated in what they do. I told them about it and they said, "Let's go." So I took them to my rock. I watched one of them go to work, and he just got down on his knees, squatted down and took the tips of his fingers and started raking in the dirt, and the dirt was soft. He started pulling up bits of ashes and charred wood and little bits of flint. To make a long story short, he got to prowling around in that thing and he could dig in the ground about a foot down right near the back. He would pull up chunks of pottery that were as large as your hand. He was just ecstatic. He could not believe that. Surely enough, Indians had been under that rock many, many times. That's kind of a sacred ground to me. I feel like some modern-day Moses. As we found pottery, I take it to mean that they had been there for an extended period, perhaps an entire season or maybe longer.

I can remember as a little boy when the river was not nearly as polluted as it is now, that we had freshwater mussels, which you cannot find any more in this region, and they were four or five inches long. My dad would take me along the river, and we'd see where the raccoons had pulled the mussels up on the bank and had cracked them open and eaten the mussels, which I'm sure were edible to the Indians. They were long, slender, black-looking things. We don't have those any more.

The Shawnees were called northern Indians because they came from Ohio. They would have come down the Kanawha River, which I call the New. They would have just come on down all the way here. As far away as upper New York, there were the Iroquois Indians who would come this way to fight the Cherokee.

I teach my children about the Teays River and how it was the master stream of North America, so huge, it started in the Appalachians and came out in the Gulf. The Gulf then would have stretched up to present-day St. Louis, Missouri. That river was so big that it was 12 miles wide. The Mississippi was a tributary of it and our New River is the only thing left of it. At one time it was the master stream of North America. I can recall years ago, Mr. Gale Hurley, who was my science teacher in high school, talked a little bit about that. Someone had remarked that they had seen the mountains and the river gorge down in Ashe County where they thought the river had been at one time because it was a huge river in that period. Kids find that fascinating.

At dry times, my father said you could walk across the river over here and not get your feet wet. You'd just bounce from rock to rock. But at one time it was a huge river, and it is referred to as the Teays. That's the name given to it by some geologist, college professor, I think. That was a huge river, and now the only thing we have left is the New River. Kids say, "Well, Mr. Jackson, if it's such an old river, why in the world did they call it the New River?" I say, "The only explanation I can give you is that it was new to the people who didn't know it was here." I've been reading that it was called the Woods River at one time, named after Abraham Woods who was an early Virginia explorer. I've often wondered what the Indians called it.

The Indians had a name for the rivers just as we do. Take the Catawba River, for instance, a prong of it heads in Watauga. I understood that that's an Indian word that means "high banks." The Yadkin, you can go to Green Park Inn and look in a storm grate and right there it begins, and technically it flows to the Atlantic Ocean, whereas the New River flows to the Gulf of Mexico. I understand Yadkin is a word that means "tall tree." It's a Sioux Indian word. Watauga is a Cherokee word that means beautiful waters, or flowing waters, or whispering waters. I've often wondered what the New River was called. I tempt my students. I say, you can go down here to Riddle's Fork and drop a ping pong ball in and if that ping pong ball does not hang up on something, you could catch it as it comes out of the Gulf of Mexico. That just blows their minds to bring in the concept of the watershed and tributaries.

As to the future of this river, though it is polluted now, I see a change for the better, I really do. I'll just tell you this. When I was little we didn't have dumpsters or we didn't have a landfill. You know what we had? My mother called it a "river box." What it was was a wooden box and if we didn't want something, we took it to the river. Well, those days have passed. We still are very bad polluters and we don't have a good record. But if you'll notice, farmers have started to fence along the river to keep the cattle out. We have really gotten environmentally interested people who are running for office in this day and time. I look for a better track record. We're beginning to introduce species of wildlife in our part of the country that have been extinct for a couple of centuries. We're talking about bringing elk back now, which is just wonderful. We had them here at one time. The wolves are coming back perhaps and it would really be nice to have that river so clean that you could put muskies or pike or big trout in it. I look for a better track record on that. We're taking better care of our rivers and we're better managers and we're better organized and people don't have river boxes any more, although people do pollute. When that river gets up, you'll see all sorts of milk cartons. But we'll do better and we'll continue to do better because our children are going to be environmentally conscious. We'll have more people, a higher population, but I believe that we'll do better environmentally. So I look for something good.

The river here, if you go from bridge to bridge, for example, if you go from the Roby Greene bridge, which is over here on the Roby Greene Road, to the Castle Ford bridge or the last bridge on the way to Todd, you see some really interesting places. You know, these people who lived there had a name for every bend in that river and every deep hole in that river and every big rock in that river and every cliff; they had a name for it. My father, before he passed away, would go along and say, "Right there's the Yellow Rock, over there's the Camping Rock, up there's the Flying Shoal, there's the Goat Rock, and there's the Pine Hole." They had names for them. I've often thought how neat it would be to get students in a canoe and take them down and map that river and go around and visit the last people who can vividly recall the old days and how people named those holes and places and map them for future use. That would really be a good oral history project. Are you acquainted with the Peggy Hole?

About half a mile before you get to Todd, there's a massive rock wall on the far side of the river. When I was a little boy, there used to be a deep hole right at the foot of that rock called the Peggy Hole. It was named for Peggy Clawson. Right across from the rock cliff across the river on the road side is a big house. I can remember when it was a smaller house and there was a lady that lived there. I don't think it was Peggy Clawson, but my aunt took me there one time when I was really little and that lady had a pet groundhog. That thing would just crawl all over her. Anyway, the Clawsons lived right where that house sits today. One day Peggy Clawson had gotten in a johnboat and poled, not paddled, but poled across the river. She was the sort who would collect herbs and dig ginseng. Her husband must have been a little on the lazy side. She was over there by herself and the story goes that she was rolling moss. You could take moss off of a log and roll it up in a roll and sell it. She had a little old cur dog that was with her. That dog went up above that big rock and brought a bear down. The bear ran right beside her and hopped in the river. She quickly jumped in her boat and drowned that bear with a pole, and didn't think anything about it. The next day her husband went to Todd. Todd was a boom town then. His remark as he walked in the general store was, "Did you hear about that bear we killed?" His wife had killed it. That was called the Peggy Hole. There's a story behind every one of those holes or places.

My dad and his father were hunters and they had a black squirrel/'possum dog. Someone bought that dog and they took it in a crate to Todd on the New River, put it on the train, and sent it at least to Abingdon, Virginia, and from thence to parts unknown. I want you to know that about three months later, they went out one morning after breakfast and that dog was lying in the front yard. He had come home. Dad said he was so sore, he laid in the grass for a week; he wouldn't move.

You asked how many dogs I have. Well, it's bad luck to count, but I believe I have 11 right now. We don't usually kill the 'coon, not any more. We just listen to the dogs. We're after the music. Some people say, "I don't hear any music, it sounds like a dog barking to me." It's music to the houndsman's ear. You can tell your dog, you can tell what he's doing and how he's running and separate your dog from all the rest. That's part of our heritage, that's part of the New River. It's part of growing up here.

Every once in a while we'll go down to the river and picnic. But when we hunt, we don't really picnic or anything like that. We'll take a snack. Sometimes we camp out along the river. It's cold.

Of course, during the Civil War, there was a lot of Union sentiment here in this county. I guess this region was about equally divided or maybe more pro–Union than Confederate. When my great-grandfather came back here, there was a lot of animosity and lots of old wrongs were being righted. A lot of vengeance took place, and it was not a good time to be around. You couldn't let people run over you. One of the things that he brought back with him was his horse, which was a splendid animal, I understand. Some of the local Tories, a name for Union sympathizers, knowing that he had been a Confederate veteran, came to take his horse. He was crippled, but he did not let them have that horse. He stood them off. He shot with a left-handed gun; the hammer was on the side away from him and he was left-handed. They said that he was willing to use that gun to keep his horse. It was a really rough time. During the Civil War, you heard about Antietam and Gettysburg and Manassas. People would say, "Yes, we know there's a big battle going on at so and so, but we're in a war right here, too!"

I've got to tell you this. Jesse W. Jackson was in Lee's Army and so was my great-great-grandfather on my mother's side. His name was Elbert Wiles. He was wounded at Fredricksburg. I did some research years ago. I took a Civil War course and I loved it. I had this professor from Mississippi. He would just sit back and talk and I would be entranced by what this man told me. I would take notes so rapidly, I'd come out of there with my hand cramped. I did a research paper on Union sentiment in Western North Carolina. I went to the archives in Raleigh and sat down and pulled out some data and manuscripts. I found that one night an entire company from Ashe County left Lee's Army and walked away, deserted, and went home, an entire company from Ashe County. One of those had to be Elbert Wiles, my great-great-grandfather. He went home, stayed a little while, then went back. Nine months later my great-grandfather, John Mack Wiles, was born. Anyway, after the war, Elbert Wiles came home to stay. One of the ways that he earned a living, he had a stallion that he would breed to other people's mares and get paid for it. He drowned in the New River riding that stallion across at flood stage. He was my great-great-grandfather on my mother's side. This gentleman here in the picture was my great-grandfather on my father's side. He was a Jackson. My mother's mother, my grandmother, was a Wiles and they were part Indian. Their hair was black and their eyes were so dark they were like coal, and they wore turbans. Their skin was just about bronze and that's who he was, he was Elbert Wiles.

I had a student in school, and she lived right over here on the Buckeye. One of my mini-courses that year was the Civil War. She said, "Mr. Jackson, have you ever heard about the Meat Rock?" I said, "No, I don't believe I have. Tell me about the Meat Rock." She said, "When my great-great-grandfather and grandmother were living here, there were Union Army soldiers that came through and they were stealing everything. My great-great-grandparents hid their meat under the Meat Rock so the Yankees couldn't get it."

You asked about my own family. I have four children. They're the four J's: Jessica, Justyn, Johnna, and Jordan (three girls and one boy), and my wife's name is Glenda. She was a Gentry. She was from Avery County, but her roots go back to Baldwin in Ashe County, the Gentrys there. We met when she was the student secretary at Avery County High School over the summer, and I did my student teaching there. We set up housekeep-

Left to right: Johnna, Jessica, John, and Justyn Jackson; Piney, Missy, and Hammer, AKC-registered big game Plotts, Crocket strain, late 1980's.

ing in the little house below. That was my mom and dad's house. They built it in 1940. It cost $1,200. When we had our first child, we added on. Then when my father passed away we moved in downstairs here and when my mother passed away we occupied the whole house.

About six years ago I was called into the ministry of the Primitive Baptist Church. I was a Methodist, but my mother was a Primitive Baptist. I was just always attracted to their doctrine, their beliefs. One of the first things I could remember was my mother taking me to Senter Primitive Baptist Church in Ashe County.

Have you ever heard the Primitive Baptists sing? It's uniquely Appalachian. You've never heard anything quite like it before. It's truly beautiful. Before I could ever understand anything about the doctrine or the word, I remember how they sang. For six years I've tried to pastor some churches and I had four. Now I'm down to three. It's been quite a change that's come over me and I can look at a lot of things like I never have before. I can recall when I was a freshman in college, my dad came and picked me up one Thursday afternoon. No one lived on this place here except my Uncle Tom and his wife, Ella Mae. My grandparents who had lived down here below me had passed away in '64 and '65. This would have been '66. My dad had an old Army Jeep that was torn up down here at the bottom and we changed a tire on it. He had gotten me from Appalachian to come out here to help him and it was in the late afternoon and it was the fall of the year, the leaves were changing and the shadows were really dark. There was a cool wind. The wind always comes from the north and it was blowing down that valley, and there was just such a feeling that came over me. I don't know, I've thought of it many, many times. I just think that was the hand of God saying, this is where you need to be. You go on off and get your education, sow your wild oats, and then come on home. This is where you need to be. In effect, I guess that's what I did.

When my mother was dying of cancer I said, "Mama, God has called me to preach." She said, "Well, that doesn't surprise me." I just look at where I am and what I've had a chance to see and experience in life and I see nothing but the hand of God and how great and good and graceful He has been to me to give me these mountains and to give me this river and to give me this home place and to give me my family. It's remarkable, it really is. I feel mighty humble. So I get misty-eyed when I hear an old mountain ballad or something like that. One night my mother and I were in here watching television and they had a news scene from Kentucky and they were carrying a coffin up a steep hill to a mountain graveyard, and you could hear them sing. She said, "Listen, listen, they're the old Baptists." Sure enough, they were singing just like the Primitive Baptists.

John Jackson and Missy, Most Outstanding Female Plott, Dixie Plott Classic, April, 1993.

In one of my churches they still sing the same way, and I'm working on the other two. They don't use a piano. The hymnbook doesn't have music. The songs are metered by syllables. Anything, for example, in common meter can be sung to the tune of Amazing Grace. There's long meter and short meter and common meter and two or three other meters. You can just about adapt any tune to the system you can imagine if you know what the meter is supposed to sound like. I don't ever want the Primitive Baptist way of singing to die out. Before there were hymnals, they would line them, line the songs. There weren't enough hymnals to pass around and so the pastor would line the hymn. He would say the line of the hymn and then the people would sing it. He would line one line at a time and then they would sing it and go to the next line. [John then illustrates singing a hymn by "lining."]

I've enjoyed every minute of this. Oral history is such a fabulous thing.

My dogs are Plott dogs, that's the state dog of North Carolina. Of course, they're mountain dogs and they were raised by the Plott family in western North Carolina. For about the last 20 years I've been infatuated by the Plott dogs. It's been my hobby to take my tape recorder and just take off to the wilds and if I can run into an old gentleman and sometimes an elderly lady who can tell me about their daddy's Plott dogs, I'll sit right down and I'll turn that recorder on and I will feed upon every word that they say. I've gone into homes and they'll get up ever so slowly out of their rockers, ease over to the cupboard, pull out a drawer, and there'll be an old faded hunting photograph and they'll start. It's fascinating.

Thomas J. Smith, 45

October 17, 1999

At the home of his mother, Mrs. Sue Smith,
on Round House Road, in Alleghany County,
North Carolina, near the North Carolina–Virginia line
and near the New River after the joining of
the North Fork and the South Fork.

This is how my mother and I granted an easement to the National Committee for the New River. The process started in the early 1990's. I went to high school with Thomas Worth, who is the secretary of the National Committee for the New River. He is an estate planning attorney whose main office is in Greensboro. He had been over here several times and knew about this property and knew about its proximity to the park. At that time, the idea of conservation easements was not something that was widely known around here and it's not something that we had heard of before.

Our family has always been very protective of our property rights and eventually when this idea was suggested to us we weren't too interested in it. In fact, at one point we said, "No, we're not going to do this," and it remained that way for a couple of years in the very early stages. I think that if we had more fully understood how conservation easements worked, and the tax advantages associated with conservation easements, then our original misunderstanding would not have been so great. Primarily, the reason that we undertook this was because, due to the fact that we have so much of this development around us here, the real estate values over in this area have skyrocketed. This was going to leave me with a huge estate tax problem when Mom passes away. Because of the value of this property, I was going to end up having to sell probably a large portion of it to pay estate tax. As it was finally explained to us, how an easement helps to ease that situation is, by placing an easement on property, you can reduce the value of the property significantly, perhaps as much as one-third.

One of the most valuable rights to owning property is the right to develop and if you give that right up, it makes the property worth less. We needed some money because we wanted to pay for some adjoining property in Virginia that we had just bought. So we sold a conservation easement on 97 acres of property which borders the New River and donated an easement on about 70 additional acres. This offset much of the capital gains tax associated with the sale of the original easement. Of course, you can't offset all of it, but you can deduct up to 30 percent of your gross income each year for a period of six years. In North Carolina, the state tax credit is not a deduction, it's a dollar for dollar credit. So, for several years, Mom's not going to be paying any state income tax at all. The reason that donating easements is attractive is because most people can recover most of the value of the donation through savings on estate taxes and income taxes. Of course, the reason that we sold the majority of our easement is that we needed money at the time to pay for this Virginia property which we'd recently bought. So basically we got that property paid for.

The Virginia property is right on the other side of the state line and on the other side of the road. Those tall pines over there, the other side of the state line, that's what we bought. We bought that in '94, and then in '96 we bought our house down there and the nine acres that went with that. Also, we were able to reduce the value of this farm significantly so that we can keep it under or at least down near the $675,000 estate tax exemption limit. That limit, by the way, increases $25,000 a year now as a result of the tax relief bill that was passed several years ago. However, it's not really much relief because the value of the property is going up faster than the upper limit of the cap is going up. But at least that helps a little bit. We didn't want the property developed. Tom Worth kept telling us, "You've got to protect the property." I kept saying, "Tom, it is protected." He said, "No, it's not." I'd say, "Yes, it is. It's protected by me." He said, "Yeah, but that's only as long as you're living, though."

If my kids or grandkids or somebody on down the line wants to sell it, that portion of the property can't be developed. Of course, this portion over here can still be developed. Where we're sitting now can still be developed, so we've given up the development rights on approximately 190 acres of our property, about 170 in North Carolina and then 20 in Virginia. When we bought the Virginia property, we granted an easement on 20 acres of that that borders the river between the state line and the Shady Shack Campground.

An easement has to be in perpetuity in order for the tax advantages to be valid. There is no tax advantage to a temporary easement. Although there is such a thing, you don't see very many of them because you don't get the tax breaks. I'm not a tax attorney, but in the process I've learned a whole lot about it.

Thomas J. Smith looks over his mother's farm in Alleghany County.

We were the first large acreage easement, I believe I'm correct in saying this, in the North Carolina portion of the river. When I say large acreage, I'm talking about 100 or more acres. There were some smaller ones before, but this was the first easement project along the New River in North Carolina of this magnitude. In some ways, I think it was kind of a ground-breaking thing. Now several other people have followed suit. It's no longer a new and novel idea. People have heard of it now. You go talk to somebody about conservation easements and it's no longer something that nobody's ever heard of. Our original response was, "What do you mean, you can sell some of the rights to the property without selling the whole thing?" We didn't understand that, and it took a lot of education to get us to where we understood how it worked. Once you reach that understanding, there's really nothing very complicated about it.

To summarize the can-dos and can't-dos with easements: the big advantage to it, to a large extent, that's up to the land owner. The land owner is in the driver's seat. They don't have to give up any rights that they don't want to, because they've got all the rights to begin with. So, they're the ones that are really negotiating from the position of power. However, there are certain things that do have to be given up in order for an easement to have any tax value. In order to qualify for tax exemptions, you have to give up, or at least severely limit, the right to develop non-agricultural structures such as commercial buildings, residential buildings, or industrial buildings, or any other kind of non-agricultural building. You have to give up the right to do things like surface mining or any kind of drastic alteration to the landscape that would be a permanent eyesore on the land or significantly damage water quality. You have to give up the right to use the property for any sort of a waste disposal facility or anything like that. Those are the basic things that are required in terms of being able to qualify for tax advantages.

In addition, there are some state and federal criteria that specify that the property must protect a wildlife habitat, must protect a scenic viewshed, or perhaps provide open space, or protect plant or animal habitat. Those criteria are very general and basically anything along the Blue Ridge Parkway or along the New River usually qualifies. You do not have to allow other people on your property. See, there's no public access to this property. I can prosecute trespassers on the easement just the same as I could before. I do not have to allow anybody to come on the property, except a representative of the National Committee for the New River who comes over about once a year, looks at it, and says, "Okay, the easement's being abided by." That's all. There's no trespassing. I still retain the right to do agricultural things, harvest crops. I can harvest timber on all portions except a no-timber zone which is really close to the river.

The main thing a property owner has to do, if they're thinking about doing an easement, is you have to have a plan for how that property is going to make you money in the future. A farmer or a landowner, the way property taxes are now, can't afford to own property that's not producing income. You have to make sure that you retain the right to produce that income, whether it's forest products, farm products, whatever. A landowner that doesn't insure that he retains those rights could be headed for trouble down the road, because he's going to have a piece of property that's not making him any money. One of the things that the landowner has to watch out for, is to make sure that his rights are adequately protected and then make sure that the language is clear that he retains the certain rights that he needs to retain. I retain the right to hunt, fish, do recreational things. Generally, a conservation easement should not contain restrictions that are not specifically related to conservation.

The other thing that has to be limited is subdivision. The easement portion of our farm can only be divided into four parcels, maximum, and none of those parcels can be smaller than five acres. We have one portion of the easement that is sold and another portion that's donated. Now on certain portions of that easement, I can build two houses. So, you don't have to totally give up the right to build houses, but it has to be limited so that basically those houses are not ecologically or scenically intrusive. I can build two houses, but they can't be within sight of the river. The more rights you give up, the more value your easement has and the bigger tax advantage you're going to get. The reason you have to limit subdivision is because there has to be a qualified holder for this easement, which in our case is the National Committee for the New River. The National Committee for the New River doesn't want to deal with 50 or 100 different landowners; it wants to deal preferably with only one. But it's willing to live with four, if I choose to subdivide it four different ways.

I have become a board member of the National Committee. The last part of our easement that we did was the Virginia portion. After that I was invited to be on the Board of Directors. I've been on the board now for a little over a year and a half. One of the things that I do with the Committee, and I've done this a number of times, is go around and give presentations about conservation easements. Usually I go in and I will do one with a tax attorney. One of the things that I would recommend, if a landowner is interested in the possibility of doing a conservation easement, before he gets into that process, he should be involved with working with a competent estate planner, maybe a CPA or a tax attorney that will represent his interests and make sure that he's working out a deal that fulfills his needs from an estate planning standpoint.

There are several tax advantages to a conservation easement and the most important one is the estate tax exemption. The importance of working with a good estate planner cannot be overstated, because the landowner has to make sure that he's working out a deal that's going to meet his estate planning needs. Again, you need to make sure that your tax advantages are done in a way that suits your needs and also, you have to watch out and make sure that your right to continue producing income on the property is maintained.

What we believe is that with the timber — and I'm really a proponent of sustainable forestry — we could sell this property one time and make a bundle of money, give the government 20 percent of it, and after we did that, we couldn't buy back what we just turned loose of. But, if you grow trees, every 40 years or so each generation of your family can sell a crop of trees that's going to be worth just about as much as the land is, and they get to do that every generation. They get to keep the land and manage the land and continue to be a steward of the land. You make your money selling the trees. That way you don't have to sell your property. These trees that we planted out there, they're not going to make me any money. But they'll make my kids some money. Then they can turn around and plant another crop that's going to make their kids some money.

We've got other farmers in the area that are into beef cattle or they're into dairy and if they're making a good living doing that, that's fine, too. That can be accommodated under a farm easement or a conservation easement just as well. I think you're going to see, and this is a prophetic statement here — and this is just mine, this doesn't come from anybody else — within the next 25 to 50 years, all the farm and forest land that you're going to find in private ownership is going to be under some kind of conservation agreement. It's because the financial incentive to develop is going to be so strong that there's going to have to be a financial incentive not to develop. A conservation easement is one of the leading ways that that incentive can be presented to a landowner.

I also would like to point out that conservation easements can be done in such a way that they don't totally prohibit development. Like I said, I can build a couple of houses on our easement. But there are certain ways that that can and cannot be done. There are certain statements in that easement that govern how that can be done. For example, they can't be sold off on a lot. I can only build a maximum of two. They can't be within sight of the river. Conservation easements can be done in certain ways that allow for some responsible development. Responsible development that's done in a way that's not too dense, that's not too ecologically damaging, and does not detract from the viewshed of the area you're trying to preserve, that can actually be worth more in the long run than development that is done in too dense a fashion. If you take an area where, let's say that you've got one house on a ten-acre tract and that house is not within sight of the river, it's not degrading the viewshed of the area, that estate is going to continue to hold its value. But if you put houses on one-acre lots all the way down to the river, what you have done there is you have degraded your viewshed by the houses themselves. When those houses are no longer new and they fall into disrepair, that area is not going to retain its scenic value and there's going to be no incentive to replace those with new houses because the area is no longer scenically valuable. That's what we're seeing done too much around here. It's not a very sustainable type of development. Once all those houses go in, it's no longer a scenic area.

When I go and I do one of these presentations, that's pretty much what I say. People say, "Do you have slides or do you have audiovisual material?" I don't have any of that, it's just totally off the cuff. It always just comes out.

In 1999, Dr. Smith became president of the National Committee for the New River.

APPENDIX:
THE PROCLAMATION

Designation of American Heritage Rivers
by the President of the United States of America

In celebration of America's rivers, and to recognize and reward grassroots efforts to restore them, last year I announced the American Heritage Rivers initiative. My goal was to help communities realize their visions for their rivers by making it easier for them to tap existing programs and resources of the Federal Government. From across the country, hundreds of communities answered my call for nominations, asking that their rivers be designated American Heritage Rivers. I applaud all of the communities that have drawn together and dedicated themselves to the goal of healthy rivers, now and forever.

Having reviewed the recommendations of the American Heritage Rivers Initiative Advisory Committee, I am pleased to be able to recognize a select group of rivers and communities that reflect the true diversity and splendor of America's natural endowment, and the tremendous energy and commitment of its citizenry.

Pursuant to Executive Orders 13061, 13080, and 13093, I hereby designate the following American Heritage Rivers: The Blackstone and Woonasquatucket Rivers, in the States of Massachusetts and Rhode Island; The Connecticut River, in the States of Connecticut, Massachusetts, New Hampshire, and Vermont; The Cuyahoga River, in the State of Ohio; The Detroit River, in the State of Michigan; The Hanalei River, in the State of Hawaii; The Hudson River, in the State of New York; The Upper Mississippi River, in the States of Illinois, Iowa, Minnesota, Missouri, and Wisconsin; The Lower Mississippi River, in the States of Louisiana and Tennessee;

The New River, in the States of North Carolina, Virginia, and West Virginia; The Rio Grande, in the State of Texas; The Potomac River, in the District of Columbia and the States of Maryland, Pennsylvania, Virginia, and

West Virginia; The St. Johns River, in the State of Florida; The Upper Susquehanna and Lackawanna Rivers, in the State of Pennsylvania; The Willamette River, in the State of Oregon.

IN WITNESS WHEREOF, I have hereunto set my hand this thirtieth day of July, in the year of our Lord nineteen hundred and ninety-eight, and of the Independence of the United States of America the two hundred and twenty-third.

WILLIAM J. CLINTON

BIBLIOGRAPHY

Ashe County Bicentennial Commission Historical Committee. *Rambling Through Ashe: Stories and Facts About Ashe County, North Carolina.* Carolina Printing, Jefferson, North Carolina, 1976.

Blackmun, Ora. *Western North Carolina: Its Mountains and Its People to 1880.* Boone, N.C.: Appalachian Consortium Press, 1977.

Fletcher, Arthur. *Ashe County, A History.* Jefferson, N.C.: Ashe County Research Association, 1960.

Foster, Stephen William. *The Past Is Another Country: Representation, Historical Consciousness, and Resistance in the Blue Ridge.* Berkeley: University of California Press, 1988.

Greene, Mrs. Ivery C. "A Brave Little Boy of a Disastrous Flood of July 13, 1940" (pamphlet).

Hyde, Arnout, Jr. *New River: A Photographic Essay.* Charleston, W.V.: Cannon Graphics (418 Lehigh Terrace; 25302), 1991.

New River News. Official Publication of the National Committee for the New River, Inc. P. O. Box 1480, West Jefferson, N.C. 28694-1480.

Reeves, Eleanor Baker. *A Factual History of Early Ashe County, North Carolina: Its People, Places and Events.* Dallas, Texas: Taylor Publishing Company, 1986.

Schoenbaum, Thomas J. *The New River Controversy.* Winston-Salem, N.C.: John F. Blair, Publisher, 1979.

Smith, Phil. *The Century Speaks: Recollections of Lancashire Over the Last 100 Years.* Lancaster [England]: Carnegie Publishing, Ltd., 1999.

Taylor, Mildred. "Grandpa's River." Unpublished, undated manuscript in Ashe County Public Library (1964 is mentioned as "this year" on page 168).

Thom, James Alexander. *Follow the River, a Novel Based on the True Ordeal of Mary Ingles.* New York: Ballantine, 1981.

ABOUT THE AUTHORS

Leland Ross Cooper, Sr., educated at Clemson College and the University of North Carolina, Chapel Hill, holds the doctor of education degree from the University of Florida. He is professor emeritus of leadership and higher education at Appalachian State University, Boone, N.C. He has also taught in the public schools of South Carolina and North Carolina and in community colleges in Florida. He is co-author of *Hungarians in Transition*.

Mary Lee Lambert Cooper was educated at the Woman's College of the University of North Carolina, Greensboro. She has worked at the University of North Carolina's School of Business Administration, Appalachian State University's College of Education, the University of Florida's Teaching Hospital, and *Horn in the West* outdoor drama in Boone. She has participated in various community and church organizations.

In 1998, as number 2 in its series Contributions to Southern Appalachian Studies, McFarland published *The Pond Mountain Chronicle: Self-Portrait of a Southern Appalachian Community,* an oral history edited by Leland R. and Mary Lee Cooper.

INDEX